MANCHESTER UNITED
OFFICIAL REVIEW
OF THE 94/95 SEASON

MANCHESTER UNITED

OFFICIAL REVIEW
OF THE 94/95 SEASON

First published in Great Britain in 1995 by

Manchester United Football Club plc
Old Trafford
Manchester
M16 0RA

in association with

Virgin Publishing Ltd
332 Ladbroke Grove
London
W10 5AH

A catalogue record for this book is available from the British Library

ISBN: 086369 814 X

Produced by **Zone Ltd**

Editor: Rachel Jervis
Design: Tim Barnes/Annie Gleadow
Contributors: Andy Mitten, Justyn Barnes, Roland Jones, Alex Whiteside

Main cover photograph: Paul Massey/FSP
Photography: Action Images (unless otherwise stated)

Printed in Italy

CONTENTS ✳

review of the 94/95 season

Introduction	8
United on Tour >July 1994	10
BLACKBURN ROVERS >Wembley 14 Aug (FA Charity Shield)	12
QUEENS PARK RANGERS >Old Trafford 20 Aug	14
NOTTINGHAM FOREST >City Ground 22 Aug	16
TOTTENHAM HOTSPUR >White Hart Lane 27 Aug	18
WIMBLEDON >Old Trafford 31 Aug	20
August >statistics	23
LEEDS UNITED >Elland Road 11 Sep	24
IFK Gothenburg >[EC #1] 14 Sep	26
LIVERPOOL >Old Trafford 17 Sep	28
PORT VALE >Vale Park [CCC R2 1L] 21 Sep	32
IPSWICH TOWN >Portman Road 24 Sep	34
GALATASARAY >[EC #2] 28 Sep	36
September >statistics	39
EVERTON >Old Trafford Oct	40
PORT VALE >Old Trafford [CCC R2 2L] 5 Oct	42
SHEFFIELD WEDNESDAY >Hillsborough 8 Oct	44
WEST HAM UNITED >Old Trafford 15 Oct	46
BARCELONA >Old Trafford [EC #3] 19 Oct	50
BLACKBURN ROVERS >Ewood Park 23 Oct	52
NEWCASTLE UNITED >Old Trafford [CCC R3] 29 Oct	56
October >statistics	59
BARCELONA >Nou Camp [EC #4] 2 Nov	60
ASTON VILLA >Villa Park 6 Nov	62
MANCHESTER CITY >Old Trafford 10 Nov	64
CRYSTAL PALACE >Old Trafford 19 Nov	68
IFK GOTHENBURG >Ullevi Stadium [EC #5] 23 Nov	70
ARSENAL >Highbury 26 Nov	72
November >statistics	75
NORWICH CITY >Old Trafford 3 Dec	76
GALATASARAY >Old Trafford [EC #6] 7 Dec	78
QUEENS PARK RANGERS >Loftus Road 10 Dec	80
NOTTINGHAM FOREST >Old Trafford 17 Dec	82
CHELSEA >Stamford Bridge 26 Dec	84
LEICESTER CITY >Old Trafford 28 Dec	86
SOUTHAMPTON >The Dell 31 Dec	88
December >statistics	91
COVENTRY CITY >Old Trafford 3 Jan	92
SHEFFIELD UNITED >Bramall Lane [FAC R3] 9 Jan	94
NEWCASTLE UNITED >St. James Park 15 Jan	96
BLACKBURN ROVERS >Old Trafford 22 Jan	100
CRYSTAL PALACE >Selhurst Park 25 Jan	102
WREXHAM >Old Trafford [FAC R4] 28 Jan	104
January >statistics	107
ASTON VILLA >Old Trafford 4 Feb	108
MANCHESTER CITY >Maine Road 11 Feb	110
LEEDS UNITED >Old Trafford [FAC R5] 19 Feb	112
NORWICH CITY >Carrow Road 22 Feb	114
EVERTON >Goodison Park 25 Feb	116
February >statistics	119
IPSWICH TOWN >Old Trafford 4 Mar	120
WIMBLEDON >Selhurst Park 7 Mar	122
QUEENS PARK RANGERS >Old Trafford [FAC R6] 12 Mar	124
TOTTENHAM HOTSPUR >Old Trafford 15 Mar	126
LIVERPOOL >Anfield 19 Mar	128
ARSENAL >Old Trafford 22 Mar	130
March >statistics	133
LEEDS UNITED >Old Trafford 2 Apr	134
CRYSTAL PALACE >Villa Park [FAC Semi Final] 9 Apr	136
CRYSTAL PALACE >Villa Park [FAC R6 Semi Final Replay] 12 Apr	138
LEICESTER CITY >City Ground 15 Apr	140
CHELSEA >Old Trafford 17 Apr	142
COVENTRY CITY >Highfield 1 May	144
April >statistics	147
SHEFFIELD WEDNESDAY >Old Trafford 7 May	148
SOUTHAMPTON >Old Trafford 10 May	150
WEST HAM UNITED >Upton Park 14 May	152
May >statistics and season summary	154
EVERTON >Wembley [FAC Final] 20 May	156

player portraits

PETER SCHMEICHEL >goalkeeper	22
PAUL PARKER >defender	30
DENIS IRWIN >defender	31
STEVE BRUCE >defender	38
LEE SHARPE >winger	48
GARY PALLISTER >defender	49
ERIC CANTONA >forward	58
PAUL INCE >midfield	66
BRIAN MCCLAIR >forward	67
RYAN GIGGS >winger	74
DAVID MAY >defender	90
GARY WALSH >goalkeeper	98
ANDREI KANCHELSKIS >forward	99
ROY KEANE >midfield	106
ANDY COLE >forward	118
MARK HUGHES >forward	132
GARY NEVILLE >defender	146

*INTRODUCTION
>A season review

Alex Ferguson: the man at the heart of one of the most dramatic seasons in football history

Faraway, so close... at the end of a traumatic, rollercoaster season, 1994/95 hasn't yielded any major trophies for Manchester United FC. After United's comprehensive, almost routine, Charity Shield victory over Blackburn Rovers in the season's traditional curtain-raiser, who could have predicted the surprises and shocks that lay in store for the reigning Premier League champions in the coming months?

At the time, everyone involved in the Old Trafford scene was brimful of **confidence** for the challenges that lay before them in league, cup and European competitions. Although United were ultimately denied in their quest for even more glory, even the most hardened critic of the club could not question the commitment of all United's staff to the cause. By the impossibly high standards which are expected of Britain's biggest club, 1994/95 will be considered a failure. With only the slightest twist of good fortune, United could have secured an unprecedented second successive League and FA Cup double. The simple fact that such an achievement is heralded as a disaster for United by the media only serves to confirm the club's massive reputation in the world of football. Next year, any team with aspirations to win the Premiership will know that MUFC is still **the** club to beat.

Manchester United: Official Review Of The 94/95 Season is the definitive record of United's remarkable season. No other Premiership club can boast such a comprehensive book covering their season's exploits: this is officially Red Devils only territory! Record-breaking triumphs and desperate disappointments are all listed, match-by-match. Statistics from each game give you the lowdown on United's relentless chase for honours and action photographs allow you to relive the vital moments of the season. There are specially compiled match reports and Alex Ferguson gives his verdict on the players' performance which may or may not agree with the press comments which are also featured.

In addition, Timeline provides a day-by-day diary of world events away from Old Trafford.

No match involving Manchester United is overlooked. From relaxed pre-season friendlies in Ireland in July 1994 to the tense FA Cup Final against Everton in May 1995, each match is analysed in extraordinary detail.

After retaining the Charity Shield on a roasting, summer's day at Wembley, courtesy of a cool penalty conversion by Cantona and a spectacular overhead kick by Ince, United's season began in earnest. Although success in all competitions is important to Manchester United, it was hoped that the club could mount a serious challenge for the European Champions' Cup. To this end, Alex Ferguson bought David May and encouraged the drive to maturity of young Englishmen in the squad in order to limit the damage of the foreigners' rule. Despite the best efforts of all the players called upon by Fergie, too many goals leaked at the back generally and a disastrous 4-0 defeat in Barcelona halted Red ambitions for this year. However, there were encouraging signs: the 2-2 draw at home to Barcelona clearly demonstrated United's ability to cut it in the highest company and goals from youngsters David Beckham and Simon Davies in a consolation 4-0 win over Galatasaray proved that the Old Trafford youth policy is paying rich dividends.

Perhaps the most comforting aspect of a frustrating season was the emergence of 'Fergie's Fledglings' who have come in and shown great composure in the absence of more established players: for example, Nicky Butt has cemented himself in the first team and has the potential to become one of the best midfielders in Europe; Gary Neville is versatile and his outstanding performances for United earnt him an England call-up for the summer's Umbro Cup tournament; Paul Scholes is a proven goalscorer who has drawn admiring comparisons with Eric Cantona

for his creative style. United's daunting fixture list encouraged the Boss to field youthful-looking sides in Coca-Cola Cup ties where the boys gave a good account of themselves before losing to an inspired Newcastle side.

The dizzy expectations of United fans for the club to win a third consecutive Premiership and retain the FA Cup were reduced by serious injuries to key players and the suspension of fiery Frenchman Eric Cantona following the Selhurst Park incident. Ultimately, Blackburn fell over the line defying a brave late burst by the Red Devils which was finally thwarted at Upton Park on the last Sunday of the Premiership season. A week later, relegation survivors Everton came to Wembley to defend and pinch a breakaway goal. Joe Royle's tactics worked perfectly and Fergie's men couldn't lift themselves to penetrate the Toffees' tight defences. Ludek Miklosko and Neville Southall have a lot to answer for!

At distressing times like this, when something so close is snatched away, it is as well to reflect on happier times. Who will ever forget United's 5-0 thrashing of Manchester City, which included a Kanchelskis hat-trick in a game dubbed the 'Demolition Derby'? Remember Eric Cantona's flash of Gallic intuition in the FA Cup match played in a swirling wind at Bramall Lane against Sheffield United? Eric spotted Blades' keeper Alan Kelly off his line before delicately lifting the ball beyond the stranded goalie. What about the record-breaking 9-0 Old Trafford execution of hapless Ipswich Town when £6 million signing Andy Cole showed his true form with five magnificent goals?

All in all, it has been a memorable season which has seen Manchester United embroiled in both controversy and glory. Despite the problems, everyone at United has pulled together and produced a brand of football that has brought global support for the club during its distinguished history.

Finally, we would like to thank Alex Ferguson, the coaching staff and the players for allowing our photographer to travel with the team and capture unique images from the dressing room and the Cliff training ground.

[Pre-Season Tour 1994]

> DUNDALK 2 UNITED 4
Saturday 30 July 1994
[Att: 12,000]

The very first game of United's pre-season tour got off to a bad start as Dundalk were allowed to score two goals. The Irish side included ex-United reserve Joe Hanrahan and played some tidy football – fully deserving their lead.

However, United have a habit of retrieving themselves from sticky situations. In the end they overcame Dundalk by displaying the kind of football that won them the Double last season.

Emotions were mixed in the stadium, but when United eventually took the lead there was no doubting that the support was mainly red. Tickets, at £22, were pricey – but our massive Irish following would've paid anything to watch Fergie's lads in action.

The action heros were rooming partners, Paul Ince and Ryan Giggs. Giggs' international teammate, Hughesey, managed to score the other two in his first match since his testimonial.

After the summer break it took United a little while to get out of neutral. Once they were in first gear though, everyone present knew it wouldn't be long before they were cruising in overdrive.

> SHELBOURNE 0 UNITED 3
Saturday 30 July 1994
[Att: 12,000]

Walking down O'Connell Street in Dublin, you will see more United replica shirts than all other teams combined. In Tolka Park the United fans were there in their thousands. The crowd consisted mainly of the Irish, but a minority of around two hundred had made the journey over the water. As no tickets had been supplied to United, the majority of the English had to pay about £45.

Ince, Cantona and McClair provided just reward of three goals for these loyal reds. The atmosphere was electric; overwhelmingly in favour of United. Some supporters even likened the occasion to a Take That concert, and the younger generation certainly laid on a massive welcome – for Ryan Giggs in particular! To the amusement of most of the crowd, he also received a kiss from an admiring Giggsette whilst preparing to take a corner. He kept his cool and appeared unaffected.

United may have said farewell to Ireland by dispatching Shelbourne 3-0, but the two Irish sides went largely unnoticed in this pre-season jaunt, and without them it wouldn't have been possible.

> WOLVES 1 UNITED 2
Saturday 3 Aug 1994
[Att: 28,000]

All things new at Molineux, following the Wolves stadium's redevelopment. The turnstiles spin to a capacity crowd for the unveiling of the new Manchester United home kit.

Wolves' supporters were friendly towards the reds, as was manager Graham Taylor. Chants of "Turnip, turnip give us a wave" were well-

received by the ex-England boss. He obliged with a wave to the 2,000 mickey-taking United fans.

The United fans were soon silenced, however. Wolves made an impressive start to the match, then sent their fans into ecstasy by opening the scoring.

The lead was short-lived. Though Wolves defender Blades did continue the scoring, he did so at the wrong end of the pitch. United fans didn't care how the team equalised, just so long as they did – and they were elated when Paul Ince later scored the winning goal. United's new kit could've been a flop. Had they lost this match, anyone superstitious amongst the potential buyers may not have found this replica a wise purchase!

Incey modestly accepts all the credit for the Dundalk win from Pally

John Peters

Ibrox International Tournament

Glasgow Rangers played host to Sampdoria, Newcastle United and Manchester United.

The hosts found themselves outclassed by the Italian side on the first day of the two-day event.

> RANGERS 1 UNITED 0
Saturday 6 Aug 1994
[Att: 29,000]

This was United's fifth match in seven days, which dictated Ferguson's team selection. The team consisted mainly of reserve players, which annoyed supporters who'd paid £22.50 for a ticket for the second day.

New signing David May was eager to impress his new team-mates. But his heading ability was without doubt the skill he'll be remembered for – he headed past our own 'keeper. The fans were understanding and supported him for the rest of the match, aiming to boost his and the team's morale. Things gradually got worse as the devils began to emerge from the reds and Cantona was sent off. The decision was undisputed; the television screens in the concourses giving supporters the opportunity to make their own minds up.

The match finished 1-0, and United finished fourth in the tournament. The majority of United fans waited to support Sampdoria in their match against Newcastle. The Italians won, much to the satisfaction of all those patient reds.

Sparky in full flow takes on Newcastle on the first night of the tournament held at Ibrox, Glasgow

> NEWCASTLE 1 UNITED 2
Saturday 5 Aug 1994
[Att: 27,000]

You couldn't say the atmosphere was as hospitable as some recent fixtures. Nevertheless United went out to win at Ibrox against Newcastle. Playing their attractive and normally successful style of football, United were unlucky not to score in the first half-hour. Newcastle, in contrast, were lucky to score in the first half, when they took the lead.

Cantona broke the ice for United, scoring with a cool header on the stroke of half time. It was fully deserved after an impressive start.

The second half saw all the football and all the goalmouth action – but no goals. This resulted in a penalty shoot-out, which doesn't inspire the reds' support with confidence.

The man who had earlier saved the day, Cantona, missed a penalty. He was too cool, and he knew it. Never mind, United lost 6-5 – but the losers' match against Rangers

Paul Ince gives David May a head-start in their race for the dressing room following another reverse for the reds

meant that the 'Battle of Britain' could, at last, commence.

[FA Charity Shield 1994]

team lineups

united

		rating
1.	Peter Schmeichel	7
12.	David May	7
4.	Steve Bruce	7
6.	Gary Pallister	7
5.	Lee Sharpe	7
14.	Andrei Kanchelskis	7
9.	Brian McClair	7
8.	Paul Ince	8
11.	Ryan Giggs	7
7.	Eric Cantona	8
10.	Mark Hughes	7

on the bench

31.	Keith Gillespie
25.	Kevin Pilkington
19.	Nicky Butt
20.	Dion Dublin
22.	Chris Casper

blackburn

1.	Tim Flowers
20.	Henning Berg
5.	Colin Hendry
2.	Tony Gale
6.	Graeme Le Saux
16.	Robbie Slater
22.	Mark Atkins
4.	Tim Sherwood
11.	Jason Wilcox
7.	Stuart Ripley
25.	Ian Pearce

on the bench

19.	Peter Thorne
13.	Bobby Mimms
18.	Andy Morrison
3.	Alan Wright
21.	Paul Harford

word up

The season kicks off!

English referees have now got to adapt to new rule changes concerning tackling from behind. An instant yellow card for such an offence will surely mean Carling Premiership matches will be littered with yellow and red confetti this season. In this match there were no red cards, and the seven yellow cards seemed a little over-zealous for such a good-natured match. Even **Giggs'** name was taken in the referee's book!

United's chosen opponents Blackburn weren't able to cope with United's fluency on the pitch. The Red Devils' attacking style seemed to overpower the Lancastrians from Ewood Park. They succeeded in giving away a penalty in only the 22nd minute, which **Cantona** slotted home for his third at Wembley this year.

United's second came late on in the match, **Paul Ince** supplying a classy finishing touch to a curling Cantona corner. His overhead kick left stunned Rovers 'keeper Flowers stranded as the ball flew into the net. Outclassed by you-know-who!

Enigmatic Eric evades Le Saux

John Peters

in the book

Referee:
P Don,
Middlesex
Rating: 7

Bookings:
Bruce,
Sharpe,
Giggs,
Hendry,
Le Saux,
Sherwood,
Wilcox

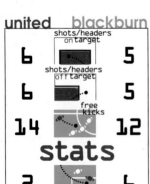

united   blackburn

stats

united		blackburn
6	shots/headers on target	5
6	shots/headers off target	5
14	free kicks	12
2	caught offside	6
3	corners	1
10	fouls	8

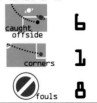

Another season begins: United fans revel in the summer sur

bite this!

"Paul Ince, scoring with a spectacular overhead kick just as a spirited but under-strength Blackburn side were beginning to threaten the lead Eric Cantona had secured for Manchester United, guaranteed that the Double winners retained the Charity Shield in the sunshine yesterday." **THE INDEPENDENT**

"When everything else is forgotten, Paul Ince will be remembered for a goal that millions dream of, but rarely see. Ince was airborne, on his back and flat as an ironing board when his shot flashed by Tim Flowers for a veritable gold-card, hundred-degree proof bicycle kick. **DAILY MIRROR**

"Once or twice Peter Schmeichel was tested by Blackburn's counter-strike reprisals and substitute Peter Thorne should have seized an equaliser.
But victory was finally established by that marvellously talented axis of Ince and Cantona nine minutes before the end. The corner flew from Giggs' boot and Cantona back-headed into the box. Waiting with an acrobatic finish was Ince." **THE SUN**

"Moneybags Rovers owner Jack Walker - who was allowed to lead out his side at the start - left the stadium to jeers of "what a waste of money" from the United terraces."

"The new rule worked very well today. I though the referee did a difficult job very well implementing it. There were quite a few bookings (seven in total), but nearly all were deserved. When you think that people have paid around £35 for a ticket to watch today's game, it's only right that they should be entertained fully.
Eric Cantona was wonderful today and didn't react badly to anything. He only does that when he feels an injustice has been done. On the whole the team played well and the winning goal has certainly put down a good marker for the rest of the goals this season. Paul was lucky, though - you're not supposed to go over to the crowd like that; he could have been booked. Let's just say the goal was more special than the celebration."

Ince **scores in spectacular style**

The two scorers share the limelight

> timeline

* **Sat 13th Aug** Bryan Robson lures 23,343 visitors to Ayresome Park to watch Middlesbrough beat Burnley 2-0

> **CANTONA TV SHOCKER — BROADCASTING WATCHDOGS BAN AN ADVERT SHOWING THE MANCHESTER UNITED BAD BOY BOASTING ABOUT HIS DIRTY TRICKS ON THE FIELD** Daily Mirror Sat 13th Aug

* **Sun 14th Aug** The Charity Shield between Manchester United and Blackburn Rovers results in no less than seven bookings. Kenny Dalglish says, "At this rate there will be no tackles at all"

> **CONVICTED DRUG DEALERS ARE HOLDING ON TO TENS OF MILLIONS OF POUNDS FROM THE PROFITS OF THEIR CRIMES THAT SHOULD HAVE BEEN SEIZED UNDER COURT ORDERS** The Observer Sun 14th Aug

* **Mon 15th Aug**
> **FATHER SEES SON DIE AFTER ATTACK BY ASIAN GANG** The Times Mon 15th Aug

* **Tue 16th Aug** Liverpool sign Phil Babb for £3.6 million

* Manchester United play Middlesbrough in Clayton Blackmore's testimonial. the ex-United player received £150,000 as a result of the match

> **FRANCE BRACED ITSELF FOR POSSIBLE TERRORIST REPRISALS LAST NIGHT AFTER THE ARREST IN SUDAN AND OVERNIGHT EXTRADITION TO PARIS OF CARLOS, THE NOTORIOUS "JACKAL."** The Guardian Tue 16th Aug

in the area

		time^	left ft	right	header	inside/outside the area	open play	set piece
7.	Eric Cantona	22		*		*		*
8.	Paul Ince	80		*	*	*		

assist: Eric Cantona

manchester united v
QUEENS PARK RANGERS 2-0
>Old Trafford
>Saturday 20 August 1994 / 3.00pm

[Att: 43,214]

[Last season :2-1]

team lineups

home team
		rating
1.	Peter Schmeichel	8
12.	David May	7
4.	Steve Bruce	7
6.	Gary Pallister	7
3.	Denis Irwin	7
14.	Andrei Kanchelskis	7
8.	Paul Ince	8
9.	Brian McClair	7
5.	Lee Sharpe	7
10.	Mark Hughes	7
11.	Ryan Giggs	7

70 mins

on the bench
2.	Paul Parker	7
25.	Kevin Pilkington	
16.	Roy Keane	7

70 mins

visitors
1.	Tony Roberts
2.	David Bardsley
4.	Steve Yates
6.	Alan McDonald
3.	Clive Wilson
7.	Andy Impey
14.	Simon Barker
8.	Ian Holloway
11.	Trevor Sinclair
9.	Les Ferdinand
20.	Kevin Gallen

82 mins · 86 mins

on the bench
12.	Gary Penrice
13.	Sieb Dykstra
16.	Danny Maddix

The flying winger takes off

bite this!

"Manchester United's quest for a third consecutive championship was eventually launched, thanks to the muscular presence of Mark Hughes..." **THE SUNDAY TELEGRAPH**

"Up to half-time United had huffed and puffed but had struggled to blow the Rangers house down until Hughes weighed in with another show-piece goal." **SUNDAY MIRROR**

"Wilson had been allocated the task of marking United's Ukrainian winger. His mission - which proved to be of the kamikaze variety - ended with Wilson looking close to tears as he departed the field after seven minutes." **THE OBSERVER**

"Queens Park Rangers are always welcome here at Old Trafford. They play good attacking football and there was certainly no bad feeling in the game, as the two sendings off seem to imply. It was played in a great spirit and even Gerry (Francis) and myself didn't fight!

Regarding Paul Parker and Clive Wilson, the only thing I would like to see happen with these new rules is consistency and the referees, after all, don't make the rules. They just have to impose them." **ALEX FERGUSON**

in the area

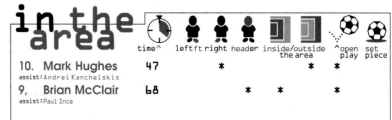

	time^	left ft	right	header	inside/outside the area		open play	set piece
10. Mark Hughes assist: Andrei Kanchelskis	47		*			*		*
9. Brian McClair assist: Paul Ince	68			*		*		*

word up

Two goals and two sendings off in the first home match of the season. The former were a result of persistence in trying to break down QPR's fragile defence. The latter is a result of the referee's new rulings handed down by the F.A. after this summer's World Cup competition.

Paul Parker and **Clive Wilson** were the two players to be dismissed but this was not a dirty game. **Cantona**, serving a two-match suspension for his pre-season red card, was not able to provide his usual service. But his modest team-mates were more than ready and able to provide the fans with the entertainment and three points that they required.

Kanchelskis racing down the right wing caused problems for **Wilson** who was the first to be walking towards the tunnel for an early bath. Once he had gone United not-so-much cruised to their victory, but merely sailed through the stormy seas QPR provided. This match never reached gale force, but Rangers certainly did make it a white water ride for the supporters.

Paul Ince lines up a right footer

John Peters

Choccy gets all the praise

John Peters

in the book

Referee: D Gallagher, Banbury
Rating: 7
Bookings:
▌ Parker
▌ Wilson

stats

united		QPR
	shots/headers on target	
5		5
	shots/headers off target	
9		4
	free kicks	
13		6
	caught offside	
1		3
	corners	
6		2
5	fouls	10

>time*line*

* **Wed 17th Aug** A FIFA representative has stated that communication between linesmen and referees needs to be improved. He suggests that two-way radios may be the answer as that system has been successful in Switzerland.

> **MENTALLY-ILL PATIENTS HAVE KILLED AT LEAST 33 INNOCENT PEOPLE SINCE NEW RULES FREEING THEM INTO THE COMMUNITY**
> DAILY EXPRESS Wed 17th Aug

* **Thu 18th Aug**

> **INFLATION HITS 27-YEAR LOW**
> THE INDEPENDENT Thur 18th Aug

* **Fri 19th Aug** Paul Ince signs a new three-year contract thought to be worth £7,500 per week.

> **STREET CHAOS AS BET IS HIT BY BUG**
> DAILY STAR Fri 19th Aug

* **Sat 20th Aug** Jürgen Klinsmann scores his first Premiership goal as the season gets underway. However a clash of heads means he is stretchered off the pitch unconscious during the game.

* Brian Horton says he doesn't blame the referee for sending off Uwe Rosler for dissent.

* Liverpool kick-start their new season by beating newly promoted Palace 6-1.

John Peters

ucial support om raving Reds

* NOTTS FOREST
> City Ground

> Monday 22 August 1994/ 8.00pm

[Att: 22,702]

v manchester united: **1-1**

team lineups

home team
1. Mark Crossley
2. Des Lyttle
3. Stuart Pearce
4. Colin Cooper
5. Steve Chettle
7. David Phillips
8. Scott Gemmill
10. Stan Collymore
11. Steve Stone
14. Ian Woan
22. Bryan Roy

on the bench _60 mins_
12. Jason Lee
23. Malcolm Rigby
9. Lars Bohinen

visitors
		rating
1.	Peter Schmeichel	7
12.	David May	7
4.	Steve Bruce	8
6.	Gary Pallister	8
3.	Denis Irwin	8
14.	Andrei Kanchelskis	9
8.	Paul Ince	9
9.	Brian McClair	9
5.	Lee Sharpe	7
10.	Mark Hughes	8
11.	Ryan Giggs	7

on the bench _55 mins_
2.	Paul Parker	
25.	Kevin Pilkington	
16.	Roy Keane	7

Bruce **head-to-head with** Collymore

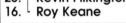

Kanchelskis **forces his way to the ball**

bite ● this!

"It required all of Paul Ince's resolve, Brian McClair's cunning, Roy Keane's hustle and Steve Bruce's bravery to prevent Forest inflicting a defeat which would have given the rest of England heart."
DAILY MAIL

"During every respite from the Forest onslaught, United themselves came up with a collection of stirring, enterprising raids." **DAILY MIRROR**

"As if they didn't know it by now, every match that Manchester United play away from Old Trafford this season will be a cup final for the opposition. That will make it desperately hard for them to lift the Championship for a third successive time, especially if Eric Cantona is not in the thick of things." **TODAY**

"Games of this heady quality are being produced partly because of the new directives on the laws which so protect the good player..."
DAILY EXPRESS

"Amazing Andrei Kanchelskis celebrated the end of his international war by scoring what is already a red-hot bet for goal of the season."
DAILY STAR

"The players showed their desire for success tonight but I'm not really happy to have come away from the City Ground with one point.
I just thought we had enough of the ball to have got a little more from the game and, after all, it was just our finishing touch that let us down. Also, Forest are so dangerous on the counter-attack that we always had to take care.
For Nottingham Forest, Stan Collymore gave us lots of trouble on the break, so as I said before, we had to be careful in defence."
ALEX FERGUSON

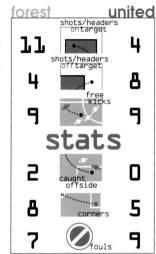

The big punch-up!

stats

forest		united
11	shots/headers on target	4
4	shots/headers off target	8
9	free kicks	9
2	caught offside	0
8	corners	5
7	fouls	9

>timeline

* **Sun 21st Aug** Newcastle beat Leicester 3-1 at Filbert Street. Bad news for Peter Beardsley, as he suffers a relapse of last year's cheek bone injury.

> **DI QUIZZED OVER PEST CALLS TO CHARLES' PAL**
> SUNDAY MIRROR Sun 21st Aug

* **Mon 22nd Aug** Reports say Bryan Robson wants to sign Gary Lineker to enhance Middlesbrough's promotion prospects.

> Paul Gascoigne admits he cannot take the pressure: "I'm a young lad and I shouldn't have to cope with it."

> **PRINCESS DIANA CLAIMED LAST NIGHT SHE HAD BEEN "FRAMED" OVER ALLEGATIONS THAT SHE IS A PHONE PEST**
> DAILY MIRROR Mon 22nd Aug

* **Tues 23rd Aug** Chris Sutton scores his first goal for Blackburn as they beat Leicester 3-0.

> **BOB FOR ITV JOB - BEEB SOCCER PRESENTER BOB WILSON IS SET TO JOIN ITV IN A BIG-MONEY TRANSFER DEAL**
> DAILY STAR Tues 23rd Aug

word up

The City ground offers little confidence to United. Not only did Forest recently have a reputation of being United's bogey team, now they have **Brian Roy** and **Stan Collymore**.

Stan the Man provided much of the entertainment for the evening's viewers both at the ground and those in their armchairs at home. He also provided Forest with their only goal of this 1-1 draw. **United's** supplier was the Ukrainian, **Andrei**

Kanchelskis, whose powerhouse right foot shot nearly burst the back of Forest's net.

Cantona's absence was conspicuous. Movement and passing between United players never seemed to connect. And when **Roy Keane** came on late in the second half, his only achievement was getting booked. In that atmosphere, though, the referee had to be seen to take action for what he judged an over-zealous challenge.

in the area

	time^	left ft right	header	inside/outside the area	^open play	set piece

14. Andrei Kanchelskis 22 — right * header * ^open play *
assist: Lee Sharpe

10. Stan Collymore. 26

in the book

Referee:
A Wilkie,
Chester-le-Street
Rating: 8
Bookings:
Keane,
Lyttle,
Woan,
Roy

Schmeichel holds a Collymore powerstrike

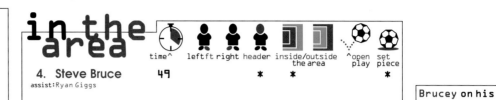

✳TOTTENHAM HOTSPUR : 0-1

> White Hart Lane   v manchester united:

[Att:24,502]

[Last season :0-1]

team lineups

home team

13.	Ian Walker
22.	David Kerslake
23.	Sol Campbell
14.	Stuart Nethercott
3.	Justin Edinburgh
9.	Darren Anderton
5.	Colin Calderwood
8.	Ilie Dumitrescu
7.	Nick Barmby
18.	Jürgen Klinsmann
10.	Teddy Sheringham

57mins

on the bench

16.	Micky Hazard
30.	Chris Day
6.	Gary Mabbutt

visitors

rating

1.	Peter Schmeichel	10
12.	David May	8
4.	Steve Bruce	8
6.	Gary Pallister	8
3.	Denis Irwin	8
14.	Andrei Kanchelskis	7
8.	Paul Ince	9
9.	Brian McClair	8
5.	Lee Sharpe	7
10.	Mark Hughes	8
11.	Ryan Giggs	7

on the bench

19.	Nicky Butt
25.	Kevin Pilkington
20.	Dion Dublin

in the area

	time^	left ft	right	header	inside/outside the area	^open play	set piece
4. Steve Bruce	49				* *		*

assist: Ryan Giggs

Brucey on his way to salute United's fans

stats

tottenham		united
8	shots/headers on target	4
2	shots/headers off target	8
16	free kicks	10
6	caught offside	4
7	corners	5
4	fouls	12

Sharpey gets past likely lad Anderton

bite this!

in the book

Referee:
K Burge, Tonypandy
Rating: 6
Bookings:
Giggs, Anderton

word up

Jürgen Klinsmann 0
Peter Schmeichel 1

The Great Dane once again saved United's bacon by saving a penalty from the German striker. **Schmeichel** was on top form pulling off at least three world-class saves as he helped United onto their first away Premier league victory of the season.

Tottenham's new formation - either due to their lack of quality defenders or excess of quality strikers - was never going to work against arguably the best defence in the league.

Paul Ince was able to roam in the middle of the pitch as Spurs lifted the ball into the air consistently trying to pick out a white shirt.

It was a supreme display of goalkeeping for one team and a deplorable display for the other, United's goal coming as an indirect result of **Ian Walker's** mishap. He tripped and fell in the six-yard box, leaving a confused Tottenham defence unable to cope with the looping goal-bound header by **Bruce**.

Calderwood holds Sparky – but not for long

manchester united v
WIMBLEDON

>Wednesday 31 August / 8.00pm

>Old Trafford

[Att:43.440]

3-0

[Last season :3-1

team lineups

home team

		rating
1.	Peter Schmeichel	7
12.	David May	7
4.	Steve Bruce	8
6.	Gary Pallister	7
3.	Denis Irwin	8
14.	Andrei Kanchelskis	7
7.	Eric Cantona	9
9.	Brian McClair	8
5.	Lee Sharpe	7
10.	Mark Hughes	8
11.	Ryan Giggs	8

on the bench

20.	Dion Dublin
25.	Kevin Pilkington
19.	Nicky Butt

visitors

1.	Hans Segers
2.	Warren Barton
12.	Gary Elkins
4.	Vinnie Jones
18.	Steve Talboys
6.	Scott Fitzgerald
26.	Neal Ardley
19.	Stewart Castledine
25.	Mick Harford
16.	Alan Kimble
20.	Marcus Gayle

on the bench

7.	Andy Clarke
21.	Chris Perry
23.	Neil Sullivan

Up where the air is clear

word up

The prospect of Wimbledon hardly sets the red heart racing, but the sight of **Eric** in a United shirt certainly does. Another capacity crowd welcomed the French genius back from suspension and his presence was immediately felt on the lush Old Trafford pitch.

With **Holdsworth**, **Earle** and the Liverpool-bound **Scales** missing, the Dons were no match for the Champions, but they nearly managed to keep the score goaless until half-time. **Eric** had other ideas, though, and when **he powerfully headed home our first goal, connecting with an inch perfect cross from the left foot of Giggs,** he re-assured United's loyal support that he was back in business.

The second half entertained an enthusiastic crowd, who created an exceptional atmosphere. They got their reward when **McClair** grabbed a second for the reds with nine minutes to play, then **Giggs** smashed home a terrific goal two minutes before time to round off a happy night for all.

in the book
Referee:
T Holbrook,
Walsall
Rating: 7

bite e this!

"Late goals by Brian McClair and Ryan Giggs ensured that United enjoyed the comfortable victory their undoubted supremacy merited..."
DAILY TELEGRAPH

"We will never be able to compete with the likes of United. Thank God we don't have to play them every week."
JOE KINNEAR

"The sensation when the whistle went was one of having stepped off the latest theme park fairground ride. Breath was short and legs were wobbly, as this roller coaster of a performance by United swooped and dashed and accelerated to the finish."
THE GUARDIAN

"United had enjoyed immense superiority of possession, without turning chances and half-chances into goals, when Cantona took aim and fired with deadly accuracy in the 40th minute." **TODAY**

"I'm pleased with the performance tonight and it was a good result. Some of the football that the team produced was excellent. We created a lot of good chances but Hans Segers has made four or five unbelievable saves. Cantona's performance was incredible and he scored a fabulous goal but, most importantly, our team spirit showed tonight with both Keane and Ince out injured. Choccy and Lee Sharpe came in for them and both contributed really well. It was a good team performance and Eric gives us that little bit extra."
ALEX FERGUSON

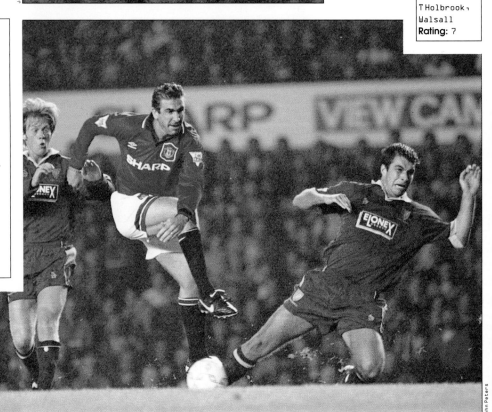

Cantona **misses due to a cunning tackle**

The 84th minute comes at last!

>time*line*

* **Sun 28th Aug** The second hat-trick of the weekend is scored by Robbie Fowler in just four minutes. Arsenal are beaten 3-0 by Liverpool.

> **SAD SOCCER STAR PAUL GASCOIGNE COMPLAINS HE IS HAVING A HARDER TIME THAN PRINCESS DIANA.**
Sunday Mirror Sun 28th Augp

* **Mon 29th Aug** Everton are set to buy Karl Heinz Reidle for £3 million.

> **ALBERT SQUARE TOLD TO LIFT THE GLOOM**
Daily Star Mon 29th Aug

* **Tues 30th Aug** Reading beat Stoke City 4-0. The match will be remembered mainly for its refereeing – nine yellow cards and two red were shown by Graham Pooley.

> **IT'S TIME FOR IRA TRUCE, SAYS ADAMS**
Daily Telegraph Tues 30th Aug

in the area

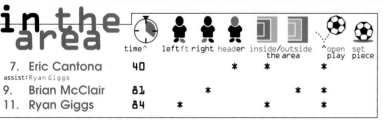

		time^	left ft	right	header	inside/outside the area	^open play	set piece
7.	Eric Cantona	40			*	*	*	
	assist: Ryan Giggs							
9.	Brian McClair	81		*			*	*
11.	Ryan Giggs	84	*			*		*

The next recipient is eagerly awaited

united   wimbledon

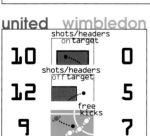

united		wimbledon
10	shots/headers on target	0
12	shots/headers off target	5
9	free kicks	7
stats		
6	caught offside	3
10	corners	2
4	fouls	3

*PETER SCHMEICHEL
> manchester united
& denmark
[Squad number: **1**]

>goalkeeper

Alan Cozzi

personal file

born: Gladsaxe, 18/11/63
height: 6'4" weight: 11st 4lb
international team: Denmark
signed pro for United: 6/8/91
transfer fee: £550,000
United league debut : 17/08/91 v Notts County (h)

appearances/goals

appearances / apps as sub / goals	Premier League (apps - goals)	FA Cup	Coca Cola Cup	European Cup	Total (apps - goals)	left ft	right	header	inside/outside the area	open play	set piece	assists	scoring rate	performance rating average
Steve Bruce	4 - 1	- -	- -	- -	4 - 1			1	1		1		25%	7.8
Ryan Giggs	4 - 1	- -	- -	- -	4 - 1	1			1	1		2	25%	7.3
Mark Hughes	4 - 1	- -	- -	- -	4 - 1		1		1	1			25%	7.8
Denis Irwin	4 -	- -	- -	- -	4 -								-%	7.8
Andrei Kanchelskis	4 - 1	- -	- -	- -	4 - 1		1		1	1		1	25%	7.5
David May	4 -	- -	- -	- -	4 -								-%	5.8
Brian McClair	4 - 2	- -	- -	- -	4 - 2	1	1	1	1	2			-%	8.0
Gary Pallister	4 -	- -	- -	- -	4 -								-%	7.5
Peter Schmeichel	4 -	- -	- -	- -	4 -								-%	8.0
Lee Sharpe	4 -	- -	- -	- -	4 -							1	-%	7.0
Paul Ince	3 -	- -	- -	- -	3 -							1	-%	8.7
Eric Cantona	1 - 1	- -	- -	- -	1 - 1		1		1	1			100%	9.0
Roy Keane	- 2	- -	- -	- -	- 2								-%	7.0
Paul Parker	- 1	- -	- -	- -	- 1								-%	7.0

Manchester United win the 1994 Charity Shield 2-0 against Blackburn Rovers

league table

FA Carling Premiership 31 August 94

	P	W	D	L	F	A	Pts
Newcastle United	4	4	0	0	15	3	12
Manchester United	4	3	1	0	7	1	10
Nottingham Forest	4	3	1	0	5	2	10
Liverpool	3	3	0	0	11	1	9
Chelsea	3	3	0	0	8	2	9
Tottenham Hotspur	4	3	0	1	9	6	9
Blackburn Rovers	4	2	2	0	8	5	8
Leeds United	3	1	1	1	3	3	4
Manchester City	4	2	0	2	7	6	6
Aston Villa	4	1	3	0	5	4	6
Norwich City	4	1	2	1	2	5	5
Sheffield Wednesday	4	1	1	2	6	7	4
Arsenal	4	1	1	2	3	4	4
QPR	4	1	1	2	5	7	4
Ipswich Town	4	1	1	2	4	6	4
Wimbledon	4	0	2	2	3	4	2
Crystal Palace	4	0	2	2	3	9	2
Southampton	4	0	2	2	3	9	2
Everton	4	0	1	3	4	10	1
Leicester City	4	0	1	3	2	8	1
West Ham United	4	0	1	3	7	7	1
Coventry City	4	0	1	3	1	10	1

* player of the month
Eric Cantona
performance rating average: 9.0

time split

	0-10 mins	11-20 mins	21-30 mins	31-40 mins	41-50 mins	51-60 mins	61-70 mins	71-80 mins	81-90 mins
Brian McClair	.	.	.	.	.	.	1	.	.
Steve Bruce	.	.	.	1	.	.	.	.	.
Eric Cantona	.	.	1	.	.	.	.	.	.
Ryan Giggs	.	.	.	.	.	.	.	.	.
Mark Hughes	.	.	.	.	.	.	.	.	.
Andrei Kanchelskis	.	.	1	.	.	.	.	.	.
TOTAL SCORED	.	.	1	2	.	1	.	.	2
TOTAL CONCEDED	.	.	1	.	.	.	.	.	.

summary

	P	W	D	L	F	A
Premier League	4	3	1	-	7	1
Total	4	3	1	-	7	1

notes

players must have played a minimum of three games in the month concerned to qualify for average performance ratings or scoring rate percentages; performance ratings are only awarded to players having played ten minutes or more in one match

>Sunday 11 September 1994 / 4.00 pm
[Att: 39,396]

LEEDS UNITED
>Elland Road v manchester united: **2-1**

[Last season :0-2]

team lineups

home team
1. John Lukic
2. Gary Kelly
6. David Wetherall
4. Carlton Palmer
15. Nigel Worthington
10. Gary McAllister
11. Gary Speed
14. David White
19. Noel Whelan
26. Phil Masinga — 30mins
8. Rod Wallace — 87mins

on the bench
9. Brian Deane
13. Mark Beeney
5. Chris Fairclough

rating

visitors
1. Peter Schmeichel — 6
12. David May — 6
3. Denis Irwin — 6
4. Steve Bruce — 7
14. Andrei Kanchelskis — 7
6. Gary Pallister — 7
7. Eric Cantona — 7
8. Paul Ince — 8
9. Brian McClair — 6
10. Mark Hughes — 7
11. Ryan Giggs — 6 — 63mins

on the bench
5. Lee Sharpe — 7 — 63mins
25. Kevin Pilkington
19. Nicky Butt — 7

John Peters

stats

leeds		united
5	shots/headers on target	6
2	shots/headers off target	10
16	free kicks	24
7	caught offside	0
5	corners	8
18	fouls	11

Wetherall takes a ride on McAllister to stop Hughesie's header

in the book
Referee: D Elleray, Harrow
Rating: 7
Bookings: May, Kelly, Palmer, Speed, Whelan, Masinga, Deane

word up

Following an eleven-day break from action due to international duty, Manchester United made their return to Premiership football at a noisy Elland Road. Leeds had not beaten the Champions in their previous twelve encounters, so few of our 1,700 fans contemplated the prospect of defeat. They certainly didn't foresee the home side taking the lead as they did after only 13 minutes.

Wetherall had the finishing touch, shooting through a crowded goalmouth, leaving **Schmeichel** un-sighted. From then on, Leeds continued to threaten **Schmeichel's** near-perfect record in the United goal throughout the first half. Disaster struck shortly after the break when Deane added a second goal for Leeds, following a lapse in the United defence. Backed by a passionate following, United refused to let their heads drop and when awarded a controversial penalty, **Cantona** coolly slotted the ball home in front of the new 'Revie Stand'.

The last fifteen minutes were frantic as the Reds pushed for an equaliser and a dream comeback was nearly complete when a **Bruce** header skimmed the Leeds crossbar.

It was definitely a case of unlucky 13 for the Reds and when the man in green finally blew the whistle, you could have thought that Leeds had won the World Cup Final, but I suppose all good things have to come to an end.

Choccy is shadowed by Giggs as he keeps an eye on the action

bite this!

"Cantona calmly converted a 74th-minute penalty given by referee David Elleray for a foul on Ince by Deane which was clearly - as Elleray himself admitted afterwards - committed way outside the box. The game became a siege, and Bruce almost levelled with a header, but Leeds would not be denied."

THE INDEPENDENT

"...Fergie's team actually got off lightly. They could have been three down by the interval and Leeds's winning margin was halved by a scandalous decision by referee David Elleray."

DAILY MIRROR

"The only way to beat them is to go for all-out attack."

CARLTON PALMER

"Palmer's dedicated marking of Hughes lay at the heart of Leeds's victory. Not until the 19-year-old Butt came on for the last 27 minutes did the Champions' momentum pick up." **THE GUARDIAN**

"For 13 years Manchester United had gone marching across the Pennines to pluck a petal from the white rose of Leeds. Yesterday all they got for their efforts was a crown of thorns." **DAILY EXPRESS**

"We wasted some chances today, especially in the last third of the pitch, and we can have no complaints about the result. Leeds were that little bit stronger and fought for their victory but our players also showed their pride, in particular for the last fifteen minutes of the second half. Mark Hughes and Paul Ince were two players that showed their determination to get a result. And although the result is a disappointment, the players have shown in the past that they can recover from setbacks and they will do it again. They'll be all right by Wednesday for the match against Gothenburg."

ALEX FERGUSON

White tries to keep a hold on Cantona

Choccy skilfully evades the challenge from Leeds

>time*line*

* **Thu 8th Sep** Joe Jordan quits from his position as Stoke's manager.

* **Fri 9th Sep** PSV Eindhoven lose two players in the same day to English clubs, Tottenham and Sheffield Wednesday. World cup star Gheorge Popescu joins Spurs for £2.9 million whilst Trevor Francis signs Klas Ingesson for £2 million.

* Dion Dublin moves to Coventry for £2 million from United.

> **CHARLES NUDE SNAP FURY**
Daily Star Fri 9th Sep

* **Sat 10th Aug**
> **MONT BLANC AVALANCHE KILLS STUDENT**
The Times Sat 10th Aug

* **Sun 11th Aug** FIFA referee David Elleray admits that Manchester United's penalty which was awarded at Elland Road was a mistake.

* Jordi Cruyff makes his debut for Barcelona.

in the area

		time^	left ft right	header	inside/outside the area	^open play	set piece
7.	Eric Cantona	74	*		*		*
6.	David Wetherall	13					
9.	Brian Deane	49					

manchester united v
IFK GOTHENBURG
>Old Trafford
4-2

>Wednesday 14 September 1994 / 8.00pm   [Att: 43,440]

team lineups

home team

		rating
1.	Peter Schmeichel	5
2.	David May	5
3.	Denis Irwin	6
4.	Steve Bruce	6
5.	Lee Sharpe	6
6.	Gary Pallister	6
7.	Andrei Kanchelskis	7
8.	Paul Ince	8
9.	Nicky Butt	7
10.	Mark Hughes	6
11.	Ryan Giggs	6

on the bench

12.	Gary Neville
13.	Kevin Pilkington
14.	Paul Scholes
15.	David Beckham
15.	Simon Davies

visitors

1.	Thomas Ravelli
2.	Pontus Kamark
3.	Magnus Johansson
4.	Joachim Bjorklund
5.	Mikael Nilsson
6.	Mikael Martinsson
7.	Magnus Erlingmark
8.	Stefan Lindqvist
9.	Jesper Blomqvist
10.	Jonas Olsson
11.	Stefan Pettersson

on the bench

12.	Dick Last
13.	Johan Anegrund
14.	Stefan Rehn
15.	Patrick Bengtsson
16.	Magnus Gustavsson

44 mins

Ravelli spreads himself well to block May's shot

bite this!

"Butt did the simple things simply and never shirked a challenge, whether of his bottle, or mettle." **THE INDEPENDENT**

"…United – even without the suspended Cantona – possessed more mobility, more fleetness, more imagination." **THE TIMES**

"On a blood and thunder Euro night, Ince unleashed a terrific 30-yarder which was brushed against the bar by Gothenburg 'keeper Tomas Ravelli to set up a second goal for his best pal Ryan Giggs." **DAILY EXPRESS**

"Ince might not have the *je ne sais quoi* of Cantona, but he's got more bottle than a French vineyard." **TODAY**

"In 1968 it was the stunning ability of George Best that powered United to glory in this competition. Twenty-six years later, Giggs looks determined to take the European stage by storm." **DAILY STAR**

"That's just what I was hoping for, though scoring four goals was a little more than I'd anticipated. There was a positive display from both teams and that was bound to show in the scoreline.

We conceded the first goal at a time when, I thought, we were doing well and then after the ball had gone in I thought we recovered well and gave Gothenburg problems, mainly at corner kicks where there was a lot of movement and a good delivery of the ball.

I was especially pleased with the display in midfield- there was good discipline and Paul Ince really distinguished himself.

The players were asked a lot of questions about their character tonight and I thought they proved themselves." **ALEX FERGUSON**

word up

Following the recent success of the Scandinavian national sides, club sides from those cold Northern parts are now treated with more respect than a couple of years ago.

IFK Gothenburg have enjoyed good runs in European competitions for many years now and it was obvious that Fergie and his team had done all the preparation necessary for our first Champions' League game.

However, all the planning in the world couldn't have stopped Petterson putting the Swedes a goal up midway through the first half. The 250 Gothenburg fans at the back of the Main Stand went crazy, and even had the cheek to sing "You're not singin' anymore" in English to the United fans!

Giggs silenced them, though, when he levelled the score soon after smashing home a clearance from close range. The Reds took the lead early in the second half courtesy of a Kanchelskis volley which sped goal-wards through a crowd of players, past Ravelli and into the back of the IFK net.

The Swedes managed to pull another goal out of the bag almost immediately, but any ideas of nicking a point went out of the window when that man Giggs grabbed his second goal of the night. A Paul Ince shot had rebounded off the crossbar before the Welsh wizard followed up for United's third. Sharpe sealed a fine victory when he seized on a defensive error to add a fourth. More European nights like this will be welcomed by all.

in the book

Referee:
G Goethals,
Belgium
Rating: ?

Kamark and Martinsson close in on Giggs

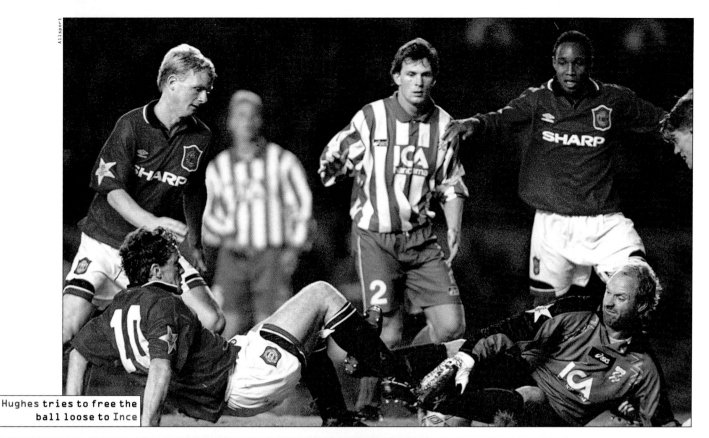

Hughes **tries to free the ball loose to** Ince

Heart-throbs in arms

united gothenberg

stats

	shots/headers on target	
11		4
	shots/headers off target	
4		3
	free kicks	
17		21
	caught offside	
6		3
	corners	
7		2
15	fouls	14

>timeline

* **Mon 12th Sep** The FA ask Ian Wright to explain what he meant when he called referee Robbie Hart "a muppet."

> **WATSON SUES FOR £1MILLION — MICHAEL WATSON IS TO SUE BOXING CHIEFS FOR THE BRAIN DAMAGE HE SUFFERED CAUSING HIS DISABILITY**
> The Sun Mon 12th Sep

* **Tue 13th Aug**

> **GANG MURDER WOMAN BOSS — BODY DUMPED IN LAY-BY AFTER WOOLWICH RAID**
> Daily Express Tue 13th Aug

* **Wed 14th Aug** George Graham is to complain about the pitch at the Arsenal v Omonia match after the players found it was littered with stones.

in the area

	time^	left ft	right	header	inside/outside the area		^open play	set piece
11. Ryan Giggs	33	*			*		*	
assist: Mark Hughes								
assist: Paul Ince	66	*			*		*	
7. Andrei Kanchelskis	48		*			*		*
5. Lee Sharpe	70	*			*		*	
assist: Andrei Kanchelskis								
11. Stefan Pettersson	27							
14. Stefan Rehn	50							

manchester united v
LIVERPOOL

>Saturday 17 September 1994 / 3.00pm

[Att:43,740]

> Old Trafford

2-0

[Last season :1-0]

team lineups

home team

		rating
1.	Peter Schmeichel	8
12.	David May	7
4.	Steve Bruce	7
6.	Gary Pallister	7
3.	Denis Irwin	7
14.	Andrei Kanchelskis	7
7.	Eric Cantona	7
8.	Paul Ince	9
5.	Lee Sharpe	7
10.	Mark Hughes	7
11.	Ryan Giggs	7

59 mins

on the bench
9.	Brian McClair	8
25.	Kevin Pilkington	
19.	Nicky Butt	

visitors

1.	David James
2.	Rob Jones
20.	Stig Inge Bjornebye
25.	Neil Ruddock
14.	Jan Molby
15.	Jamie Redknapp
17.	Steve McManaman
9.	Ian Rush
10.	John Barnes
23.	Robbie Fowler
12.	John Scales

71 mins

on the bench
6.	Phil Babb
13.	Michael Stensgaard
7.	Nigel Clough

Sharpey wins the ball on the follow-through

in the area

		time^	left ft	right	header	inside/outside the area	^open play	set piece
14.	Andrei Kanchelskis	71		*		*	*	
9.	Brian McClair	73		*		*		*

assist: Eric Cantona

Ruddock tests Ince's biceps

bite this!

"Before Babb could adjust to the electric pace of a game with enough edge to slice the Sunday roast, Scales handed United the lead with a reckless back-header."
SUNDAY EXPRESS

"United were suffering from a European Cup hangover and for long periods only the giant frame of goalkeeper Peter Schmeichel kept them in the game."
SUNDAY MIRROR

"Alex made a good decision and I made a bad one."
ROY EVANS

"...within three minutes United had claimed an undeserved triumph."
THE MAIL ON SUNDAY

"For Liverpool this was a classic case of snatching defeat from the jaws of victory. For Manchester United it was an important Premiership win, dredged out of a tumultuous contest in which they were often out-played and, dare one say it, occasionally out-classed by the team they have deposed as England's finest."
THE SUNDAY TELEGRAPH

"After a disappointing outcome on Sunday this is a brilliant result for us.

Liverpool, in the first half, had the upper hand, with both goalkeepers coming into action. And for the first twenty minutes in the second half they ran us all over the place – with Jan Molby starting to take control of the whole game. It was at that point I decided to take Mark Hughes off, who was having an unusually quiet game against Liverpool, and replace him with Brian McClair. From then on we did really well and got the result we wanted.

Our hope now is that Mark will get some treatment and return to training before the Galatasaray match."
ALEX FERGUSON

Rob Jones puts his foot on the ball as Bruce is held back

Hail Cantona!

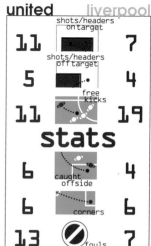

united		liverpool
	shots/headers on target	
11		7
	shots/headers off target	
5		4
	free kicks	
11		19

stats

6	caught offside	4
6	corners	6
13	fouls	7

in the book

Referee:
K Morton,
Bury St.
Edmunds
Rating: 6

Bookings:
May,
Bruce,
Cantona,
Jones,
Ruddock

word up

Liverpool's early-season form set up a classic showdown with United. Many had judged this one to be the big test for Roy Evans' team but few spoke of the importance this game held for United.

The side from the other end of the M62 **certainly impressed in the first half, with a neat passing game that caused so many problems for United.** Three times **Schmeichel** had to make flying saves to stop **Bjornebye, Ruddock** and **McManaman** grabbing the headlines, but the scoreline didn't change.

The action was fast and the atmosphere charged and it seemed that **United were starting to get the better of things when Hughes** was substituted for **McClair.**

Almost immediately United took the lead and **Kanchelskis** intercepted a back-header to **James** then calmly flicked the ball into the net. A minute later **McClair** played a neat pass with **Cantona** before steering the ball past **James.** Two-nil to the Champions and a terrific game.

>timeline

* **Thu 15th Sep** Aston Villa are beaten by a Denis Bergkamp spot-kick in the San Siro Stadium.

* **Fri 16th Sep**

> **SINN FEIN'S BROADCAST BAN TO END - GOVERNMENT MAY LIFT SIX-YEAR BROADCASTING BAN ON SINN FEIN**
The Daily Telegraph Fri 16th Sep

* **Sat 17th Sep** Blackburn Rovers are so scared of losing Alan Shearer to foreign clubs that they have given him a £2,000 per week rise. Alledigedly Shearer didn't even have to ask!

> **IT'S UP TO YOU - MAJOR PLEDGES REFERENDUM FOR ULSTER**
Daily Star Sat 17th Sep

* **Sun 18th Sep** Benfica coach Jorge undergoes surgery for a brain tumour. Concern is rising over increasing pressure on managers.

*PAUL PARKER
>defender

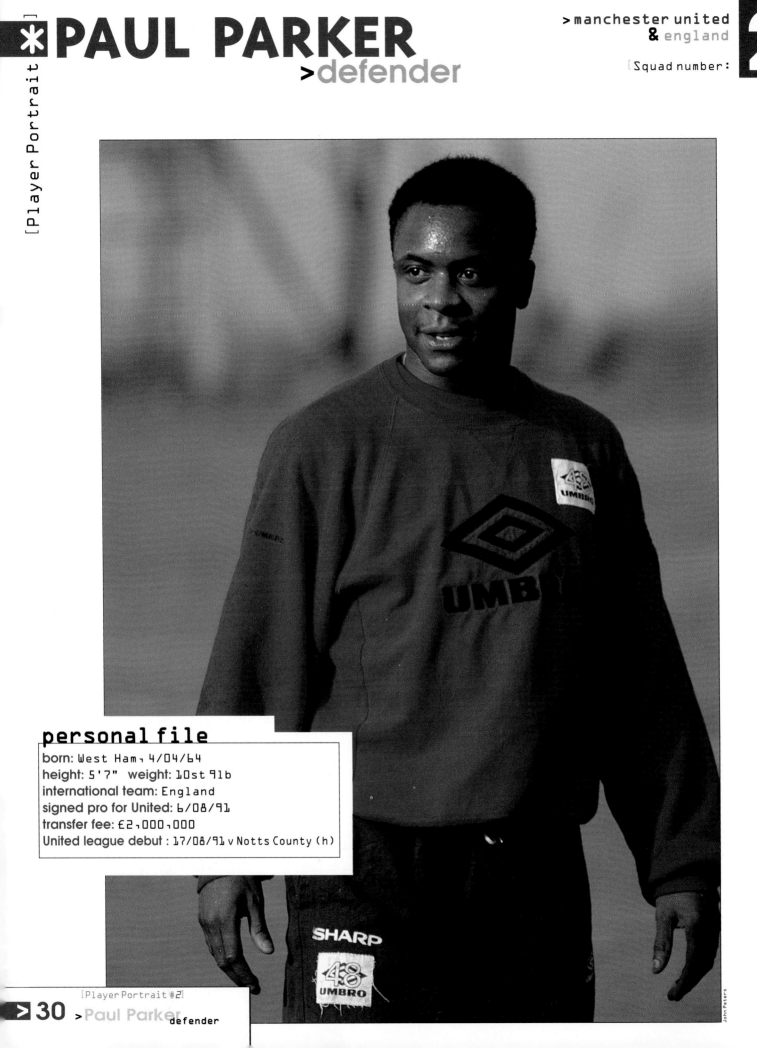

personal file

born: West Ham, 4/04/64
height: 5'7" weight: 10st 9lb
international team: England
signed pro for United: 6/08/91
transfer fee: £2,000,000
United league debut : 17/08/91 v Notts County (h)

John Peters

✳DENIS IRWIN
>defender

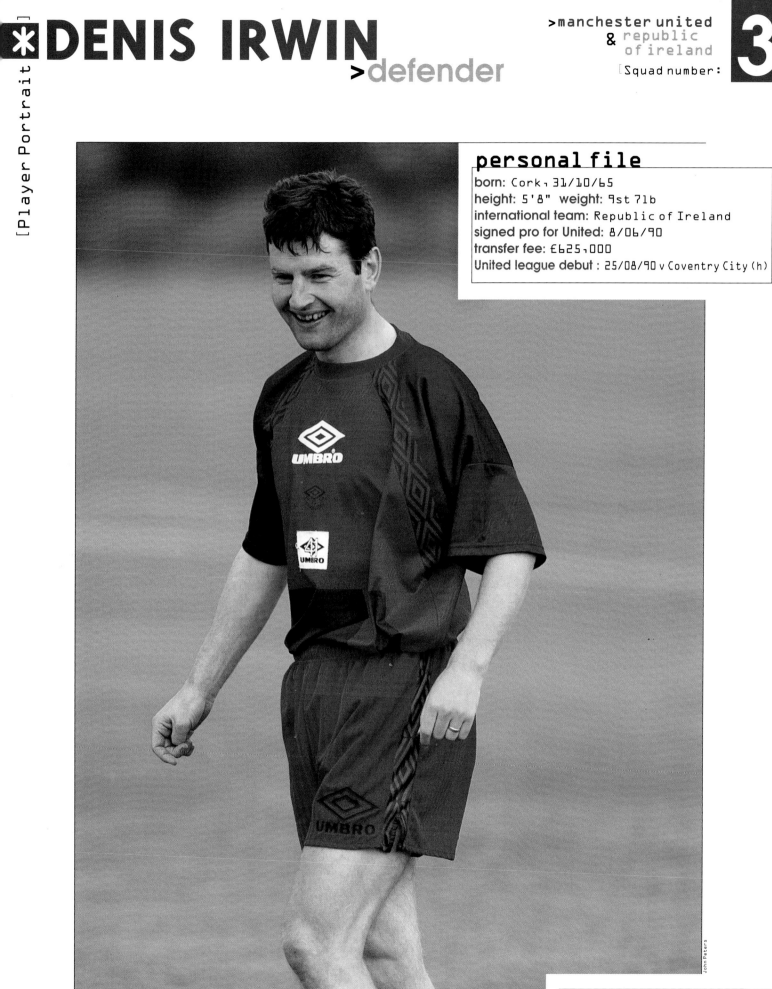

personal file

born: Cork, 31/10/65
height: 5'8" weight: 9st 7lb
international team: Republic of Ireland
signed pro for United: 8/06/90
transfer fee: £625,000
United league debut : 25/08/90 v Coventry City (h)

John Peters

PORT VALE
> Vale Park

v **manchester united:**

> Wednesday 21 September 1994 / 7.45pm

[Att: 18,605]

1-2

team lineups

home team

1. Paul Musselwhite
2. Bradley Sandeman
3. Allen Tankard
4. Andy Porter
5. Gareth Griffiths
6. Dean Glover
7. Kevin Kent
8. Robin Van der Laan
9. Martin Foyle
10. Lee Glover
11. Tony Naylor

70 mins

on the bench
12. Ray Walker
13. Arjan Van Heusden
14. Mark Burke

visitors

		rating
1.	Gary Walsh	7
2.	Gary Neville	7
3.	David May	8
4.	Roy Keane	7
5.	Denis Irwin	7
6.	Keith Gillespie	7
7.	David Beckham	7
8.	Nicky Butt	7
9.	Brian McClair	7
10.	Paul Scholes	8
11.	Simon Davies	7

75 mins

on the bench
12.	Lee Sharpe	
13.	Kevin Pilkington	
14.	John O'Kane	7

Scholes takes Beckham for a ride

stats

port vale		united
4	shots/headers on target	5
7	shots/headers off target	4
8	free kicks	10
3	caught offside	1
5	corners	8
7	fouls	7

Vale defenders run alongside Scholesy as he shoots

word up

Alex Ferguson ignored all the murmurings of punishment from the FA. He fielded his so-called under strength side at Vale Park tonight and watched them return from a goal down to take the lead.

"**Choccy** is their teacher" they shouted on the terraces tormenting the Vale fans who had apparently turned up to watch the likes of **Eric Cantona**. Instead they saw the likes of Scholes, the future of Manchester United, and what a future!

They played with as much fluency and skill as the first team do week in week out, and what's more these players can only get better. Some even said that this was the best football match they'd seen in ages. To the future!

bite ● this!

"They were the kids off the Old Trafford block that had produced nothing like it since Matt Busby's glorious era of England domination."

"In the end victory was achieved with such control and comfort, United's fans taunted Rudge's team with the powerful chorus: "They go to school in the morning."
THE SUN

"...as naked teenage ambition began to manifest itself in authoritative football in all sections of the field, United, with the barest minimum of fuss and effort, moved into the ascendancy." **THE DAILY TELEGRAPH**

"Paul Scholes proved yet again the old adage ' if they're good enough, they're old enough.'"

"David Beckham has vision and an incredible passing ability that United often lack, even in their awesome first-team line-up." **TODAY**

"Two goals from whizzkid Paul Scholes had Alex Ferguson

grinning all the way back to Old Trafford."

"...United were a class act and playing with confidence, skill and sheer determination produced a result they can brag about when they go back to cleaning the stars' boots."
DAILY STAR

"Regarding the controversy surrounding tonight's match - I think with the demand from internationals and the European game next week that people expected us to field the side that we did. That could incur the wrath of the authorities, but people expect us to do the right thing for Manchester United.

The inexperience of my side was an advantage tonight because they didn't seem to have a care and feared no-one. The boy Scholes took his goals superbly, and capped an excellent performance by the whole team."
ALEX FERGUSON

Choccy's **determined to catch the opposition unawares**

John Peters

in the area

	time ^	left ft	right	header	inside/outside the area	^open play	set piece
10. Paul Scholes	36		*		*	*	
assist: Simon Davies	53		*		*	*	
10. Lee Glover	7						

Gillespie cheekily robs Vale of the ball

>timeline

* **Tue 20th Sep** Gary Lineker, suffering from a toe injury, announces his retirement from football. He says, "It's frustrating not being able to perform as I used to."

> LIBS VOTE TO LEGALISE POT - PADDY ASHDOWN SUFFERED AN EMBARRASSING SETBACK LAST NIGHT AS THE LIBERAL DEMOCRATS VOTED TO LEGALISE CANNABIS
Daily Express Tue 20th Sep

* **Wed 21st Sep** Manchester United beat Port Vale 2-1 amidst controversy for fielding a so-called 'under-strength' side.

> SLEEP LITTLE ANGEL, SLEEP - ABANDONED BABY WHO HAD BEEN SMOTHERED DIED WITHIN A MONTH OF HER BIRTH
Daily Mirror Wed 21st Sep

*IPSWICH TOWN
> Saturday 24 September / 3.00pm

> Portman Road

v manchester united: [Att: 22,559] **3-2**

[Last season : 1-2]

team lineups

home team
1.	Craig Forrest	
19.	Frank Yallop	
6.	David Linighan	
5.	John Wark	
8.	Gavin Johnson	
4.	Paul Mason	
7.	Geraint Williams	
18.	Steve Palmer	
14.	Steve Sedgley	89 mins
12.	Claus Thompsen	
24.	Adrian Paz	77 mins

on the bench
9.	Bontcho Guentchev	
13.	Clive Baker	
24.	Simon Milton	

visitors
		rating
13.	Gary Walsh	7
3.	Denis Irwin	7
4.	Steve Bruce	7
6.	Gary Pallister	7
16.	Roy Keane	8
14.	Andrei Kanchelskis	7
8.	Paul Ince	7
5.	Lee Sharpe	6
9.	Brian McClair	7
7.	Eric Cantona	7	62 mins
11.	Ryan Giggs	7	85 mins

on the bench
24.	Paul Scholes	7
25.	Kevin Pilkington	
19.	Nicky Butt	

in the book

Referee:
P Jones, Loughborough
Rating: 6

Bookings:
Irwin, Keane, Palmer, Sedgley

Yallop fails to stop young Lee Sharpe from heading the ball goal-bound

stats

ipswich		united
4	shots/headers on target	12
1	shots/headers off target	7
10	free kicks	15
10	caught offside	3
4	corners	19
8	fouls	7

first aid box

> John Wark required stitches to head

John Peters

Roy's in possession, with Sedgley breathing down his neck

An easy tap-in for Eric thanks to help from Keano

word up

United dominated right from the kick-off in this clash against Suffolk's finest and several **Giggs** corners troubled the Ipswich defence early on. The home side, beaten convincingly at home by Bolton three days previous, had little to offer so it was surprising when they took the lead. **A further surprise was to follow when a second Ipswich goal rattled Schmeichel's net** to make the score 2-0 at half time.

United continued to attack in the second half, and when **Cantona** poached a goal from close range, everyone thought a comeback was on the cards. **Backed by a large passionate following, United grabbed a dramatic equaliser through man-of-the-moment Scholes** with ten minutes to play.

United's dominance up front left the defence exposed, and **Ipswich streaked away to score the winner much to the dismay of the players and fans**.

These things happen in football, and it was all credit to Ipswich for not giving in until the final whistle.

Giggsy weighs up his options

in the area

		time^	left ft	right	header	inside/outside the area	^open play	set piece
7.	**Eric Cantona**	71	*			*	*	
	assist: Roy Keane							
24.	**Paul Scholes**	73		*		*	*	
	assist: Roy Keane							
4.	**Paul Mason**	15						
		43						
14.	**Steve Sedgley**	80						

> Wednesday 28 September 1994 / 8.00pm

✳ GALATASARAY
v **manchester united:** 0-0

> Ali Sami Yen Stadium

[Att: 30,000]

team lineups

home team

1. Ghintaras Stauce
2. Gotz Mapeza
3. Korkmaz Bulent
4. Kaya Sedat
5. Korkmaz Mert
6. Kerinoghu Tugay
7. Alintas Yusuf
8. Sancakli Saffet
9. Sukur Hagn — 45 mins
10. Hamzaoglu Hamza
11. Turkiylmaz Kubilay — 76 mins

on the bench

12. Erdem Arif
13. Cakir Osman
14. Boiuglu Nezimi
15. Arsla Cihat
16. Buruk Okan

visitors

		rating
1.	Peter Schmeichel	9
2.	David May	7
3.	Lee Sharpe	7
4.	Steve Bruce	7
5.	Nicky Butt	7
6.	Gary Pallister	7
7.	Andrei Kanchelskis	7
8.	Paul Ince	8
9.	Roy Keane	7
10.	Mark Hughes	7
11.	Ryan Giggs	6

65 mins — on the bench

12.	Paul Parker	7
13.	Gary Walsh	
14.	Paul Scholes	
15.	David Beckham	
16.	Gary Neville	

John Peters

Manza and Hughesie tussle for supremacy

Incey with a shot destined for the woodwork

in the book

Referee:
M Van der Ende, Holland
Rating: 7
Bookings:
May, Kanchelskis, Hughes, Arif

word up

After what happened last year in Turkey, I don't think the supporters or the players were looking forward to this one. **The players were locked in their hotels like prisoners in cells, unable to walk outside the perimeter of the hotel grounds.** Once again the hate mob waited at the airport but luckily this time all seemed calm within the United camp.

When all around threatened chaos **the players kept their heads and returned home with a valuable point.**

The crowd seemed less threatening than last year. Or maybe it was us who didn't look as threatening to them. Whichever way, United managed to cope with all their emotions. This time their play was promising and **they were unlucky not to score on a couple of occasions.** Having said all that, a 0-0 draw here at the Ali Sami Yen is quite acceptable.

bite this!

"Manchester United sit proudly on top of their Champions' League today after returning to the scene of one of their darkest days."
DAILY EXPRESS

"Manchester United emerged from the 'hell' of Istanbul last night with a precious point against Galatasaray in their quest to win the European Cup." **TODAY**

"The United players strolled onto the field to see a huge banner proclaiming "Welcome to the Judgement Day". Far better than the warnings of "RIP Manchester United" on the previous occasion." **THE TIMES**

"Manchester United's European dream was full of Eastern promise last night.
DAILY STAR

"Alex Ferguson and his Manchester United heroes turned the hell-hole of Galatasaray into GalatasHooray last night.
DAILY MIRROR

"We showed a lot of composure tonight, and I felt we handled it better than last year. It was a good result for us tonight and Barcelona getting beat by Gothenburg means we have to get the eight points I originally thought we were going to need.

We have a couple of difficult European games coming up soon but we are looking forward to them; in fact we can't wait to play them.

Back to tonight's performance though, I felt it was a good, solid performance and the referee handled the situation very well. We didn't win but we're not too disapointed because we got a point in a difficult situation."
ALEX FERGUSON

Another Hughesie special

But just not to be...

galatasaray united

stats

4	shots/headers on target	4
2	shots/headers off target	2
13	free kicks	13
3	caught offside	1
5	corners	4
10	fouls	12

>timeline

* **Mon 26th Sep**
> CLARKE LAY DOWN TERMS FOR TAX CUTS - KENNETH CLARKE SIGNALS CUTS BEFORE THE NEXT GENERAL ELECTION CONFIRMING THE CABINET'S COMMITMENT TO LOWER TAXES
The Daily Telegraph Mon 26th Sep

* **Tue 27th Sep** Alex Ferguson demands discipline from United's players in order to help them get through their daunting trip to Turkey.
> FERGIE'S FURY AT TELLTALE FATHER - RIFT OVER MAJOR RON BOOK
The Sun Tue 27th Sep

* The part-time footballers of Trelleborgs threaten Rover's European dream by holding Blackburn to a 2-2 draw at Ewood Park.

* **Wed 28th Sep** Jack Walker boosts Blackburn's morale by offering more money for new players.
> DEAL REACHED TO SETTLE RAIL PAY DISPUTE - THE END OF THE SIGNALMEN'S FOUR- MONTH STRIKE
The Times Wed 28th Sep

* **Thu 29th Sep** Lou Macari returns to Stoke as manager.

* David Platt twists his ankle whilst playing for Sampdoria, leaving him a doubtful candidate for England's upcoming fixture.

*STEVE BRUCE
>defender

Sportshot

personal file

born: Newcastle-upon-Tyne, 31/12/60
height: 6'0" weight: 12st 6lb
international team: England
signed pro for United: 17/12/87
transfer fee: £800,000
United league debut : 19/12/87 v Portsmouth (a)

september 94

▽ appearances/goals →

appearances (apps as sub / goals)	Premier League			FA Cup	Coca Cola Cup	European Cup	Total		left ft	right	header	inside/outside the area	open play	set piece	assists	scoring rate	performance rating average
Steve Bruce	3	-	-	-	-	2	5	-	-	-	-	-	-	-	-	- %	6.8
Ryan Giggs	3	-	-	-	2	- 2	5	- 2	2	-	-	2	-	2	-	40%	6.4
Paul Ince	3	-	-	-	-	2	5	-	-	-	-	-	-	1	-	- %	8.0
Denis Irwin	3	-	-	1	-	2	5	-	-	-	-	-	-	-	-	- %	6.6
Andrei Kanchelskis	3	- 1	-	-	2 - 1	5 - 2	-	2	-	1	1	1	1	40%	7.0
David May	3	-	-	1	-	2	5	-	-	-	-	-	-	-	- %	6.2
Gary Pallister	3	-	-	-	-	2	5	-	-	-	-	-	-	-	-	- %	6.8
Mark Hughes	2	-	-	-	2	4	-	-	-	-	-	-	1	- %	6.8
Peter Schmeichel	2	-	-	-	2	4	-	-	-	-	-	-	-	7.0
Lee Sharpe	2	1	-	-	2	4	1 1	1	-	1	-	1	-	20%	6.6
Nicky Butt	-	2	-	-	-	3	2	-	-	-	-	-	- %	7.0
Eric Cantona	3	- 2	-	-	-	3 - 2	1 1	-	2	-	-	67%	7.0
Roy Keane	1	-	-	-	-	1	-	-	-	-	2	- %	7.3
Brian McClair	2	1 1	-	-	-	3 1 1	-	1	-	1	-	1	25%	7.0
Gary Walsh	1	-	-	-	-	2	-	-	-	-	- %	7.0
David Beckham	-	-	1	-	-	1	-	-	-	-	- %	7.0
Simon Davies	-	-	1	-	-	1	-	-	-	1	- %	7.0
Keith Gillespie	-	-	1	-	-	1	-	-	-	- %	7.0
Gary Neville	-	-	1	-	-	1	-	-	-	- %	0.0
Paul Scholes	-	1 1	-	1	-	1 1 3	-	2	1	3	-	3	100%	7.5
John O'Kane	-	-	-	1	-	1	-	-	-	- %	0.0
Paul Parker	-	-	-	1	-	1	-	-	-	- %	7.0

season to september 94

▽ appearances/goals →

appearances (apps as sub / goals)	Premier League			FA Cup	Coca Cola Cup	European Cup	Total		left ft	right	header	inside/outside the area	open play	set piece	assists	scoring rate	performance rating average
Steve Bruce	7	- 1	-	-	2	9 - 1	-	1	-	1	-	1	-	11%	7.2
Ryan Giggs	7	- 1	-	2	- 2	9 - 3	3	-	3	-	3	-	2	33%	6.8
Denis Irwin	7	-	-	1	-	1	9	-	-	-	-	- %	7.1
Andrei Kanchelskis	7	- 2	-	2 - 1	9 - 3	-	3	-	2	1	2	1	2	33%	7.2
David May	6	-	-	1	-	1	9	-	-	-	-	- %	6.0
Gary Pallister	7	-	-	-	2	9	-	-	-	-	- %	-
Mark Hughes	6	- 1	-	-	2	8 - 1	-	1	-	1	1	-	1	13%	7.3
Paul Ince	6	-	-	-	2	8	-	-	-	-	2	- %	8.3
Peter Schmeichel	6	-	-	-	2	8	-	-	-	- %	7.5
Lee Sharpe	6	1	-	1	2	8 2 1	1	-	1	-	1	-	11%	6.8
Brian McClair	6	1 3	-	1	-	7 1 3	-	2	1	2	1	3	38%	7.5
Eric Cantona	4	- 3	-	-	4 - 3	1 1	1	1	3	-	2	1	75%	7.5
Nicky Butt	-	2	-	1	2	3 2	-	-	-	- %	7.5
Roy Keane	1	2	-	1	-	3 2	-	-	-	2	- %	7.3
Gary Walsh	1	-	-	-	1	-	-	-	- %	7.0
David Beckham	-	-	1	-	1	-	-	-	- %	7.0
Simon Davies	-	-	1	-	1	-	-	-	- %	7.0
Keith Gillespie	-	-	1	-	1	-	-	-	- %	7.0
Gary Neville	-	-	1	-	1	-	-	-	- %	7.0
Paul Scholes	-	1 1	-	1 - 2	1 1 3	-	-	-	-	-	150%	7.5
John O'Kane	-	-	-	1	-	1	-	-	-	- %	7.0
Paul Parker	-	1	-	-	1	2	-	-	-	- %	7.0

league table

FA Carling Premiership 24 September 94

	P	W	D	L	F	A	Pts
Newcastle United	7	6	1	0	23	8	19
Blackburn Rovers	7	5	2	0	16	3	17
Nottingham Forest	7	5	2	0	14	5	17
Manchester United	7	4	1	2	12	6	13
Chelsea	6	4	0	2	12	8	12
Liverpool	6	3	2	1	12	4	11
Manchester City	7	3	2	2	11	8	11
Leeds United	6	3	1	2	8	7	10
Aston Villa	7	2	3	2	8	8	9
Wimbledon	7	3	0	4	12	15	9
Norwich City	7	2	3	2	3	5	9
Tottenham Hotspur	7	3	0	4	12	15	9
Southampton	7	2	3	2	9	12	9
Ipswich Town	7	2	1	4	8	12	7
QPR	7	1	3	3	9	12	6
Arsenal	7	1	3	3	5	7	5
Sheffield Wednesday	6	1	2	3	8	12	5
Leicester City	7	1	2	4	7	12	5
West Ham United	6	1	2	3	2	7	5
Coventry City	7	1	2	4	6	9	5
Crystal Palace	7	1	1	5	4	11	4
Everton	7	0	3	4	7	16	3

* player of the month
Paul Ince
performance rating average: **8.0**

⏱ time split

	0-10 mins	11-20 mins	21-30 mins	31-40 mins	41-50 mins	51-60 mins	61-70 mins	71-80 mins	81-90 mins
Eric Cantona				1				2	
Ryan Giggs				1		1		1	
Andrei Kanchelskis		1		1		1			
Brian McClair			1				1		
Paul Scholes			1			1		1	
Steve Bruce				1					
Mark Hughes						1			
Lee Sharpe						1			
TOTAL SCORED	-	-	1	3	3	2	2	5	2
TOTAL CONCEDED	1	2	2	-	2	-	-	2	-

summary

	P	W	D	L	F	A
Premier League	7	4	1	2	12	6
Coca Cola Cup	1	1	-	-	2	1
European Cup	2	1	1	-	4	2
Total	10	6	2	2	18	9

notes

players must have played a minimum of three games in the month concerned to qualify for average performance ratings or scoring rate percentages; performance ratings are only awarded to players having played ten minutes or more in one match

manchester united v
EVERTON
> Saturday 1 October 1994 / 3.00pm > Old Trafford

[Att: 43,803]

2-0

[Last season]
: 1-0

team lineups

home team | rating

1.	Peter Schmeichel	9
3.	Denis Irwin	7
4.	Steve Bruce	8
6.	Gary Pallister	7
12.	David May	7
14.	Andrei Kanchelskis	7
8.	Paul Ince	8
16.	Roy Keane	6
7.	Eric Cantona	8
10.	Mark Hughes	7
5.	Lee Sharpe	7

75 mins

on the bench
24.	Paul Scholes	
13.	Gary Walsh	
9.	Brian McClair	7

visitors

1.	Neville Southall
4.	Ian Snodin
5.	Dave Watson
26.	David Unsworth
16.	David Burrows
19.	Gary Rowett
8.	Graham Stuart
17.	Joe Parkinson
7.	Vinny Samways
3.	Andy Hinchcliffe
11.	Daniel Amokachi

86 mins

on the bench
18.	Stuart Barlow
2.	Matt Jackson
12.	Jason Kearton

word up

Struggling Everton came to Old Trafford, and like their neighbours from across Stanley Park, they left with nothing to show but a 2-0 defeat.

The Toffeemen started brightly and although *Schmeichel* was forced to make some important saves, **Pallister** and **Bruce** kept new signing Amokachi et al under close guard.

It was United who opened the scoring when **Sharpe** turned the ball past Southall from a defence splitting pass by **Ince** to make it 2-0 to the Champions. Another three points towards United's championship chase and three taken away to make Everton's slide to the bottom seem that little bit more imminent.

Cantona watches as the ball is booted clear

bite this!

"Action man Ince loaded the gun for Fergie's flying wingers Kanchelskis and Sharpe to bury a struggling Everton side who performed better than a team still searching for their first Premiership win." **THE PEOPLE**

"On a slow, staccato afternoon, its character dictated by the visitors' flooding of the midfield, the outcome was not settled when Sharpe scored two minutes from the final whistle." **THE OBSERVER**

"United had ridden uneasily on the back of a goal from Andrei Kanchelskis four minutes before the break, a searing, stooping header in full flight after Sharpe had picked him out with the kind of cross goals are made of." **SUNDAY EXPRESS**

"Lee Sharpe and Ryan Giggs may be brothers-in-arms as Manchester United continue their quest for European and domestic domination. But when it comes down to Old Trafford's treasured left wing spot, Sharpe becomes a one-man band determined to blow out his best mate in football." **DAILY MIRROR**

"It's good that we have returned from a European match to win in the Premiership. Those two goals gave us the points we needed to stay up near the top of the table especially with Newcastle winning.

We had to play people in to beat their off-side, I'm not sure how many times we got caught off-side to day but it must have been quite a few.

Schmeichel has helped us today especially with his saves from free-kicks . Kanchelskis got on the end of a wonderful cross supplied by Sharpe. It was a good goal – forwards love that kind of ball." **ALEX FERGUSON**

Best o'buddies

[Premier League #8]
> 1-10-94
Old Trafford
Everton
2-0
home * win

in the book

Referee:
G Poll,
Tilehurst
Rating: 5

Bookings:
Bruce,
Sharpe,
Snodin,
Burrows,
Amokachi,
Barlow

---

united   everton

shots/headers on target
6   6

shots/headers off target
4   3

free kicks
13   22

stats

caught offside
8   4

corners
7   3

fouls
9   14

Stuart and Sharpe get stuck in, leaving Keane on the ground

> timeline

* **Fri 31st Sep** Rumours abound that Old Trafford is to be extended when a third tier arrives, on the same day the club announce a £10.8 million profit.

* **Sat 1st Oct** Everton offer £4 million for Glasgow Rangers' Duncan Ferguson and Ian Durrant.

> **TOP TRAINER FOUND DEAD – MILLIONAIRE HORSE RACING TRAINER IS SHOT**
DAILY EXPRESS Sat 1st Oct

* **Sun 2nd Oct**

> **MARK THATCHER FACES $3 MILLION RACKETEERING LAWSUIT IN TEXAS**
THE OBSERVER Sun 2nd Oct

---

in the area

	time ^	left f right	header	inside/outside the area	^ open play	set piece
14. Andrei Kanchelskis	41		*	*	*	
assist: Lee Sharpe						
5. Lee Sharpe	88	*		*	*	
assist: Paul Ince						

manchester united v
PORT VALE
>Old Trafford

2-0

>Wednesday 5 October 1994 / 8.00pm
[Att: 31,615]

team lineups

home team

		rating
1.	Gary Walsh	8
2.	Chris Casper	7
3.	John O'Kane	7
4.	Nicky Butt	7
5.	David May	8
6.	Gary Pallister	7
7.	Keith Gillespie	7
8.	David Beckham	7
9.	Brian McClair	7
10.	Paul Scholes	7
11.	Simon Davies	7

64 mins

on the bench

12.	Graeme Tomlinson	7
13.	Kevin Pilkington	
14.	Gary Neville	7

76 mins

visitors

1.	Paul Musselwhite	
2.	Bradley Sandeman	
3.	Allen Tankard	
4.	Andy Porter	
5.	Neil Aspin	
6.	Dean Glover	
7.	Tony Kelly	
8.	Kevin Kent	
9.	Martin Foyle	
10.	Lee Glover	
11.	Mark Burke	

on the bench

12.	Robin Van der Laan	
13.	Arjan Van Heusden	
14.	Joe Allon	

73 mins

73 mins

McClair powers a shot as Vale watch helplessly

John Peters

bite this!

"Alex Ferguson made light of the £50,000 fines that are being threatened as he put out half-a-dozen 19-year-olds from the side that lifted the FA Youth Cup three years ago."
DAILY EXPRESS

"While old-timers Brian McClair and David May got the goals that wrapped up a convincing Coca Cola Cup victory against Port Vale, it was crafted by Manchester United's new kids on the block."
DAILY MIRROR

"Alex Ferguson is making a kids' game of the Coca Cola Cup and, with a little bit of help from a few seniors, the talented youngsters of Manchester United are winning." **DAILY MAIL**

"It was a difficult game tonight and I said before tonight's match that this would be far better than our previous meeting. Judging by the chances they had earlier in the game they probably deserved a better scoreline, but we had three or four good opportunities and scored twice.
The main thing that needs working on is a defensive thing; things such as one-twos. Getting caught in the last third of the pitch. Experience is obviously important and I think Nicky Butt showed that tonight after only a few games with the first team.
ALEX FERGUSON

John Peters

in the book

Referee:
A Wilkie,
Chester-Le-
Street
Rating: 7
Bookings:
Porter,
Glover L

"Choccy is their teacher."

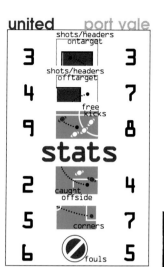

united   port vale

	shots/headers on target	
3		3
	shots/headers off target	
4		7
	free kicks	
9		8

stats

	caught offside	
2		4
	corners	
5		7
6	fouls	5

John Peters

Murmurings of punishment from the football league failed to change Fergie's policy of playing the youngsters in the Coca Cola Cup and why should he? With the likes of **Butt, Neville, Davies, Casper** and Co. firmly on the team sheet, the young red side set out to do the important thing, ensure progress to the next round of the competition and gain valuable experience in the process.

United had a chance to extend the 2-1 first leg lead when a penalty was awarded early on.

Unfortunately Butt crashed the ball against the bar, much to the amusement of the small Vale following.

Amends were made a minute later however, when **McClair** scored from close range. **With all the good football coming from the reds, it was no surprise when May headed home a second** from a corner midway through the second half.

With the aggregate score standing at 4-1 and the tie a foregone conclusion it was nice to sit and relax, and watch the immense talents that we have at United for the future years.

Scholes **pokes the ball clear of Vale's defence**

>timeline

* **Mon 3rd Oct** Alex Ferguson appeals for internationals to be played midweek, which would reduce the disruption to the domestic schedule.

> **BETRAYAL OF A PRINCESS - DIANA IS DEEPLY HURT BY HEWITT KISS-AND-TELL BOOK WHICH IS SAID TO BE THE MOST INTRUSIVE BOOK ABOUT HER YET**
> DAILY EXPRESS Mon 3rd Oct

* **Tues 4th Oct** Third division Mansfield complete their two-leg defeat of Leeds and knock them out of the Coca-Cola cup.

* The FA refuse to lift Alan Sugar's ban on Terry Venables visiting Spurs.

> **DIANA'S SECRET LOVE CODE - HER LETTERS REVEAL RED NAILS WERE A PASSIONATE SIGN TO MAJOR HEWITT**
> TODAY Tues 4th Oct

* **Wed 5th Oct** Neil Webb begins a one-month loan period at Swindon Town. The move could be made permanent if he is successful.

* Le Tissier scores all four goals in Southampton's drubbing of Huddersfield.

> **TORY MP IN WIFE DEATH PROBE - TWO-TIMING TORY TONY MARLOW IS TO BE QUIZZED ABOUT THE HOLIDAY DROWNING OF HIS WIFE CATHERINE**
> DAILY STAR Wed 5th Oct

* **Thu 6th Oct** ITV sign up Terry Venables as match analyser. The four year contract is thought to be worth £250,000.

* Kevin Keegan publicly approves of Ferguson's youth policy.

> **48 DIE IN CULT SUICIDE PACT - RELIGIOUS CULT IN SWITZERLAND**
> THE TIMES Thu 6th Oct

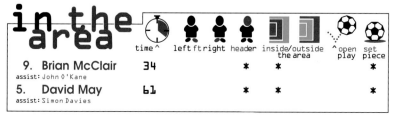

in the area

		time ^	left ft right	header	inside/outside the area	^ open play	set piece
9.	Brian McClair	34		*	*		*
	assist: John O'Kane						
5.	David May	61		*	*		*
	assist: Simon Davies						

> Saturday 8 October 1994 / 3.00pm

*SHEFFIELD WEDNESDAY

> Hillsborough   v manchester united:

1-0

[Att: 33,441]

[Last season : 2-3]

team lineups

home team

13.	Kevin Pressman	
2.	Peter Atherton	
12.	Andy Pearce	
17.	Des Walker	
3.	Ian Nolan	
29.	Lee Briscoe	
16.	Graham Hyde	
11.	John Sheriden	
14.	Chris Bart-Williams	
9.	David Hirst	65mins
10.	Mark Bright	

on the bench

4.	Ian Taylor	88mins
23.	Lance Key	
20.	Gordon Watson	

visitors

		rating
1.	Peter Schmeichel	7
2.	Paul Parker	7
3.	Denis Irwin	7
4.	Steve Bruce	8
6.	Gary Pallister	8
8.	Paul Ince	8
5.	Lee Sharpe	7
31.	Keith Gillespie	8
16.	Roy Keane	7
10.	Mark Hughes	7
9.	Brian McClair	7

60mins / 76mins

on the bench

12.	David May	7
13.	Gary Walsh	
24.	Paul Scholes	7

But ref! You've got to be kidding!

word up

Over five thousand reds made the annual trans-Pennine trek to Hillsborough hoping to see a much needed second away league victory of the season. With **Kanchelskis** and **Cantona** lost to international duty and **Giggs** out injured, things were going to be tough against a side who are always fired up for the visit of united.

Events on the pitch gave neither set of fans much to shout about but **our hopes were raised when Gillespie put the ball in the back of the net** Unfortunately the goal was ruled out and it proved to be a turning point for the worse.

With United sensing a goal they pushed forward only to be caught on the break by the Owls. **Hurst ran clear and calmly slotted the ball past an irate Schmeichel**.

The second half saw inevitable pressure from United but chances were few and far between. Nothing seemed to go right for the red shirts and a third successive away defeat in the league made our title aspirations seem distant.

bite this!

"They could have had the game won at the interval instead of being caught out on the stroke of half-time, but for all of their superiority, something of a malaise was apparent."
THE TIMES

"The impression that Manchester United left at Hillsborough was that of a team in crisis - an identity crisis..... They badly missed Andrei Kanchelskis and Eric Cantona, and while Keith Gillespie kept the starlet standard high in the absence of Ryan Giggs, Hirst's winner had its origins in the debutant's inability to accelerate away from defenders."
THE INDEPENDENT

"As the ball hit the back of the net two minutes before half-time United boss Ferguson must have wondered if it was taking his quest for a third successive title with it."
DAILY EXPRESS

"Manchester United's championship crown is wobbling after three successive away defeats."
MANCHESTER EVENING NEWS

Brian McClair, in particular, Paul Ince and Lee Sharpe must have had their manager cringing at their profligacy in front of goal."
DAILY TELEGRAPH

"Keith Gillespie made a good contribution towards the match but he got tired towards the end. Obviously we have got a few players out injured at the moment but I don't really see that as an issue and I'm not going to use that as an excuse. Sheffield Wednesday beat us fairly with a good display but I don't think we created as many chances after the break as we could have to test their defence.

People are saying that Europe is the main reason we are having a few bad results but if you look back two years ago; we made a bad start, played well from October onwards and went on to win the league."
ALEX FERGUSON

in the book

Referee:
P Danson,
Leicester
Rating: 6

Bookings:
Bruce,
Sharpe,
Hughes,
Pearce

Ince flies over a late tackle

John Peters

The race is on···

"Brian McClair, in particular, Paul Ince and Lee Sharpe must have had their manager cringing at their profligacy in front of goal."

DAILY TELEGRAPH

stats

wednesday		united
3	shots/headers on target	3
2	shots/headers off target	8
15	free kicks	22
10	caught offside	6
4	corners	11
12	fouls	9

Bruce ends up at the bottom of the pile as Pally comes out on top

in the area

time^	left ft	right	header	inside/outside the area	^open play	set piece

9. David Hirst — 44

>timeline

* **Fri 7th Oct** Keegan again talks to the press. This time he says that "Blackburn are our biggest threat in the league." He said Manchester United have other priorities.

> **BSKYB SEEKS TO GO INTO ORBIT WITH £5 BILLION FLOTATION**
THE GUARDIAN Fri 7th Oct

* **Sat 8th Oct**

> **SADDAM MENACES KUWAIT — CLINTON PUTS TROOPS ON ALERT AS UP TO 65,000 IRAQI SOLDIERS ADVANCE ON BORDER**
THE GUARDIAN Sat 8th Oct

* **Sun 9th Oct** Peter Beardsley is withdrawn from the England squad with a thigh injury.

> **REVEALED: MARK THATCHER'S SECRET PROFIT FROM £20 BILLION ARMS DEAL**
THE SUNDAY TIMES Sun 9th Oct

* **Mon 10th Oct** John Fashanu is in court after John O'Neill accused him of deliberately hurting him seven years ago with a tackle that allegedly ended his career.

* Pat Bonner is made skipper of Ireland's national team as usual captain Andy Townsend is injured.

> **US RUSHING FORCES OUT TO THE GULF**
THE TIMES Mon 10th Oct

manchester united v
WEST HAM UNITED

[Att: 43,795]

1-0

>Saturday 15 October 1994 / 3.00pm   >Old Trafford

[Last season :3-0]

team lineups

home team

		rating
1.	Peter Schmeichel	7
12.	David May	7
3.	Denis Irwin	7
4.	Steve Bruce	7
6.	Gary Pallister	7
8.	Paul Ince	8
5.	Lee Sharpe	7
14.	Andrei Kanchelskis	7
7.	Eric Cantona	8
10.	Mark Hughes	7
11.	Ryan Giggs	7

on the bench

19.	Nicky Butt	7
13.	Gary Walsh	
9.	Brian McClair	

visitors

1.	Ludek Miklosko
2.	Tim Breaker
4.	Steve Potts
5.	Alvin Martin
12.	Keith Rowland
14.	Matthew Rush
6.	Martin Allen
10.	John Moncur
26.	Don Hutchinson
19.	Mike Marsh
27.	Tony Cottee

on the bench

7.	Ian Bishop
21.	Tony Feuer
22.	Adrian Whitbread

John Peters

Sparky beats Steve Potts to the ball

A typical Hughes manoeuvre

in the book

Referee:
R Gifford,
Llanbaorach
Rating: 6

Bookings:
Sharpe,
Butt

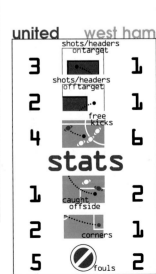

united   west ham

stats

	united		west ham
shots/headers on target	3		1
shots/headers off target	2		1
free kicks	4		6
caught offside	1		2
corners	2		1
fouls	5		2

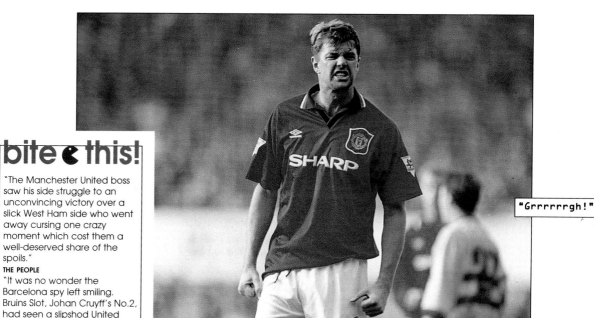

bite this!

"The Manchester United boss saw his side struggle to an unconvincing victory over a slick West Ham side who went away cursing one crazy moment which cost them a well-deserved share of the spoils."
THE PEOPLE

"It was no wonder the Barcelona spy left smiling. Bruins Slot, Johan Cruyff's No.2, had seen a slipshod United show riddled with damaging lethargy and carelessness.... "
NEWS OF THE WORLD

"Cantona was on hand to supply the coup de grace.... The Frenchman has a habit of provoking intense argument and there was considerable debate in the Hammers ranks at the breach of defensive discipline.."
THE MAIL ON SUNDAY

"Only the remarkable defensive diligence of Gary Pallister and Peter Schmeichel's supremacy in showdowns with Tony Cottee and Martin Allen prevented Newcastle disappearing over the horizon."
THE SUN

We're thankful for three points more than anything. This certainly hasn't been one of our best performances of the season so far, and West Ham will be kicking themselves for not taking the chances they had.

It was a frustrating game to watch and you have to credit the teams for trying to get forward. It was an untidy performance, and a scrappy goal won the match for us in the end. Later on in the second half we started to attack more. But then our finishing wasn't great.

There was some great play on the right wing - Andrei had an outstanding game for us, but from time to time you started to wonder where the goal would come from. Fortunately we got the decisive goal, not West Ham.

ALEX FERGUSON

"Grrrrrrgh!"

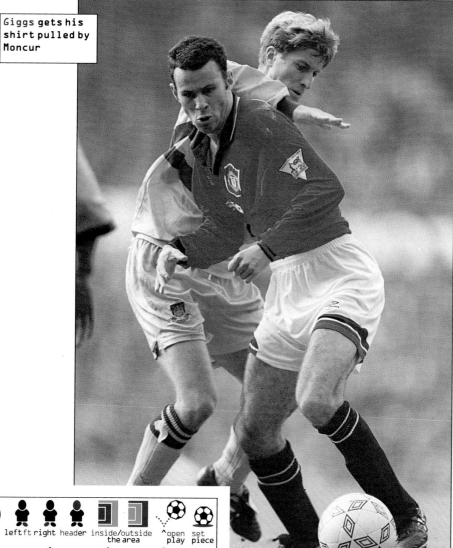

Giggs gets his shirt pulled by Moncur

word up

United's Premiership hopes were put back on course with a much needed 'no thrills' home win against the Hammers.

A single **Cantona** tap-in just before half-time was enough to separate the men from the boys but Harry Redknapp's side looked dangerous on more than one occasion. **Matthew Rush** in particular caused the Reds' defence a few problems with his sharp runs from the wing, but in the end neither **Rush** nor his team-mates could become the first team to score a league goal at Old Trafford this season, let alone get a result.

>timeline

* **Tues 11th Oct** England under-21 side beat Austria 3-1 even though Robbie Fowler is sent off.

> I STAND BY ARMS DEAL — THATCHER'S PRIDE OVER £20BN SALE
> DAILY EXPRESS Tues 11th Oct

* **Wed 12th Oct** Robert Lee makes an international dream debut equalising for England in a 1-1 draw with Romania at Wembley.

> LADY T FACES DIVORCE BLOW — MARGARET THATCHER FLIES TO AMERICA TODAY IN A DESPERATE ATTEMPT TO RESCUE HER SON'S DOOMED MARRIAGE
> DAILY EXPRESS Wed 12th Oct

* **Thu 13th Oct** Billy Bingham criticises John Fashanu for the tackle which allegedly ended John O'Neill's playing career.

> LOYALISTS ORDER A CEASE-FIRE — END TO 25 YEARS OF ULSTER TERROR
> THE GUARDIAN Thu 13th Oct

* **Fri 14th Oct**

> SINN FEIN TALKS 'BY CHRISTMAS' - LOYALISTS CEASE-FIRE YESTERDAY SPARKS HOPES FOR TALKS BETWEEN BRITISH OFFICIALS AND SINN FEIN
> THE DAILY TELEGRAPH Fri 14th Oct

* **Sat 15th Oct**

> THE GREAT LOTTERY ROBBERY — ITV PLAN RIVAL TO SPOIL BBC'S BIG NIGHT
> Today Sat 15th Oct

in the area

	time^	left ft	right	header	inside/outside the area	^open play	set piece
7. Eric Cantona	44		*		*	*	

assist: Ryan Giggs

*LEE SHARPE
>forward

>manchester united
& england
[Squad number: **5**]

Sportshot

personal file

born: Halesowen, 27/05/71
height: 5'11" weight: 11st4lb
international team: England
signed pro for United: 1/06/88
transfer fee: £185,000
United league debut: 24/09/88 v West Ham Utd

✳ GARY PALLISTER
>defender

John Peters

personal file

born: Ramsgate, 30/06/65
height: 6'4" **weight:** 13st
international team: England
signed pro for United: 28/08/89
transfer fee: £2,300,000
United league debut: 30/08/89 v Norwich City (h)

manchester united v
FC BARCELONA
[Att: 40,064] **2-2**
>Old Trafford
>Wednesday 19 October 1994 / 8.30pm

team lineups

Praise to the Gods! Someone up there likes us!

home team

		rating
1.	Peter Schmeichel	8
2.	Paul Parker	8
3.	Denis Irwin	8
4.	David May	8
5.	Nicky Butt	8
6.	Gary Pallister	8
7.	Andrei Kanchelskis	8
8.	Paul Ince	8
9.	Roy Keane	8
10.	Mark Hughes	8
11.	Lee Sharpe	9

69mins
67 mins

on the bench

12.	Steve Bruce	8
13.	Gary Walsh	
14.	Paul Scholes	8
15.	Gary Neville	
16.	Simon Davies	

visitors

1.	Carlos Busquets	
2.	Fernandez Abelardo	
3.	José Guardiola	
4.	Ronald Koeman	
5.	Sergi Barjuan	
6.	José Maria Bakero	
7.	Luis Cembranos Martinez	
8.	Hristo Stoichkov	
9.	Miguel Angel Nadal	
10.	Romario de Souza Faria	
11.	Aitor Beguiristain	

46mins
67 mins

on the bench

12.	Sanchez Jara	
13.	Julian Lope Tegui	
14.	Jordi Cruyff	
15.	Sacristán Eusebio	
16.	Guillermo Amor	

Parker side-foots to Pally

bite this!

"The 2-2 draw with Barcelona was just about everything we had been told it would be and it ended with a goal of the very highest quality - scored by an Englishman." **DAILY MAIL**

"United's opening was brilliant. They passed the ball around with accuracy and confidence and it was in keeping with the run of play when Lee Sharpe got in the perfect cross for Mark Hughes to thunder home a header."
MANCHESTER EVENING NEWS

"A draw with Barcelona's band of marauding mavericks was just reward for Ince and Co, whose efforts brought United a fourth point and the increasing likelihood of qualification for the quarter-finals of the European Cup."
DAILY TELEGRAPH

"Paul Ince took the captain's armband for Manchester

United last night and then grabbed the tiller as his side drifted towards the rocks.... Snapping and snarling like a hungry lion, he drove forward one more time to set up Lee's great goal that saved the day for United..." **DAILY EXPRESS**

"We gave away two bad goals and we can't be happy with that, because we started the game tremendously well and created several chances.

But I was pleased with the way we fought back. After Barcelona's second goal, they were playing superbly, keeping possession all the time but in the end we went for the throat and it paid off.

Paul Ince responded magnificently when we needed someone to whip us on he did it. And at one point after we'd equalised I thought we could have won the match."
ALEX FERGUSON

word up

The visit of Barça to Old Trafford was the most eagerly awaited game in recent years. A repeat of the three-nil demolition of the Catalans ten years ago would have set us up for qualification from our Champions' League group but first we had the small matter of dealing with **Romario**, **Stoichkov** and **Bakero** et al.

The reds attacked from the whistle and took the lead when **Sharpe** sent a perfect cross over to **Hughes**, who headed past the stranded **Busquets**. The roof nearly lifted from Old Trafford's stands as expectations of another European glory night were high.

Barça clawed their way back into a United-dominated game and **when the world class Romario** grabbed a crucial equaliser just before the break, things went a bit flat.

The Catalans took the game to United after the break and took the lead through the lively **Bakero** to deflate the reds even more.

The added presence of **Bruce** seemed to spur United on to better things and almost immediately chances were created. Barça didn't look so confident now, and when **a brilliant move involving Ince, Keane** and finally **Sharpe** yielded an equaliser, it was a fitting end to a superb game with an atmosphere to match.

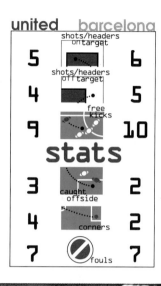

united   barcelona

stats

united		barcelona
5	shots/headers on target	6
4	shots/headers off target	5
9	free kicks	10
3	caught offside	2
4	corners	2
7	fouls	7

Professional Sport

Andrei Kanchelskis gains complete control

Koeman fears the worst, as Hughes connects to make it 1-0

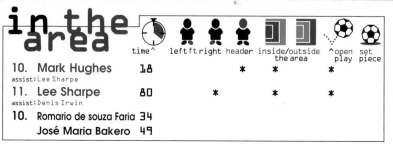

in the book

Referee:
I Craciunescu, Romania
Rating: 8
Bookings:
May

in the area

	time^	left ft	right	header	inside/outside the area	^open play	set piece
10. Mark Hughes	18			*	*	*	
assist: Lee Sharpe							
11. Lee Sharpe	80	*		*	*	*	
assist: Denis Irwin							
10. Romario de souza Faria	34						
José Maria Bakero	49						

>timeline

* **Sun 16th Oct** Bryan Robson – ruled out of contention for his team's match against Luton with a calf-strain – watches from the bench as they concede five goals whilst only managing to score one.

> **I NEVER LOVED DIANA - CHARLES CONFESSES**
SUNDAY MIRROR Sun 16th Oct

* **Mon 17th Oct** Johan Cruyff's verdict on the outcome of United's qualifying group is that both they and Barça will proceed to the quarter-finals.

> **I CAN'T BELIEVE HE NEVER LOVED ME - PRINCESS DIANA**
DAILY MIRROR Mon 17th Oct

* **Tues 18th Oct** Bobby Charlton plays host to Ronald Koeman for a game of golf the day before United's match against Barcelona at Old Trafford.

> **CLARKE TO SLASH BACK TREASURY - MORALE PLUM METS AS POLICY REVIEW TAR GETS MANDARINS**
THE GUARDIAN Tue 18th Oct

* **Wed 19th Oct**

> **SLAVE BOYS - NINE YEAR OLD BOYS HAVE BEEN DISCOVERED HACKING OUT STONE TO PAVE BRITAIN'S STREETS**
DAILY STAR Wed 19th Oct

* **Thu 20th Oct**

> **'NORTH'S NOT SO NICE' BLUNDER BY QUEEN - QUEEN SAYS MANCHESTER IS 'NOT SUCH A NICE PLACE'**
DAILY MIRROR Thu 20th Oct

*BLACKBURN ROVERS

> Sunday 23 October 1994 / 4.00pm

v manchester united:

> Ewood Park [Att: 30,260]

1-1

[Last season :1-2]

team lineups

home team

1.	Tim Flowers	
20.	Henning Berg	
2.	Tony Gale	
5.	Colin Hendry	
6.	Graeme Le Saux	
7.	Stuart Ripley	
24.	Paul Warhurst	
22.	Mark Atkins	
11.	Jason Wilcox	
9.	Alan Shearer	
16.	Chris Sutton	

84mins

on the bench

25.	Ian Pearce
13.	Bobby Mimms
17.	Robbie Slater

visitors

rating

1.	Peter Schmeichel	6
16.	Roy Keane	7
3.	Denis Irwin	7
4.	Steve Bruce	8
6.	Gary Pallister	7
8.	Paul Ince	8
5.	Lee Sharpe	7
14.	Andrei Kanchelskis	8
7.	Eric Cantona	7
10.	Mark Hughes	7
19.	Nicky Butt	7

82mins

on the bench

9.	Brian McClair
13.	Gary Walsh
31.	Keith Gillespie

in the area

		time^	left ft	right	header	inside/outside the area	^open play	set piece
7.	Eric Cantona	45		*	*	*		*
14.	Andrei Kanchelskis	52	*		*	*	*	
		82		*		*	*	
10.	Mark Hughes	67		*		*	*	
5.	Colin Hendry	51						
24.	Paul Warhurst	13						

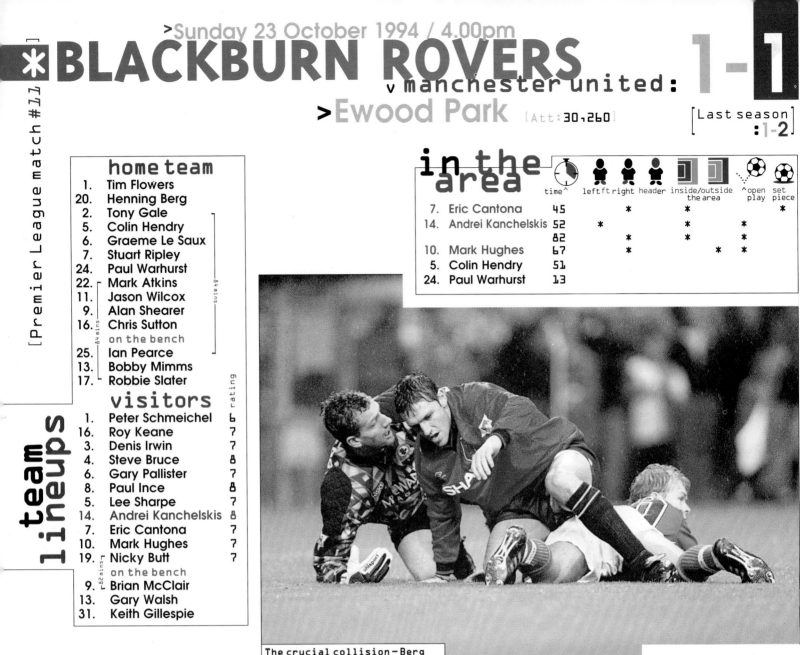

The crucial collision – Berg awaits his marching orders

Nicky Butt streaks away from Atkins

stats

blackburn		united
	shots/headers on target	
5		11
	shots/headers off target	
2		4
	free kicks	
12		10
	caught offside	
4		3
	corners	
11		5
	fouls	
6		9

word up

Last season, fans paid £100 on the black market to watch this match confident of seeing United pull away from rivals Blackburn for the title; they went home disappointed.

This season, with a near 7,000 ticket allocation, fans paid £14 desperate to see United win an away league game and they went home happy, very happy.

Warhurst put Rovers ahead early on, then Cantona smashed home an equaliser from the penalty spot following the controversial sending off of Berg.

Hendry put Rovers back in front, but less than a minute later Kanchelskis levelled affairs as he knocked in a rebound of his own shot.

Hughes lobbed home a third to stun Blackburn and the watching millions on television, and when Kanchelskis raced clear and rounded Flowers for a fourth, the execution was complete. Ecstasy.

Watch out Newcastle, United are back.

bite this!

"It was appropriate that on the day the clocks went back Manchester United turned back the calendar to last winter, when they established an unstoppable momentum to carry them to the title..."

TODAY

"Manchester United's awesome attacking machine roared back into lethal top gear - kick-started by a spot of luck. They won the battle of Ewood Park with a clinical and ruthless second half goal spree against 10-man Rovers.... It was no surprise when Mark Hughes gave United the lead after 66 minutes. The goal was a personal disaster for the impressive Le Saux, who had his hands full all afternoon with the speed of Kanchelskis."

DAILY STAR

"Blackburn are never an easy team to beat and I had wondered how our players would cope after the big European game mid-week.

Credit to Blackburn - they got off to a great start. The penalty decision was talked about as being the turning point of the match, but I don't think it was. The actual turning point was when we equalised; from then on we started to play some good football and created good openings, although we still let Blackburn score."

ALEX FERGUSON

Keano **lets fly**

John Peters

"It was as if a smooth saloon had suddenly had the bodywork dented and **United** began to remove the tyres and steal the engine, as Paul Ince once again took total control."

DAILY EXPRESS

Just another penalty

>timeline

* **Sat 22nd Oct** Blackpool beat Swindon and continue their home run of unbeaten matches, which started on the opening day of the seasons

> **BIRDMAN BURT DIES AGED 80 - TOUGH GUY ACTOR BURT LANCASTER DIED YESTERDAY**
DAILY EXPRESS Sat 22nd Oct

* **Sun 23rd Oct**

> **TORY PARTY PACKS NHS TRUSTS - NEARLY £2M HAS BEEN GIVEN TO THE CONSERVATIVE PARTY AND TORY "FRONT" ORGANISATIONS WHOSE DIRECTORS NOW SIT ON NHS TRUSTS**
INDEPENDENT ON SUNDAY
Sun 23rd Oct

* **Mon 24th Oct** Alex Ferguson has finally been given approval from the Football League to field a younger side.

> **DEMANDS FOR INQUIRY INTO MPS' CONDUCT - THE PRIME MINISTER WAS UNDER MOUNTING PRESSURE LAST NIGHT TO SET UP AN INDEPENDENT INQUIRY INTO THE RULES GOVERNING MPS' CONDUCT AS A WAY OF DEFUSING THE "CASH FOR QUESTIONS ROW."**
THE TIMES Mon 24th Oct

in the book

Referee:
G Ashby, Worcester
Rating: 4
Bookings:

Bruce
Berg,
Sutton

*NEWCASTLE UNITED

[Att: 34,718]

>St. James' Park   v manchester united: 2-0

>Wednesday 26 October 1994 / 8.00pm

[Last season :1-1]

home team

1. Pavel Srnicek
12. Marc Hottiger
6. Steve Howey
15. Darren Peacock
3. John Beresford
27. Phillipe Albert
19. Steve Watson
8. Peter Beardsley
11. Scott Sellars
9. Andy Cole — 63mins
28. Paul Kitson

on the bench

10. Lee Clark — 63mins
30. Mike Hooper
18. Steve Guppy

visitors

rating

1. Gary Walsh — 7
2. Gary Neville — 7
3. Denis Irwin — 7
4. Steve Bruce — 7
5. Nicky Butt — 8
6. Gary Pallister — 7
7. Keith Gillespie — 8
8. David Beckham — 7
9. Brian McClair — 52 mins — 7
10. Paul Scholes — 7
11. Simon Davies — 7

on the bench

12. Graeme Tomlinson — 7
13. Kevin Pilkington — 52 mins
14. Lee Sharpe — 7

Hughes holds up play for a while...

word up

Just, **Bruce**, **Pallister** and **Sharpe** kept their regular places in the squad for the Coca-Cola cup tie at a packed St. James' Park. **Fergie** had stuck to his word and played the youngsters in their biggest test yet.

For 85 minutes United were more than a match for a full-strength top of the league Newcastle side, but in the end ran out of steam. Belgian international, **Phillipe Albert** broke the deadlock with a powerful header and the Geordies added a second a minute before the whistle.

Full praise to the youngsters, who are now rapidly maturing – giving United's faithful assurance that their time will come. **We are out of the cup but if there was disappointment in the United camp it couldn't be detected.**

newcastle   united

stats

newcastle		united
	shots/headers on target	
7		3
	shots/headers off target	
8		4
	free kicks	
11		10
	caught offside	
4		2
	corners	
5		4
6	fouls	9

in the area

time^

| 27. | Phillipe Albert | 82 |
| 26. | Paul Kitson | 87 |

...and he flies through the air with the greatest of ease...

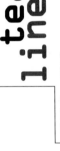

first aid box

> **Lee Sharpe** ligament and small fracture to ankle

* **Tues 25th Oct**
> DOLE SYSTEM TO BE REPLACED BY 'WORKFARE' – A NEW SCHEME AIMED TO REJECT LONG-TERM UNEMPLOYED OFF THE DOLE
THE TIMES Tues 25th Oct

* **Wed 26th Oct** Tottenham's fans voice their displeasure at the continued employment of Ossie Ardiles.

> BLACKMAIL PROBE INTO MR HARRODS – HARRODS BOSS MOHAMED AL FAYED FACES BLACKMAIL INVESTIGATIONS AFTER JOHN MAJOR ORDERS THE DIRECTOR OF PUBLIC PROSECUTIONS FOR AN INQUIRY
THE SUN Wed 26th Oct

* **Thu 27th Oct** According to the press Mark Hughes has laid down an ultimatum to Manchester United. Either he receives an acceptable offer within two weeks or he leaves Old Trafford.

> £5 A GALLON DEATH KNELL FOR DRIVERS – A ROYAL COMMISSION ON ENVIRONMENTAL POLLUTION RAISED THE REAL PROSPECT OF THE £5 GALLON OF PETROL BY THE YEAR 2000
DAILY EXPRESS Thu 27th Oct

* **Fri 28th Oct** Bobby Robson is rumoured to be in line for the Tottenham manager's job. Ossie Ardiles is still at Spurs and the club have not made any announcement concerning the position.

in the book

Referee:
T Holbrook, Walsall

Rating: 6

Bookings:
Butt, Scholes, Howey

Gillespie prepares to dribble past Howey

bite this!

"Fresh, when linked with faced, was the right word for the visitors. Pallister, Irwin, Bruce and McClair were familiar; the rest of the starting line-up had the red supporters rapidly scanning their programmes before launching into "There's only one...."
THE INDEPENDENT

"The Manchester United manager had the bare-faced cheek to march into Kevin Keegan's kingdom with virtually his second team." **THE SUN**

"Newcastle's vastly more experienced line-up had more then their share of the early play, but it was the sweet, uninhibited football of Fergie's Fledglings that made the senses tingle." **DAILY EXPRESS**

"Newcastle learned the hard way last night that there is more than one Manchester United..." **THE GUARDIAN**

"The pleasing aspect of this match is that we knew that the lads had the talent. What we didn't know was whether they had the temperament as well, but now we do.
They deserved the chance because of how they played against Port Vale.
I wish Newcastle well because I think they've been a breath of fresh air in the Premiership."
ALEX FERGUSON

Scholes puts in a shot despite the challenge from Peacock

manchester united v
NEWCASTLE UNITED 2-0
>Old Trafford
>Saturday 29 October 1994 / 3.00pm

[Att: 43,785] [Last season :1-1]

team lineups

home team

		rating
1.	Peter Schmeichel	8
16.	Roy Keane	8
3.	Denis Irwin	8
4.	Steve Bruce	9
6.	Gary Pallister	9
8.	Paul Ince	9
14.	Andrei Kanchelskis	9
9.	Brian McClair	8
7.	Eric Cantona	8
10.	Mark Hughes	9
11.	Ryan Giggs	8

on the bench
19.	Nicky Butt	66 mins
13.	Gary Walsh	
31.	Keith Gillespie	

visitors

1.	Pavel Srnicek
12.	Marc Hottiger
6.	Steve Howey
15.	Darren Peacock
3.	John Beresford
27.	Phillippe Albert
19.	Steve Watson
11.	Scott Sellars
7.	Robert Lee
5.	Ruel Fox
8.	Peter Beardsley

on the bench
10.	Lee Clark	75 mins
30.	Mike Hooper	
14.	Alex Mathie	

Ince turns and deceives Newcastle's defence

in the book
Referee:
J Worrall, Warrington
Rating: 6
Bookings:
Bruce

Eric refuses to give away possession

word up

The big one. **On Wednesday it was men against boys, today it was men against men.** As champions, United had to prove that the Premiership trophy wasn't just residing at old Trafford for the fun of it.

As early as the 11th minute, **Pallister** met a **Giggs** cross and headed past keeper **Srnicek**. Newcastle were a good side and came back at United, but in the second half the reds really turned on the style. **Kanchelskis** was rampant as ever and United were consistently causing problems. The killer second goal came when substitute **Gillespie** skilfully worked his way past three defenders before firing home a terrific shot.

"2-0 to the champions" sang the red masses, if the team continues to play as today then no one is going to stop us from winning our third league title in a row.

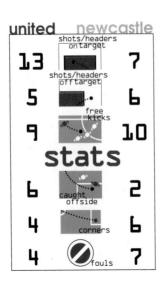

united   newcastle

united		newcastle
	shots/headers on target	
13		7
	shots/headers off target	
5		6
	free kicks	
9		10
	stats	
	caught offside	
6		2
	corners	
4		6
	fouls	
4		7

bite this!

"Back to full strength the champions looked the part again, ending Newcastle's unbeaten start and trimming the gap between them at the top of the League to a manageable four points in their best performance of the season." **THE SUNDAY TIMES**

"Against Newcastle, Eric Cantona was the sorcerer once more to the gallant knights of Paul Ince, Mark Hughes and Andrei Kanchelskis...." **TODAY**

"If Manchester United have a talisman, it is Ince the battler, the ball-winner and prompter. How unsettling it must be to play against him, to know that any small error, any infinitesimal clumsiness, and there is Ince in at you, flat on his back, foot slashing at what is - momentarily - a loose ball. "
THE TIMES

"I expected a fabulous game today and I wasn't disappointed. A marvellous result won by a marvellous football team. Newcastle certainly played their part in it. By having a positive attitude and by trying to win they made us sweat, some of the one-touch football they produced was terrific.

Pavel Srnicek has probably played his best game for the club and pulled off six or seven superb saves.

Let's just say you'll have to go a long way before seeing a game as good as that."
ALEX FERGUSON

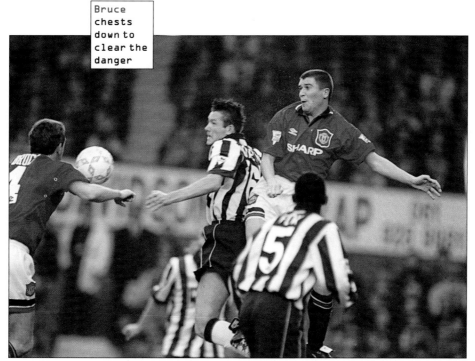

Bruce chests down to clear the danger

>timeline

* **Sat 29th Oct**

> **ANGER AS WIFE-KILLER IS FREED – HUSBAND RECEIVES SUSPENDED SENTENCE AFTER STRANGLING HIS WIFE TO DEATH**
THE GUARDIAN Sat 29th Oct

* **Sun 30th Oct** Sunderland face a midfield crisis. Due to injuries the only players available selection are defenders and forwards.

* Newcastle lead the Premiership by four points as Manchester United climb into third place.

> **TUNNEL TURNS BIG BEN INTO LEANING TOWER OF LONDON - TUNNELLING WORK 30 YARDS FROM BIG BEN PUTS THE TOWER IN DANGER ACCORDING TO EXPERTS**
THE SUNDAY TIMES Sun 30th Oct

* **Mon 31st Oct** 2,000 United fans are alleged to be travelling to Barca without tickets, leaving the Spanish club with security problems.

> **VENABLES CHEATED SPURS OUT OF £400,000 - TV DOCUMENTARY REVEALS DETAILS THAT COULD COST THE ENGLAND MANAGER HIS JOB**
DAILY MIRROR Mon 31st Oct

in the area

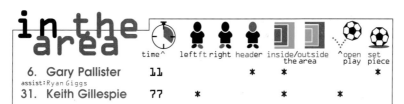

	time^	left ft	right	header	inside/outside the area	^open play	set piece
6. Gary Pallister	11			*	*		*
assist: Ryan Giggs							
31. Keith Gillespie	77	*			*	*	

*ERIC CANTONA
>forward

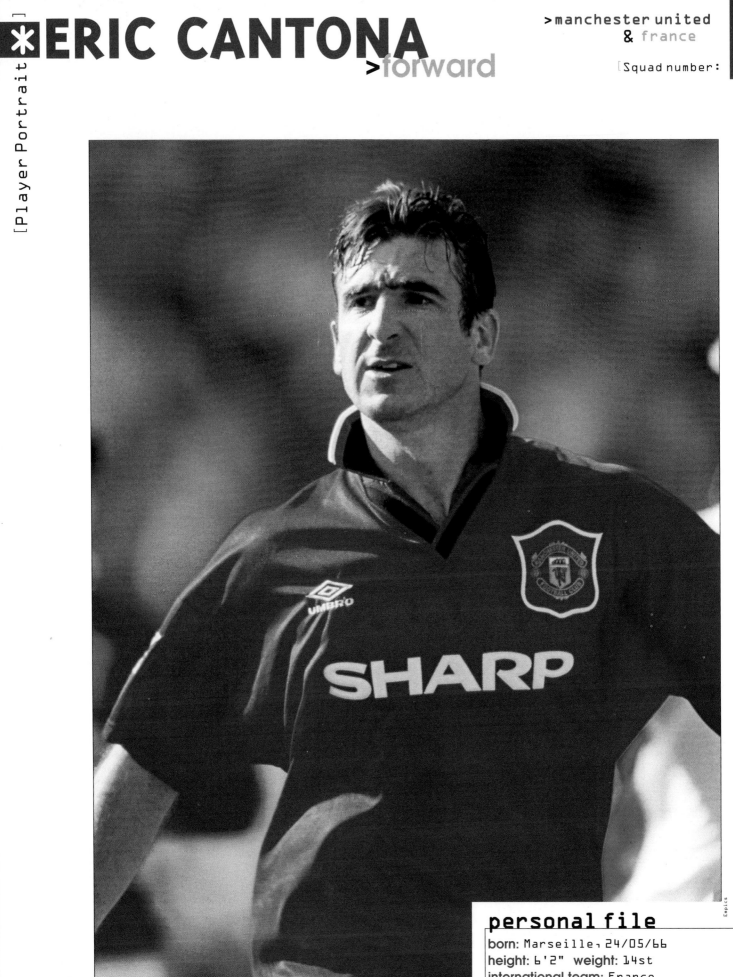

personal file
born: Marseille, 24/05/66
height: 6'2" weight: 14st
international team: France
signed pro for United: 27/10/92
transfer fee: £1,000,000
United league debut : 6/11/92 v Manchester City (h)

▾ appearances/goals ➤

Apps are shown as appearances / apps as sub / goals for each competition; Total is shown as total appearances / goals.

Player	Premier League	FA Cup	Coca Cola Cup	European Cup	Total	left ft	right	header	inside/outside the area	open play	set piece	assists	scoring rate	performance rating average
Gary Pallister	5 / – / 1	–	2	1	8 / 1	–	1	1	–	–	1	–	13%	7.4
Denis Irwin	5	–	1	1	7	1	–	–	–	–	–	–	–%	7.3
Steve Bruce	5	–	– / 1	1	6 / 1	1	1	–	–	–	–	–	–%	7.7
Mark Hughes	5 / – / 1	–	1	1 / 1	6 / 2	–	1	1	1 / 1	2	–	–	33%	7.5
Paul Ince	5	–	1	–	6	–	–	–	–	–	–	1	–%	8.2
Peter Schmeichel	5	–	1	–	6	–	–	–	–	–	–	–	–%	7.5
Andrei Kanchelskis	4 / – / 3	–	1	–	5 / 3	1	1	1	3	3	–	–	60%	7.8
Roy Keane	4	–	1	–	5	–	–	–	–	–	–	1	–%	7.2
Lee Sharpe	4 / – / 1	–	1	–	5 / 1	1	–	–	2	2	–	2	33%	7.3
Nicky Butt	1 / 1	–	2	–	2	–	–	–	–	–	–	–	–%	5.8
Eric Cantona	4 / – / 2	–	–	–	4 / 2	–	2	–	2	1	1	–	50%	7.8
David May	2 / 1	–	1 / – / 1	1	4 / 1	–	1	1	1	–	–	–	20%	7.4
Brian McClair	2 / 2	–	2	–	4 / 2	2	1	–	–	–	–	–	20%	5.8
Keith Gillespie	1 / 1 / 1	–	2	–	3 / 1	1	–	–	1	1	–	–	25%	7.5
David Beckham	–	–	2	–	2	–	–	–	–	–	–	–		7.0
Simon Davies	–	–	2	–	2	–	–	–	–	–	–	–		7.0
Ryan Giggs	2	–	–	–	2	–	–	–	–	–	–	2		7.5
Paul Parker	–	–	–	1	2	–	–	–	–	–	–	–		7.5
Paul Scholes	– / 1	–	2	1	2 / 2	2	–	–	–	–	–	–	–%	7.3
Gary Walsh	–	–	1	–	1	–	–	–	–	–	–	–	–%	7.5
Chris Casper	–	–	1	–	1	–	–	–	–	–	–	–		7.0
Gary Neville	–	–	1	1	1	1	–	–	–	–	–	–		7.0
John O'Kane	–	–	1	–	1	–	–	–	–	–	–	–	–%	7.0
Graeme Tomlinson	–	–	2	–	2	–	–	–	–	–	–	–	–%	7.0

▾ appearances/goals ➤

Player	Premier League	FA Cup	Coca Cola Cup	European Cup	Total	left ft	right	header	inside/outside the area	open play	set piece	assists	scoring rate	performance rating average
Gary Pallister	12 / – / 1	–	2	3	17 / 1	–	1	1	–	–	1	–	6%	7.2
Denis Irwin	12	–	2	3	16	–	–	–	–	–	–	–	–%	7.2
Steve Bruce	12	–	2 / 1	3	15 / 1	1	1	–	1	–	–	–	6%	7.4
Mark Hughes	11 / – / 2	–	3	3 / 1	14 / 3	–	2	1	1 / 2	3	–	1	21%	7.4
Paul Ince	11	–	3	–	14	–	–	–	–	–	–	3	–%	8.2
Andrei Kanchelskis	11 / – / 5	–	3	–	14 / 6	1	4	–	5 / 1	5	1	2	43%	7.4
Peter Schmeichel	11	–	3	–	14	–	–	–	–	–	–	–	–%	7.5
David May	8 / 1	–	2	3 / 1	13 / 1	1	1	–	1	–	–	–	7%	6.5
Lee Sharpe	10 / 1 / 1	–	2 / 2	3 / 2	13 / 3	3	1	2	3	3	–	3	20%	7.0
Ryan Giggs	9 / – / 1	–	2	3	11 / 2	3	–	–	3	3	–	4	27%	6.9
Brian McClair	8 / 3 / 3	–	3	3	11 / 3	3	4	–	2 / 2	3	–	4	31%	6.8
Eric Cantona	8 / – / 5	–	–	–	8 / 5	1	3	1	5	3	2	1	63%	7.6
Roy Keane	5 / 2	–	2	–	8 / 2	2	–	–	–	–	–	3	–%	7.2
Nicky Butt	1 / 3	–	3	–	7 / 3	–	–	–	–	–	–	–	–%	6.3
Keith Gillespie	1 / 1 / 1	–	3	–	4 / 1	1	–	–	1	1	–	–	25%	7.4
Gary Walsh	1	–	3	–	4	–	–	–	–	–	–	–	–%	7.3
David Beckham	–	–	3	–	3	–	–	–	–	–	–	–		7.0
Simon Davies	–	–	3	–	3	–	–	–	–	–	–	–	1%	7.0
Paul Scholes	– / 2 / 2	–	3 / 2	1	3 / 3	3	–	2	1 / 3	3	–	–	100%	7.3
Gary Neville	–	–	2 / 1	1	2	–	–	–	–	–	–	–	–%	7.0
Paul Parker	1 / 1	–	–	1	1	–	–	–	–	–	–	–	–%	7.3
Chris Caspar	–	–	1	–	1	–	–	–	–	–	–	–		7.0
John O'Kane	–	–	1 / 1	–	1	–	–	–	–	–	–	–	–%	7.0
Graeme Tomlinson	–	–	2	–	2	–	–	–	–	–	–	–	–%	7.0

league table

FA Carling Premiership 31 October 94

Team	P	W	D	L	F	A	Pts
Newcastle United	12	9	2	1	29	12	29
Nottingham Forest	12	8	3	1	25	13	27
Manchester United	12	8	1	3	21	9	25
Blackburn Rovers	12	7	3	2	25	12	24
Liverpool	11	7	2	2	27	11	23
Leeds United	12	6	3	3	18	13	21
Chelsea	11	6	1	4	21	14	19
Norwich City	11	5	4	2	12	10	19
Manchester City	12	5	4	2	21	14	19
Arsenal	12	5	3	4	17	13	18
Tottenham Hotspur	12	5	3	4	21	18	18
Southampton	12	4	3	5	18	22	15
Coventry City	12	4	3	5	14	20	15
West Ham United	12	4	2	6	8	14	14
Sheffield Wednesday	12	3	4	5	15	21	13
Crystal Palace	12	3	4	5	8	14	13
QPR	12	2	4	6	17	22	10
Aston Villa	12	2	4	6	11	18	10
Leicester City	12	2	3	7	14	24	9
Wimbledon	11	2	3	14	24	18	9
Ipswich Town	12	2	1	9	11	24	7
Everton	12	0	8	8	24	4	

* player of the month
Paul Ince performance rating average: 8.2

⏱ time split

Player	0-10 mins	11-20 mins	21-30 mins	31-40 mins	41-50 mins	51-60 mins	61-70 mins	71-80 mins	81-90 mins
Andrei Kanchelskis	–	–	–	2	–	–	–	1	–
Eric Cantona	–	–	1	2	–	–	–	–	–
Brian McClair	–	–	1	–	1	–	–	–	–
Ryan Giggs	–	–	1	–	–	1	–	–	–
Mark Hughes	–	–	–	1	–	1	–	–	–
Paul Scholes	–	–	1	–	1	–	–	–	–
Lee Sharpe	–	–	–	–	–	–	–	2	–
Steve Bruce	–	1	–	–	–	–	–	–	–
Keith Gillespie	–	–	–	1	–	–	–	–	–
David May	–	–	–	–	–	1	–	–	–
Gary Pallister	–	1	–	–	–	–	–	–	–
TOTAL SCORED	–	2	1	4	6	3	4	7	4
TOTAL CONCEDED	1	3	2	1	3	3	2	2	2

summary

	P	W	D	L	F	A
Premier League	12	8	1	3	21	9
Coca Cola Cup	3	2	–	1	4	3
European Cup	3	1	2	–	6	4
Total	18	11	3	4	31	16

notes

players must have played a minimum of three games in the month concerned to qualify for average performance ratings or scoring rate percentages↓ performance ratings are only awarded to players having played ten minutes or more in one match

BARCELONA

> Nou Camp

> Wednesday 2 November 1994 / 7.45pm

[Att: 115,000]

v **manchester united :** 4-0

team lineups

home team

1. Carlos Busquets
2. Albert Ferrer
3. Fernandez Abelardo
4. Ronald Koeman
5. Sergi Barjuan
6. Guillermo
7. José Maria Bakero
8. José Guardiola
9. Hristo Stoichkov
10. Romario
11. Jordi Cruyff

on the bench

12. Francisco Jara
13. Angoy
14. Ivan Iglesias
15. Altor Beguiristain
16. Luis Cembranos Martinez

75 mins → 62 mins

visitors

		rating
1.	Gary Walsh	6
2.	Paul Parker	5
3.	Steve Bruce	6
4.	Gary Pallister	6
5.	Denis Irwin	5
6.	Andrei Kanchelskis	6
7.	Nicky Butt	6
8.	Roy Keane	5
9.	Paul Ince	7
10.	Mark Hughes	6
11.	Ryan Giggs	7

on the bench   79 mins

12. Paul Scholes
13. David Beckham
14. Gary Neville
15. Simon Davies
16. Kevin Pilkington

stats

barcelona — united

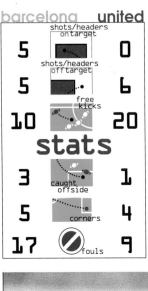

barcelona		united
5	shots/headers on target	0
5	shots/headers off target	6
10	free kicks	20
3	caught offside	1
5	corners	4
17	fouls	9

Ince drives forward in sheer desperation

Everything to play for – the proud pre-match line-up

bite & this!

"For this season at least, Ferguson's footballing fantasy might just have been bludgeoned into oblivion by the destroyers of Barcelona. They smashed his English champions to the very edge of humiliation with a four-goal destruction that Fergie has never suffered before on a foreign field..."
THE SUN

"Terry Venables returned to the scene of his greatest glories here last night - only to witness the daunting magnitude of his England task. The former Barcelona boss saw World Cup star Hristo Stoichkov help his old club rip England's finest to pieces.... realism came hurtling in to smash United's self-deception like a sledgehamer crushing a melon."
DAILY STAR

"The English champions were put to the sword 4-0 on a night as black as their shirts by the rapier-like skills of Barcelona's awesome strike force of Hristo Stoichkov and Romario." **TODAY**

"It was an humiliating experience. All I can say is that it was a bad, bad performance.

In these matches you hope you get a good start but their early goal was a killer.

In the second half we tried to play Ryan Giggs through the middle and change it around, but you leave gaps then and the high speed attacks of Romario and Stoitchkov stretched us.

We just couldn't handle them at all - all night. I have no complaints, world-class players like them are absolutely fantastic."
ALEX FERGUSON

in the area

		time^
9.	Hristo Stoichkov	9
		52
10.	Romario	45
2.	Albert Ferrer	88

word up

In arguably our biggest game for five years, **Barcelona** gave United a European lesson to remember in front of a capacity 115,000 Nou Camp crowd along with an 800 million television audience. It was never going to be easy with **Cantona**, **Sharpe** and **Schmeichel** absent, but the reds were systematically torn apart by a team of genuine world-class players for ninety minutes.

The sight of **Bakero**, **Romario**, **Stoitchkov** et al outclassing the reds was too much for the 7,000 travelling United fans to take, but deep down they and the players knew this was the standard needed should we really have a chance of winning the European Cup.

At the end of the ninety minutes, the huge video scoreboard at the top of the stadium told the sad story, "Barcelona 4 Manchester 0," with two goals from **Stoichkov**, and one each from **Ferrer** and **Romario**.

in the book

Referee:
J Quiniou, France
Rating: 5
Bookings:
Parker, Ince, Koeman

Nicky Butt runs himself into the ground

Giggs — turns a blind eye to his pursuer

>timeline

* **Tue 1st Nov** Division One sees Tranmere beat Barnsley by seven goals to one. Ex-Kop hero John Aldridge scored four.

> **68 DEAD IN AIR HELL – A THUNDERSTORM CAUSES A PLANE TO CRASH WHILST APPROACHING CHICAGO AIRPORT**
THE SUN Tue 1st Nov

* **Wed 2nd Nov** Manchester United lose 4-0 in the Champions' league. Stoichkov scores two of Barça's goals.

> **ANGER AS PINT OF MILK RISES BY 3p**
THE DAILY TELEGRAPH

* **Thu 3rd Nov** Chelsea and Arsenal proceed to the next round of the European Cup Winners' Cup beating FK Austria and Brondby respectively.

* Southampton's Nicky Banger joins Oldham for £225,000.

> **POST OFFICE SELL-OFF TO BE SHELVED**
THE DAILY TELEGRAPH Thu 3rd Nov

* **Fri 4th Nov** The Serious Fraud Office announce they will not be investigating the allegations made towards Terry Venables. The ex-Spurs chief says he is "not relieved" because he always knew he had "nothing to worry about."

ASTON VILLA
> Villa Park

[Att: 32,136]

v manchester united: **1-2**

[Last season : 1-2]

team lineups

home team

1.	Nigel Spink	
2.	Earl Barrett	
5.	Paul McGrath	
16.	Ugo Ehiogu	
15.	Phil King	
7.	Ray Houghton	
6.	Kevin Richardson	
11.	Andy Townsend	
3.	Steve Staunton	78 mins
9.	Dean Saunders	
10.	Dalian Atkinson	58 mins
	on the bench	
14.	Garry Parker	
13.	Mark Bosnich	
18.	Dwight Yorke	

visitors

		rating
13.	Gary Walsh	7
16.	Roy Keane	7
4.	Steve Bruce	7
6.	Gary Pallister	7
3.	Denis Irwin	7
14.	Andrei Kanchelskis	7
19.	Nicky Butt	
8.	Paul Ince	7
7.	Eric Cantona	7
24.	Paul Scholes	7 / 8 mins
11.	Ryan Giggs	7
	on the bench	
9.	Brian McClair	7 / 78 mins
25.	Kevin Pilkington	
31.	Keith Gillespie	7

Giggsy glides past Houghton

Denis Irwin takes on Barrett

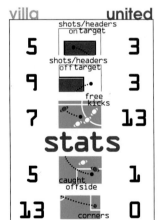

stats

villa — united

5	shots/headers on target	3	
9	shots/headers off target	3	
7	free kicks	13	
5	caught offside	1	
13	corners	0	
8	fouls	5	

first aid box

> Nicky Butt lost tooth after a clash of heads

bite this!

"Walsh enjoyed an afternoon of marvellous athletic saves - interspersed with skittish false rushes - and brilliantly turned away another Bruce deflection, from Staunton's shot. Later on, he was a goalkeeper redeemed." THE TIMES

"Champions Manchester United grabbed a fourth successive league victory to keep Villa chained in the relegation zone prison - and struggling for their lives.... United equalised seconds before the interval after gradually upping the tempo. Paul Scholes flighted a perfect ball for Kanchelskis to cross from the right and Ince struck a 25-yard effort that slipped past 'keeper Nigel Spink." TODAY

"Giggs failed to turn it on as he can, and so often does, so it was left to hard-working Kanchelskis to snatch a victory." THE SUN

A relief after Wednesday's match but we did have to defend very tightly to hold on to the result, especially in the second half, when Villa had us under the cosh.

I'm pleased for Gary Walsh. He is a very good 'keeper and a few years ago I thought he was destined to play for England until injury stopped him. He had some bad luck in Barcelona, so today will be a bit of a morale booster.

Aston Villa have had their problems but their lowly league position does not reflect on their performance. In fact, Villa are a very good side.

ALEX FERGUSON

in the area

		time^	left ft	right	header	inside/outside the area	^open play	set piece
8.	Paul Ince	44		*		*	*	*
14.	Andrei Kanchelskis	51		*		*		*
	assist: Denis Irwin							
10.	Dalian Atkinson	29						

Sportshot

in the book
Referee:
P Don, Middlesex
Rating: 7
Bookings:
Bruce, Gillsepie, McGrath

word up

United's rehabilitation after the shock in Barcelona came at the expense of ex-United manager Ron Atkinson and his Aston Villa side.

Villa pounded the United defence for the majority of the game but it was a day when God was wearing a United shirt. Villa had taken the lead after half an hour, when a **Dalian Atkinson** shot looped off **Bruce** over **Walsh's** head. The champions hit back when Ince produced a low half-volley past **Spink** from 20 yards a minute before half-time.

A surprise second goal was added early in the second half when a stunning run by Irwin resulted in a cross which **Cantona** left for **Kanchelskis** to control; the Ukrainian calmly stroked the ball past **Spink** and the five hundred United fans in the away end, plus many more dotted around the ground, were ecstatic.

Guess who stole the show?

>timeline

* **Sat 5th Nov**
> **TERRORIST DUD CASH KILLINGS – TWO MEN ARE SHOT AND KILLED IN A SUBURBAN STREET BY A TERRORIST HITMAN**
TODAY Sat 5th Nov

* **Sun 4th Nov** Dundee goal keeper Michel Pageaud is attacked by a fan as dozens of others invade the pitch.

> **MURDER AT WOOLWORTHS – STORE BOSS KNIFED TO DEATH FOR JUST TWO 50P PIECES**
DAILY MIRROR Sun 6th Nov

* **Mon 7th Nov** Forest 0 Newcastle 0. Doubts now surround Andy Cole, as he has only scored one goal since returning from injury four games ago.

> **MELLOR: WHAT'S THE BIG DEAL? – TORY MP SHRUGS OFF HIS BREAK DOWN OF MARRIAGE**
DAILY EXPRESS Mon 7th Nov

* **Tue 8th Nov** Bruce Grobbelaar does not fly on his previously arranged flight to Zimbabwe. Instead he leaves Gatwick to see his solicitors concerning match-fixing allegations made by journalists who were waiting at the airport.

manchester united v
MANCHESTER CITY
5-0

[Att:43,738]

>Old Trafford

>Thursday 10 November 1994 / 8.00pm

[Last season :2-0

home team

rating

1.	Peter Schmeichel	9
16.	Roy Keane	9
4.	Steve Bruce	9
6.	Gary Pallister	9
3.	Denis Irwin	9
14.	Andrei Kanchelskis	10
9.	Brian McClair	9
8.	Paul Ince	9
7.	Eric Cantona	9
10.	Mark Hughes	8
11.	Ryan Giggs	8

74mins

81mins

on the bench

24.	Paul Scholes	8
13.	Gary Walsh	
27.	Gary Neville	

visitors

32.	Simon Tracey
22.	Richard Edgehill
12.	Ian Brightwell
6.	Michael Vonk
3.	Terry Phelan
16.	Nicky Summerbee
10.	Garry Flitcroft
21.	Steve Lomas
11.	Peter Beagrie
8.	Paul Walsh
9.	Niall Quinn

on the bench

18.	David Brightwell
33.	John Burridge
24.	Adie Mike

team lineups

word up

The 5-1 derby defeat of 1989 was finally laid to rest tonight. United were simply rampant throughout, and from the minute **Cantona** put the reds ahead there was only going to be one result.

Kanchelskis added a second just before the break and the red masses erupted in fine voice. The magical Ukrainian, playing his best football at Old Trafford since he arrived in 1991, added his second just after the break.

When **Hughes** added a fourth, the City fans were doubly gutted, for no longer could they sing, "4-0 to Barcelona" at the reds in K-Stand and wave their Barça scarves which they had gone to the trouble of buying – thinking that would jerk the tears from their red rivals.

"We want five" echoed around Old Trafford, and when **Hughes** had an easy chance to oblige, it looked like our dream was coming true. Unfortunately his effort went wide, and everyone was ready to settle for four.

Kanchelskis, on a hat-trick, had other ideas when he sprinted clear of the City defence and smashed the ball home. His hat-trick was completed, as was a dream for the red half of Manchester.

United 5 City 0, the scoreboard said it all.

Giggs bamboozles
Ian Brightwell

John Peters

Denis and Brucey
congratulate the
hat-trick hero

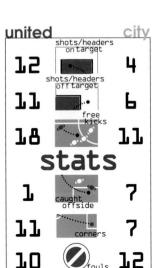

stats

united / city

united		city
	shots/headers on target	
12		4
	shots/headers off target	
11		6
	free kicks	
18		11
	caught offside	
1		7
	corners	
11		7
	fouls	
10		12

Schmikes attempts to wrest the ball from Quinn

>timeline

* **Wed 9th Nov** FIFA demand a report from the FA concerning Bruce Grobbelaar.

* Graham Taylor considers spending £1 million on Liverpool's Paul Stewart.

> **DISASTER FOR CLINTON IN US ELECTIONS - 2.30 AM NEWS: REPUBLICAN HOPE TO CAPTURE BOTH HOUSES OF CONGRESS FOR THE FIRST TIME IN 40 YEARS** THE INDEPENDENT Wed 9th Nov

* **Thu 10th Nov**

> **HUMILIATED CLINTON IN STRUGGLE FOR SURVIVAL - TAX CUT PLEDGE AS US LURCHES RIGHT** THE GUARDIAN Thu 10th Nov

* **Fri 11th Nov**

> **GROB LIBEL: I WON'T LET THIS ONE DROP - BRUCE GROBBELAAR ISSUES A WRIT TO THE SUN NEWSPAPER OVER MATCH FIXING ALLEGATIONS** DAILY STAR Fri 11th Nov

* **Sat 12th Nov**

> **MURDERED FOR £5,99 VIDEOS - SHOP ASSISTANT STABBED FOR A PACK OF BLANK VIDEO CASSETTES** DAILY EXPRESS Sat 12th Nov

bite this!

"Few events in English football provide a better antidote to the game's supposed poisons than a frantic derby. City were soon silenced, the Blue Moon spectacularly eclipsed by the Rampant Reds."
DAILYT TELEGRAPH

"Kanchelskis left a pile of blue-shirted debris strewn across Old Trafford... and up on Tyneside you sensed that Newcastle could hear the roar of the approaching engine."
DAILY EXPRESS

"It was an enthralling performance, a display of sheer, graceful beauty. These games are big time, and City showed that they don't quite have the players for the show just yet. United on the other hand were all-singing, all-dancing."
TODAY

"Andrei completed his first hat-trick in four years at Old Trafford as United, inspired by a revived Eric Cantona, frolicked on the wide open spaces left by a retreating City defence."
THE GUARDIAN

"It was a great performance - we looked sharp from the start.

Derbies are so important because they mean so much to local people. At the time Eric scored the first goal we were easing into the game but some of the football after that was absolutely brilliant.

That result has kept our momentum going in the league.

With all that we are now trying to build up some good form to take us into December."
ALEX FERGUSON

in the area

		time^	left ft	right	header	inside/outside the area		^open play	set piece
7.	Eric Cantona	24	*			*		*	
	assist: Andrei Kanchelskis								
14.	Andrei Kanchelskis	43	*			*		*	
	assist: Eric Cantona								
14.	Andrei Kanchelskis	47		*		*		*	
	assist: Eric Cantona								
14.	Andrei Kanchelskis	88		*		*		*	
	assist: Eric Cantona								
10.	Mark Hughes	70		*		*		*	

first aid box

> Ryan Giggs injured ankle

"Here I come..."

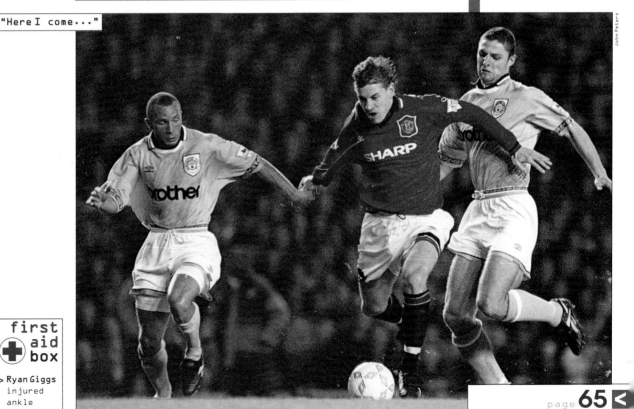

John Peters

*PAUL INCE
>midfielder

John Peters

personal file

born: Ilford, 21/10/67
height: 5'10" weight: 12st 2lb
international team: England
signed pro for United: 13/09/89
transfer fee: £1,250,000
United league debut : 16/09/89 v Millwall (h)

✳BRIAN McCLAIR
>forward

[Player Portrait

John Peters

personal file

born: Airdrie, 8/12/63
height: 5'10" **weight:** 12st 9lb
international team: Scotland
signed pro for United: 1/07/87
transfer fee: £850,000
United league debut: 15/08/87 v Southampton (a)

manchester united v
CRYSTAL PALACE
[Att: 43,738]
3-0
>Saturday 19 November 1994/ 3.00pm
>Old Trafford

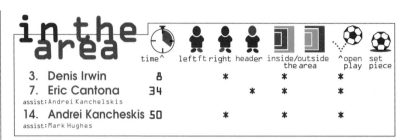

team lineups

home team
		rating
1.	Peter Schmeichel	7
27.	Gary Neville	9
6.	Gary Pallister	8
12.	David May	7
3.	Denis Irwin	8
14.	Andrei Kanchelskis	9
9.	Brian McClair	9
8.	Paul Ince	8
7.	Eric Cantona	8
10.	Mark Hughes	8
18.	Simon Davies	8

on the bench
24.	Paul Scholes	8
25.	Kevin Pilkington	8
31.	Keith Gillespie	7

7mins
52mins
72mins

visitors
1.	Nigel Martyn
22.	Darren Patterson
6.	Chris Coleman
14.	Richard Shaw
3.	Dean Gordon
2.	John Humphrey
4.	Gareth Southgate
23.	Ricky Newman
11.	John Salako
9.	Chris Armstrong
18.	Andy Preece

on the bench
15.	Bobby Bowry
16.	Darren Pitcher
19.	Rhys Wilmot

in the area

		time^	left ft	right	header	inside/outside the area	open play	set piece
3.	Denis Irwin	8	*			*	*	
7.	Eric Cantona	34		*		*	*	
	assist: Andrei Kanchelskis							
14.	Andrei Kancheskis	50	*			*	*	
	assist: Mark Hughes							

first aid box
> Peter Schmeichel back injury during warm-up
> Andrei Kanchelskis pulled stomach muscle

John Peters

Hughesie fends off Southgate

stats
united / palace

united		palace
13	shots/headers on target	5
8	shots/headers off target	6
17	free kicks	16
3	caught offside	9
8	corners	6
13	fouls	8

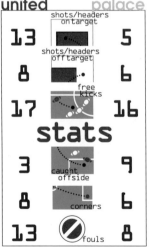

Old friends Cantona and Shaw

John Peters

in the book
Referee: B Hill, Market Harborough
Rating: 6
Bookings: Patterson, Southgate

word up

With seven straight wins, no draws or defeats at the Theatre of Dreams so far this season, on-form Crystal Palace can't have fancied their chances against the champions in the Old Trafford fortress.

The United side had an unfamiliar look about it due to injuries but despite this they seemed to gel well together. **Irwin** shot the reds ahead when his free-kick deflected past **Martin** into the Palace net.

Just before half-time **Kanchelskis** whipped over a great cross which **Cantona** met and headed high into the net for our second of the afternoon.

Schmeichel went off only minutes into the first half after a back injury occurred during the warm-up. **Pilkington**, his replacement, pulled off a fine series of saves, mainly from **Armstrong**, to keep yet another clean sheet at Old Trafford.

The three points were secured and the defeat for Newcastle ensured that we went back to the top of the league.

Darren Patterson needs to know if Simon Davies is ticklish

John Peters

bite this!

"Like any god worth his salt, Cantona has awesome, destructive powers and he used them to wreak terrible damage on the wide-eyed savages from Crystal Palace.... Cantona frightened Palace to death with his swaggering presence." **TODAY**

"Palace boss Alan Smith held his hands up after the champions had destroyed his youngsters and reckoned Cantona was "priceless"..." **DAILY STAR**

"Here were Palace, facing what was virtually United's Coca-Cola Cup side, only to find novices such as Neville, Davies and Gillespie looking ominously like the real thing." **THE OBSERVER**

"Suddenly United hit the form that destroyed Manchester City, their pace and accuracy dissecting Palace's defence. Cantona powered in a low shot, Paul Ince tried a spectacular volley and Mark Hughes gave a rendition of his overhead kick routine." **THE SUNDAY TELEGRAPH**

"We saw some terrific football being played today. The youngsters did a marvellous job. In the last few weeks all the players have risen to the challenge that has confronted them. We needed consistency in our performances and we got it.

We are now at the top of the table but it's early days, obviously we want to stay there but it won't be easy.

Unfortunately we have got a few injured players at the moment and Peter became another victim today. He pulled his back in the warm-up, and even the strongest painkillers couldn't help him. As soon as he kicked the ball for the first time he knew he had to come off." **ALEX FERGUSON**

Andrei tucks home the third

John Peters

>timeline

* Thu 17th Nov

> NHS CHIEF'S PRICE OF LOYALTY - MILLIONAIRE HEALTH BOSS WHO SLAMMED DOCTORS FOR LACK OF LOYALTY WALKED AWAY FROM A COMPANY JUST WEEKS BEFORE IT CRASHED OWING £1 MILLION
Today Thu 17th Nov

* Fri 18th Nov

CROPS AND GROBBERS - GROBBELAAR QUIZZED BY POLICE OVER MATCH-FIXING ALLEGATIONS
Today Fri 18th Nov

* Sat 19th Nov Grobbelaar plays in the first match since his 'nightmare' began and says it was "the hardest game of my life." Even though Southampton managed to overcome Arsenal by one goal to nil.
Daily Express Sat 19th Nov

* Media reports suggest Alex Ferguson is going to propose a £4 million transfer deal to buy Teddy Sheringham.

* Sun 20th Nov Brian Little's managerial future is under question as Villa are said to want him.

*GOTHENBURG
>Ullevi Stadium

>Wednesday 23 November 1994 / 7.30pm

v **manchester united:**

[Att: 36,350]

3-1

[Last season : 1-2]

team lineups

home team

1. Thomas Ravelli
2. Pontus Kamark
3. Joachim Bjorklund
4. Magnus Johansson
5. Mikael Nilsson
6. Mikael Martinsson
7. Jesper Lindquist
8. Stefan Rehn
9. Jesper Blomqvist
10. Magnus Erlingmark
11. Steffan Pettersson

on the bench

12. Erik Wahlstedt
13. Dick Last
14. Thomas Andersson
15. Johan Anegrund
16. Patrick Bengston

visitors

		rating
1.	Gary Walsh	7
2.	David May	5
3.	Denis Irwin	5
4.	Steve Bruce	8
5.	Andrei Kanchelskis	8
6.	Gary Pallister	7
7.	Eric Cantona	6
8.	Paul Ince	6
9.	Brian McClair	7
10.	Mark Hughes	7
11.	Simon Davies	7
	on the bench	
12.	Gary Neville	7
13.	Kevin Pilkington	
14.	Nicky Butt	7
15.	David Beckham	
16.	Paul Scholes	

Gary Walsh at full stretch during training before the Gothenburg match

Empics

Sparky misses the target

John Peters

stats

gothenburg united

shots/headers on target

7   5

shots/headers off target

3   4

free kicks

22   27

caught offside

3   8

corners

8   9

fouls

24   14

 **word up**

Following the slaughter in Barcelona, United desperately needed a win against the Swedish champions to restore any hopes of progressing in the European Cup.

The situation was only to reach nightmare proportions as group leaders Gothenburg justified their position with a competent 'English style' performance which left United second best in every department.

Youngster **Blomqvist**, apparently a United fan himself, gave the Swedes the lead as early as the tenth minute and from then on it was an uphill struggle for United.

A **Hughes** goal, our first away goal in Europe this season, raised the hopes of the 2,500 travelling fans, but before they had even stopped celebrating, United were a goal behind again.

Gothenburg added a third goal to wrap the game up and if we thought that things couldn't get any worse we were wrong, as **Ince** was sent off for dissent.

The result virtually confirmed our exit from Europe – for this season at least – but it was no more than we deserved.

Hopes are raised as Andrei sprints through

Eric misses out

bite this!

"Gothenburg star Jesper Blomquist, who plays with the same style and flair as Giggs, will be cursed by United for ever and a day. In the space-age Ullevi Stadium, this latter-day Viking brought devastation and ultimate destruction to Alex Ferguson's European Cup dream..."
THE SUN

"The measure of their disarray came in two colours - yellow cards for Cantona and Hughes, a red for Ince - and, although they may point to the absence through injury of Schmeichel, Giggs, Parker, Keane and Sharpe, there can be no excuse..."
THE TIMES

"Let's not beat about the bush... this was a rubbish performance. The chips were down and Manchester United again failed miserably to rise to the European challenge..."
MANCHESTER EVENING NEWS

"Ferguson's English champions were tortured by the blistering skills of the Swedes, who carved through United's defending at will. When they needed heroes, they were simply not good enough."
DAILY STAR

We were well beaten and I suppose you can use all kinds of excuses but, on the night, we just weren't good enough.
I feel terribly disappointed with our performance but I don't want to take any credit away from Gothenburg. We had worked for hours on what happened in Barcelona, but we defended terribly.
It's difficult to believe that we could let in goals like that, but when we got the equaliser I thought we would have a chance.
I think we are out. We are capable of beating any team at Old Trafford, but I don't think Barcelona will lose to the Swedes.
ALEX FERGUSON

in the area

	time^	left	ft	right	header	inside/outside the area	^open play	set piece
10. Mark Hughes assist: Eric Cantona	64				*		*	*
9. Jesper Blomquist	10							
10. Magnus Erlingmark	64							
2. Pontus Kamark	71							

*ARSENAL

> Saturday 26 November 1994 / 3.00pm

v **manchester united:**
> **Highbury** [Att: 38,301]

0-0

[Last season]
:2-2

team lineups

home team

1. David Seaman
2. Lee Dixon
12. Steve Bould
6. Tony Adams
3. Nigel Winterburn
21. Steve Morrow
17. John Jensen
11. Eddie McGoldrick
19. Jimmy Carter   66mins
8. Ian Wright
9. Alan Smith   45mins

on the bench

14. Martin Keown
13. Vince Bartram
27. Paul Dickov

visitors

		rating
13.	Gary Walsh	7
27.	Gary Neville	7
12.	David May	8
6.	Gary Pallister	7
3.	Denis Irwin	7
14.	Andrei Kanchelskis	6
9.	Brian McClair	7
8.	Paul Ince	7
7.	Eric Cantona	7
10.	Mark Hughes	7
31.	Keith Gillespie	7 56mins

on the bench   73mins

18.	Simon Davies	7
25.	Kevin Pilkington	
19.	Nicky Butt	7

word up

When two teams who have won three out of the last four league titles meet, you come to expect top quality football. Manchester United and Arsenal have presented us with some great matches recently but this wasn't one of them.

Good pals **Paul Ince** and **Ian Wright** spent the afternoon snapping and snarling at each other in an angry match where six players were booked and **Mark Hughes** was sent off.

The midweek defeat in Gothenburg had quashed the morale of the reds and I suppose the last thing they needed was a game against bore-draw specialists Arsenal.

Of course a tedious 0-0 draw was what we got.

McClair did come close for United but **David Seaman** was far from being the busiest man on the pitch. Instead referee **Kelvin Morton** had that honour for all the wrong reasons.

McClair collides with Wright and the ball goes flying

Eric Cantona swerves to evade Bould

bite ◖ this!

"In the Premiership, most sides eschew Arsenal-style attrition for United's adventure, but such attitudes court disaster in Europe. Ask Newcastle United. Arsenal, negatively but intelligently, shut up shop more quickly than bailiffs in a recession." **THE DAILY TELEGRAPH**

"In the first half Arsenal undoubtedly had the edge... The second half began in Metropolitan darkness, the air was rawer and so, alas, was the play."
SUNDAY EXPRESS

"We had quite a bad result on Wednesday night and Arsenal have also had a bad week. So I suppose, in that respect, a draw is probably the best result for both of us and unfortunately there are no goals to talk about...

Despite the fact we drew, I am very pleased with the character we showed today. Arsenal are never an easy team to play and today's match at Highbury was certainly a tough one." **ALEX FERGUSON**

in the book

Referee: K Morton, Bury St. Edmunds
Rating: 6
Bookings:
☐ Ince,
☐ Hughes,
☐ Gillespie,
☐ Butt,
☐ McGoldrick,
☐ Dickov
■ Hughes

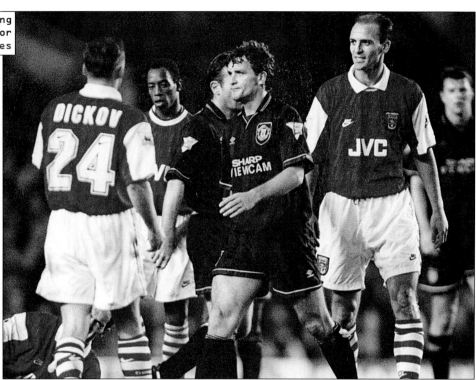

Marching orders for Hughes

stats

arsenal | united

shots/headers on target
4 | 3

shots/headers off target
3 | 4

free kicks
19 | 28

caught offside
4 | 7

corners
6 | 5

fouls
24 | 12

No shortage of concentration – and no goals

>time*line*

* **Fri 25th Nov**
> **MAJOR CLEARS FIRST HURDLE – BUT LEADERSHIP CHALLENGE IS STILL LOOMING FROM TORY REBELS**
DAILY EXPRESS Fri 25th Nov

* **Sat 26th Nov** Joe Royle tries to prise Duncan Ferguson with a £4 million offer.

> **BT SECRETS STILL PUBLICLY AVAILABLE – THOUSAND OF PHONE NUMBERS INCLUDING THOSE OF 10 DOWNING STREET ARE REVEALED TO BE ACCESSIBLE THROUGH INTERNET**
THE INDEPENDENT Sat 26th Nov

* **Sun 27th Nov** Tottenham are reported to have made attempts to buy Ruddock back from Liverpool.

> **BIHAC FEARS MASSACRE – SERB FORCES THREATEN BIHAC WHICH CONTAINS AT LEAST 70,000 RESIDENTS**
INDEPENDENT ON SUNDAY Sun 27th Nov

* **Mon 28th Nov** Peter Schmeichel faces six weeks out of action with a bad back.

> **SHOT DOWN BY JILTED GROOM ON WHAT SHOULD HAVE BEEN THEIR WEDDING DAY**
TODAY Mon 28th Nov

*RYAN GIGGS
>forward

[Player Portrait]

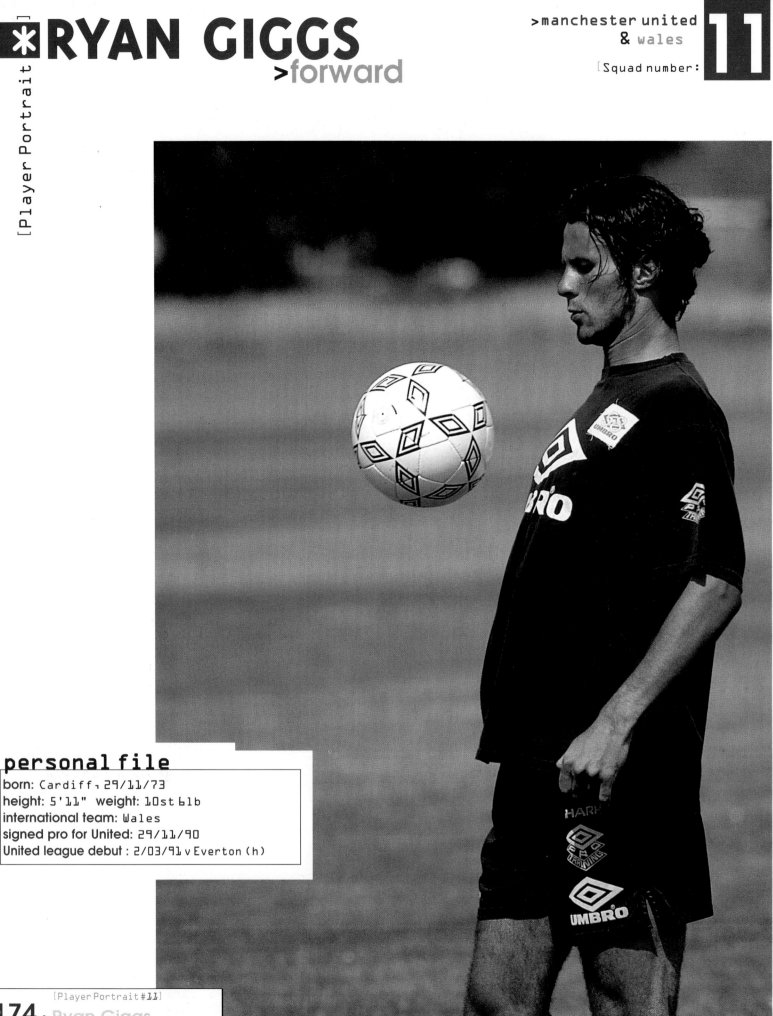

personal file

born: Cardiff, 29/11/73
height: 5'11" weight: 10st 6lb
international team: Wales
signed pro for United: 29/11/90
United league debut : 2/03/91 v Everton (h)

november 94
monthly statistics *

▽ appearances/goals

appearances apps as sub / goals	Premier League	FA Cup	Coca Cola Cup	European Cup	Total	left ft	right	header	inside/outside the area	^open play	set piece	assists	scoring rate	performance rating average
Paul Ince	4 - 1	- - -	- - -	2 - -	6 - 1	-	1	-	- 1	-	-	-	17%	6.2
Denis Irwin	4 - 1	- - -	- - -	2 - -	6 - 1	-	1	-	1 -	1	-	1	17%	7.0
Andrei Kanchelskis	4 - 5	- - -	- - -	2 - -	6 - 5	1	4	-	5 -	5	-	2	83%	7.7
Gary Pallister	4 - -	- - -	- - -	2 - -	6 - -	-	-	-	- -	-	-	-	-%	7.3
Eric Cantona	4 - 2	- - -	- - -	1 - -	5 - 2	1	-	1	2 -	2	-	4	40%	7.4
Mark Hughes	3 - 1	- - -	2 - 1	- - -	5 - 2	-	2	-	2 -	2	-	1	40%	7.2
Steve Bruce	2 - -	- - -	- - -	2 - -	4 - -	-	-	-	- -	-	-	-	-%	7.5
Brian McClair	3 1 -	- - -	1 - -	2 - -	4 1 -	-	-	-	- -	-	-	-	-%	7.8
Gary Walsh	2 - -	- - -	- - -	2 - -	4 - -	-	-	-	- -	-	-	-	-%	6.8
Ryan Giggs	2 - -	- - -	- - -	3 - -	3 - -	-	-	-	- -	-	-	-	-%	7.3
Roy Keane	2 - -	- - -	- - -	3 - -	3 - -	-	-	-	- -	-	-	-	-%	7.0
David May	2 - -	- - -	- - -	3 - -	3 - -	-	-	-	- -	-	-	-	-%	6.7
Nicky Butt	1 1 -	- - -	1 - -	2 2 -	2 2 -	-	-	-	- -	-	-	-	-%	6.8
Simon Davies	1 - -	- - -	1 - -	2 1 -	2 1 -	-	-	-	- -	-	-	-	-%	7.3
Gary Neville	2 - -	- - -	1 - -	2 1 -	2 1 -	-	-	-	- -	-	-	-	-%	7.7
Peter Schmeichel	2 - -	- - -	- - -	2 - -	2 - -	-	-	-	- -	-	-	-	-%	8.0
Keith Gillespie	1 2 -	- - -	1 2 -	- - -	1 2 -	-	-	-	- -	-	-	-	-%	7.0
Paul Parker	- - -	- - -	- - -	- - -	- - -	-	-	-	- -	-	-	-	-%	5.0
Paul Scholes	1 2 -	- - -	1 2 -	- - -	1 2 -	-	-	-	- -	-	-	-	-%	9.7
Kevin Pilkington	- - -	- - -	- - -	- - -	- - -	-	-	-	- -	-	-	-	-%	7.5

season to november 94
cumulative statistics *

▽ appearances/goals

appearances apps as sub / goals	Premier League	FA Cup	Coca Cola Cup	European Cup	Total	left ft	right	header	inside/outside the area	^open play	set piece	assists	scoring rate	performance rating average
Gary Pallister	16 - 1	- - -	2 - -	5 - -	23 - 1	-	-	1	1 -	-	1	-	4%	7.3
Denis Irwin	16 - 1	- - -	2 - -	4 - -	22 - 1	-	1	-	1 -	1	-	1	5%	7.1
Paul Ince	15 - 1	- - -	- - -	5 - -	20 - 1	-	1	-	- 1	1	-	3	5%	7.6
Andrei Kancheskis	15 - 10	- - -	- - -	5 - 1	20 - 11	2	8	1	10 -	10	-	4	55%	7.5
Steve Bruce	14 - 1	- - -	1 - -	4 1 -	19 1 1	-	-	1	1 -	-	1	-	5%	7.5
Mark Hughes	14 - 3	- - -	- - -	5 - 2	19 - 5	-	4	1	3 2	5	-	2	26%	7.3
David May	10 1 -	- - -	2 - 1	4 - -	16 1 1	-	1	-	1 -	-	1	-	6%	6.5
Peter Schmeichel	13 - -	- - -	- - -	3 - -	16 - -	-	-	-	- -	-	-	-	-%	7.6
Brian McClair	11 4 3	- - -	3 - -	1 - -	15 3 4	-	2	2	3 1	3	1	-	22%	7.1
Ryan Giggs	11 - 1	- - -	- - -	3 - 2	14 - 3	3	-	-	3 -	3	-	4	21%	7.0
Eric Cantona	12 - 7	- - -	- - -	1 - -	13 - 7	2	3	2	7 -	5	2	5	54%	7.5
Lee Sharpe	10 1 1	- - -	2 - -	1 - 2	13 3 3	1	2	-	3 -	3	-	3	20%	7.0
Roy Keane	7 2 -	- - -	1 - -	3 - -	11 2 -	-	-	-	- -	-	-	3	-%	7.2
Nicky Butt	2 4 -	- - -	3 - -	- - -	4 4 -	-	-	-	- -	-	-	-	-%	6.5
Simon Davies	1 - -	- - -	3 - -	1 1 -	5 1 -	-	-	-	- -	-	-	-	-%	7.2
Keith Gillespie	2 3 1	- - -	3 - -	- - -	5 3 1	1	-	-	1 -	1	-	-	20%	7.3
Gary Neville	2 - -	- - -	2 1 -	1 - -	4 2 -	-	-	-	- -	-	-	-	-%	7.3
Paul Scholes	1 4 1	- - -	3 - 2	2 - -	4 6 3	-	2	1	3 -	3	-	-	75%	8.1
David Beckham	- - -	- - -	3 - -	- - -	3 - -	-	-	-	- -	-	-	-	-%	7.0
Paul Parker	1 1 -	- - -	- - -	2 - -	3 2 -	-	-	-	- -	-	-	-	-%	6.8
Chris Casper	- - -	- - -	1 - -	- - -	1 - -	-	-	-	- -	-	-	-	-%	7.0
John O'Kane	- - -	- - -	1 1 -	- - -	1 1 -	-	-	-	- -	-	-	-	-%	7.0
Kevin Pilkington	- 1 -	- - -	- - -	- - -	- 1 -	-	-	-	- -	-	-	-	-%	7.5
Graeme Tomlinson	- - -	- - -	2 - -	- - -	- 2 -	-	-	-	- -	-	-	-	-%	7.0
Gary Walsh	3 - -	- - -	3 - -	2 - -	8 - -	-	-	-	- -	-	-	-	-%	7.0

league table

FA Carling Premiership	30 November 94						
Blackburn Rovers	16	11	3	2	35	13	36
Manchester United	16	11	2	3	31	10	35
Newcastle United	16	10	4	2	34	17	34
Liverpool	16	9	3	4	33	17	30
Nottingham Forest	16	8	4	4	25	16	28
Leeds United	16	8	3	5	24	19	27
Manchester City	16	7	4	5	27	25	25
Chelsea	16	7	3	6	25	20	24
Norwich City	16	6	6	4	15	14	24
Coventry City	16	6	4	6	19	26	22
Southampton	16	5	6	5	23	26	21
Arsenal	16	5	5	6	18	16	20
Crystal Palace	16	5	5	6	15	18	20
Tottenham Hotspur	16	5	4	7	25	31	19
Wimbledon	16	5	3	8	17	28	18
Sheffield Wednesday	15	4	5	6	14	17	17
West Ham United	16	5	2	9	17	17	17
QPR	16	4	4	8	23	31	16
Everton	16	3	5	8	12	24	14
Aston Villa	15	3	4	8	19	27	14
Leicester City	16	3	3	10	17	29	12
Ipswich Town	16	3	2	11	15	31	11

* player of the month
Paul Scholes
performance rating average: **9.7**

⏱ time split

	0-10 mins	11-20 mins	21-30 mins	31-40 mins	41-50 mins	51-60 mins	61-70 mins	71-80 mins	81-90 mins
Andrei Kanchelskis	-	-	1	-	5	2	-	1	2
Eric Cantona	-	-	1	2	2	-	-	2	-
Mark Hughes	-	1	-	1	-	3	-	-	-
Brian McClair	-	-	-	1	-	1	-	-	1
Ryan Giggs	-	-	-	1	-	1	-	-	-
Paul Scholes	-	-	-	1	-	-	-	-	1
Lee Sharpe	-	-	-	-	-	-	-	2	1
Steve Bruce	-	-	-	-	1	-	-	-	-
Keith Gillespie	-	-	-	-	1	-	-	-	-
Paul Ince	-	-	-	-	-	1	-	-	-
Denis Irwin	1	-	-	-	-	-	-	-	-
David May	-	-	-	-	1	-	-	-	-
Gary Pallister	-	1	-	-	-	-	-	-	-
TOTAL SCORED	1	2	2	5	10	4	6	7	5
TOTAL CONCEDED	3	3	3	1	4	3	1	3	3

summary

	P	W	D	L	F	A
Premier League	16	11	2	3	31	10
Coca Cola Cup	3	2	-	1	4	3
European Cup	5	1	2	2	7	11
Total	24	14	4	6	42	24

notes

players must have played a minimum of three games in the month concerned to qualify for average performance ratings or scoring rate percentages; performance ratings are only awarded to players having played ten minutes or more in one match

manchester united v
NORWICH CITY

[Att: 43,789]

1-0

>Old Trafford

>Saturday 3 December 1994 / 3.00pm

[Last season]
:2-0

team lineups

home team

		rating
1.	Gary Walsh	7
27.	Gary Neville	7
3.	Denis Irwin	7
12.	David May	7
14.	Andrei Kanchelskis	7
6.	Gary Pallister	7
7.	Eric Cantona	9
8.	Paul Ince	7
9.	Brian McClair	8
10.	Mark Hughes	7
11.	Simon Davies	7

88mins

on the bench
19.	Nicky Butt	7
25.	Kevin Pilkington	
31.	Keith Gillespie	7

88mins

visitors

1.	Bryan Gunn
2.	Mark Bowen
3.	Rob Newman
4.	Ian Crook
5.	Jon Newsome
16.	Carl Bradshaw
15.	Darryl Sutch
18.	Robert Ullathorne
9.	Mark Robins
10.	John Polston
11.	Jeremy Goss

63mins

on the bench
8.	Mike Milligan
25.	Jamie Cureton
24.	Andy Marshall

in the book

Referee:
T Holbrook,
Walsall
Rating: 5

Bookings:
Neville

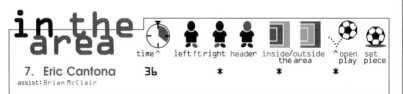

Andrei slips past Bowen with the greatest of ease

Sportshot

in the area

	time^	left ft	right	header	inside/outside the area		^open play	set piece
7. Eric Cantona assist: Brian McClair	36		*			*	*	

bite this!

"United were considerably below their best but still managed to beat a spirited Norwich City side through a goal by Eric Cantona."
DAILY TELEGRAPH

"Cantona, Giggs, Sharpe, Kanchelskis, Hughes and Ince receive the plaudits, but Manchester United's title pursuit is being built on an outstanding defence."
THE TIMES

"Ince played in severe pain from his two-year-old shoulder injury… But everyone who witnessed the sheer power of his display knows he is the best guv'nor around and that without him the genius of Cantona would be submerged."
DAILY STAR

"I have to say that this is a good result for us. The first half saw a good performance from Norwich and then in the second half they went went straight for our throats - tackling like tigers and fighting for every loose ball.
It was a game of two halves - Norwich playing some excellent football, and every one of their players distinguished themselves admirably throughout the match. As I said before - a very good result."
ALEX FERGUSON

Before Eric can react, Gunn smothers

word up

The French genius that is **Eric Cantona** showed once again that on his day there is no better player in this country.

He scored the only goal of the game just before half-time, and the three points gained ensured that we stayed in touch at the top with leaders Blackburn.

Bryan Gunn, the popular Norwich 'keeper, was a busy man in the first half as United played some thrilling football. **Hughes**, **Ince** and **Cantona** all came close, but **Gunn** resisted all their efforts with a string of outstanding saves.

However, **Gunn** was well and truly beaten when Ince and **McClair** combined well, leaving **Cantona** free to place the ball inside the far post; a fine goal.

The Canaries pressurised United in the second half, but a defence which included **May** at centre-back and young **Gary Neville** stood firm to keep our 100 per cent home record intact.

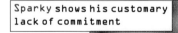
Simon Davies drives into the side-netting

John Peters

>time*line*

* **Tue 29th Nov** If rumours are true that Paul Merson made money from selling "his story" to a national newspaper. He will be asked to make a sizeable donation to an appropriate charity.

> MASS MURDERER KILLED IN PRISON - JEFFREY DAHMER, SELF-CONFESSED AMERICAN SERIAL KILLER, KILLED WHILST SERVING 16 LIFE SENTENCES
The Independent Tue 29th Nov

* **Wed 30th Nov**

> PHIL SOBS OVER PAL BUSTER - THE GREAT TRAIN ROBBER COMMITS SUICIDE AT THE AGE OF 62
The Sun Wed 30th Nov

* **Thu 1st Dec** Paul Merson is told of the outcome of his hearing. He is to spend six weeks in a rehabilitation centre whilst Arsenal will continue to pay his £5,000 weekly wage.

> UN CHIEF MEETS WALL OF INSULTS IN BOSNIA
The Independent

Sparky shows his customary lack of commitment

united   norwich

	shots/headers on target	
1		1
	shots/headers off target	
12		5
	free kicks	
10		7

stats

	caught offside	
1		3
	corners	
2		3
	fouls	
6		7

manchester united v
GALATASARAY

[Att: 39,220]

4-0

> Old Trafford

> Wednesday 7 December 1994 / 7.30pm

team lineups

home team

		rating
1.	Gary Walsh	8
2.	Gary Neville	8
3.	Denis Irwin	8
4.	Steve Bruce	8
5.	Roy Keane	8
6.	Gary Pallister	8
7.	Eric Cantona	8
8.	Nicky Butt	8
9.	Brian McClair	8
10.	David Beckham	9
11.	Simon Davies	8

on the bench

12.	David May
13.	Kevin Pilkington
14.	Paul Scholes
15.	John O'Kane
16.	David Johnson

visitors

1.	Gintaras Stauce
2.	Penbe Ergün
3.	Korkmaz Bulent
4.	Balkanli Sedat
5.	Korkmaz Mert
6.	Kerimoglu Tugay
7.	Erdem Arif
8.	Hamzaoglu Hamza
9.	Sukur Hakan
10.	Suat Kaya
11.	Kubilay Türkyilmaz

on the bench

12.	Bologlu Nezihi
13.	Tütüneker Ugur
14.	Tepekule Usuf
15.	Sancakli Saffet
16.	Gür Bekir

Eric strides away from his marker

David Beckham's scoring debut was one highlight on an anti-climactic night

word up

United finally went out of the European Cup on a night of mixed emotions at Old Trafford. There was pride in the young red side, which was seven short of the team that won the league in May.

Sadly, the four goals, and it could have been more, meant nothing as Barcelona got the point they needed at home to Gothenburg to qualify for the final stages of the Champions League.

Young pretenders **Neville, Butt, Davies** and **Beckham** blended in superbly with older talents like **Keane** and **Cantona**. **Davies** put the reds a goal up after just two minutes when he angled a left-foot shot past keeper **Stauce**.

Beckham, in vibrant form, added a second after 38 minutes with a speculative low shot from twenty yards. **Keane** added a third and an own goal made the scoreline 4-0. United had clearly done enough at Old Trafford but what mattered was the result in Barcelona.

From nowhere a cheer went up; everyone thought Gothenburg had done the impossible and taken the lead in Nou Camp... suddenly the biting Mancunian wind didn't seem so bad. Was there an opposing fan in the crowd somewhere, because the rumours were soon confirmed as being false? It was cruel, very cruel on the young reds who perhaps deserved to show their talents to the rest of Europe in the latter rounds.

There's always next year.

united galatasaray

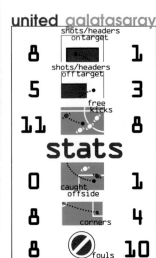

united		galatasaray
	shots/headers on target	
8		1
	shots/headers off target	
5		3
	free kicks	
11		8

stats

united		galatasaray
	caught offside	
0		1
	corners	
8		4
	fouls	
8		10

Keano's finishing earns him a Becks

bite this!

"If the Theatre of Dreams is the catwalk of football, then there were four young models who strutted their stuff along it with a swagger and a sway that eased the pain of United's exit.
Although Gary Neville, David Beckham, Nicky Butt and Simon Davies might not yet carry the same resonance as Eric Cantona, Ryan Giggs, Andrei Kanchelskis and Lee Sharpe."

DAILY EXPRESS

"For what it was worth, Alex Ferguson's weakened though youthfully-buoyant team beat a semi-interested Galatasaray side 4-0.

THE GUARDIAN

"I was delighted with our performance. The young players went out and enjoyed themselves. The early goal settled them, but it was an outstanding performance and I'm proud of them. They grew up out there.

Roy Keane showed great determination and character, and set the pattern from the very first tackle. Our front men's display was an object lesson to any young player who was watching. Their movement was fantastic.

We'll be back. Even with half-a-dozen players unavailable because of the rules, we have still finished with as many points as Barcelona and we can build on that next year.

ALEX FERGUSON

Nicky Butt shows the Turks the way to go

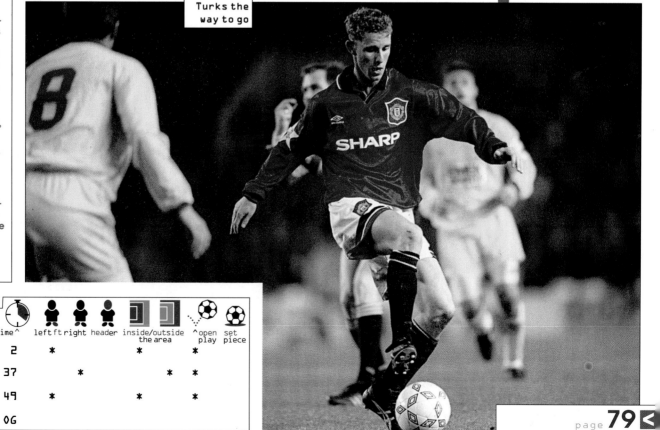

in the area

		time^	left ft	right	header	inside/outside the area	^open play	set piece
11.	Simon Davies	2	*			*	*	
	assist: Brian McClair							
10.	David Beckham	37		*		*	*	
	assist: Eric Cantona							
5.	Roy Keane	49	*			*	*	
	assist: David Beckham							
10.	Korkmaz Bulent	OG						

QUEENS PARK RANGERS 2-3

> Loftus Road v **manchester united:** [Att: 18,948]

> Saturday 10 December 1994/ 3.00pm

[Last season :2-3]

team lineups

home team

13.	Sieb Dykstra
3.	Clive Wilson
16.	Danny Maddix
2.	David Bardsley
6.	Alan McDonald
7.	Andy Impey
25.	Steve Hodge
14.	Simon Barker
9.	Les Ferdinand
20.	Kevin Gallen
11.	Trevor Sinclair

on the bench

8.	Ian Holloway
23.	Peter Caldwell
10.	Bradley Allen

visitors

		rating
13.	Gary Walsh	8
27.	Gary Neville	7
3.	Denis Irwin	7
4.	Steve Bruce	7
6.	Gary Pallister	7
16.	Roy Keane	8
14.	Andre Kanchelskis	7
8.	Paul Ince	7
9.	Brian McClair	9
24.	Paul Scholes	9
18.	Simon Davies	8

on the bench

19.	Nicky Butt
25.	Kevin Pilkington
31.	Keith Gillespie

Incey battles it out with Les Ferdinand

stats

	qpr	united
shots/headers on target	12	6
shots/headers off target	3	3
free kicks	9	19
caught offside	5	0
corners	10	5
fouls	14	9

in the area

	time^	left ft	right	header	inside/outside the area	^open play	set piece
24. Paul Scholes assist: Denis Irwin	34			*	*	*	
assist: Simon Davies	47		*	*			*
16. Roy Keane assist: Brian McClair	44	*		*	*		
9. Les Ferdinand	23						

Salford's Paul Scholes comes of age

in the book

Referee:
G Poll, Reading
Rating: 6

Bookings:
Neville, Irwin, Keane, Ince, McDonald, Ferdinand

bite  this!

Pally does his best to restrain Kevin Gallen

word up

The midweek exit from Europe gave United a chance to intensify their domestic efforts, starting at Loftus Road. As usual, United fans amassed at Sheperds Bush in their thousands, expecting victory.

The scene was clearly set but Les Ferdinand wasn't reading it; he smashed a shot home past **Gary Walsh** from 30 yards after 23 minutes. With **Cantona** and **Hughes** absent for the reds it was up to **Scholes** and **McClair** to provide the firepower and they didn't disappoint. **Scholes** levelled the scoreline after 34 minutes, **Keane** made it 2-1 after 44 minutes and **Scholes** added his second just after the break. Three United goals in the space of fifteen blistering minutes destroyed Rangers.

The talents of **Paul Ince** in midfield were clear for all to see, the Guv'nor was simply inspirational. **Ferdinand** and the lively **Kevin Gallen** keep battling for QPR and their efforts were rewarded with another goal for the England striker after 64 minutes. The home side could muster no more goals and the reds returned to Manchester with three points firmly in the bag.

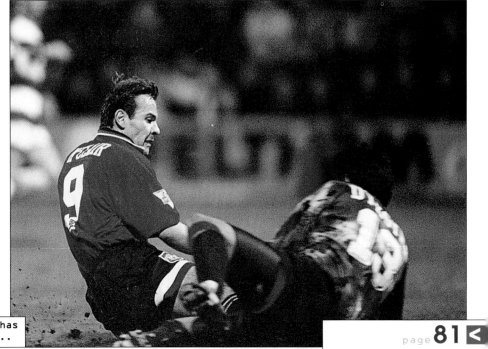

Choccy has a rest...

manchester united v
NOTTS FOREST
[Att: 43,744]
1-2
>Old Trafford

>Saturday 17 December 1994 /3.00pm

team lineups

home team
		rating
13.	Gary Walsh	7
16.	Roy Keane	9
3.	Denis Irwin	7
4.	Steve Bruce	7
14.	Andrei Kanchelskis	7
6.	Gary Pallister	7
7.	Eric Cantona	8
8.	Paul Ince	9
9.	Brian McClair	8
10.	Mark Hughes	8
11.	Ryan Giggs	7

87 mins
75 mins

on the bench
19.	Nicky Butt
25.	Kevin Pilkington
27.	Gary Neville

visitors
1.	Mark Crossley
2.	Des Lyttle
18.	Alf-Inge Haaland
5.	Steve Chettle
3.	Stuart Pearce
7.	David Phillips
11.	Steve Stone
8.	Scott Gemmill
14.	Ian Woan
10.	Stan Collymore
22.	Bryan Roy

on the bench
85 mins
20.	Paul McGregor
13.	Tommy Wright
9.	Lars Bohinen

bite this!

"An inability to cope with counter-attacks, centres and Stan Collymore debunked theories of Manchester United's invincibility at Old Trafford. The damage inflicted by Forest was invested with a statistical significance, too. This proved not only United's first home defeat of the season, but involved Alex Ferguson's team conceding their first home goal in Premier League action since April." **SUNDAY TIMES**

"Referee Keith Burge booked eight players, six from Forest, and at times the game threatened to explode into a full-scale brawl as United saw defeat looming." **THE PEOPLE**

"...United struggled for supremacy always beyond them once Forest buttressed the back four with tuck-in protectors Steve Stone and Ian Woan." **THE SUN**

"Forest were worth their win simply because more of their players produced the kind of performances demanded in this kind of setting, and with these stakes involved." **DAILY EXPRESS**

"We started off quite slowly in this match and then we went a goal down to a superb hit by Stan Collymore, those kind of goals are his speciality. Stuart Pearce's shot, however, took a deflection and it was then that I thought this wasn't going to be our day.
These were the first league goals conceded at Old Trafford this season and I suppose all good things have to come to an end. We have a good run in our league matches at home, but it's a pity that Forest felt they had to foul us and waste time to beat us. We showed a lot of commitment today, especially in the second half, and we were unlucky in the end not to get a point." **ALEX FERGUSON**

Gemmill is kept at bay by a touch of 'magique'

word up

Counter attacks and **Stan Collymore**, that's what Nottingham Forest brought to Old Trafford, and it was enough for Frank Clark's men to inflict United's first home Premier defeat of the season.

Hughes came close for the reds early on but it was a matter of time before that man **Collymore** made his mark.

Benefiting from excellent service from **Stone** on the right, he created space once again outside the United area, before letting fly, curling a twenty-yard strike that gave Walsh no chance.

United did have their fare share of chances, but Forest stood firm in defence- with **Lyttle** marking **Giggs** out of the game.

Cantona did pull a goal back for United, but his role in the match was firmly overshadowed by that of **Collymore**; a class player.

Incey strives for the breakthrough

Stone closes Sparky down

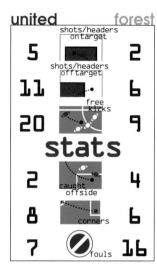

	united	forest
shots/headers on target	5	2
shots/headers off target	11	6
free kicks	20	9

stats

	united	forest
caught offside	2	4
corners	8	6
fouls	7	16

>timeline

* **Fri 16th Dec** Ryan Giggs returns from a six-match lay-off due to an ankle injury.

* **Sat 17th Dec** George Graham fails to convince an FA inquiry that he is innocent of receiving an illegal payment. The allegation has been made in connection with the signing of John Jensen.

* **Sun 18th Dec** Stuart Pearce is accused by Paul Ince of racial abuse during United's match against Nottingham Forest.

> **IT WAS HIM - NEWS OF THE WORLD REVEALS £18M LOTTERY-WINNER [AGAINST HIS WILL]** News of the World Sun 18th Dec

* **Mon 19th Dec** The PFA are appealing to Stuart Pearce to apologise to Paul Ince for racist remarks.

> **LOTTS FOR MY MATES - LOTTERY WINNER GIVES £40,000 TO EACH OF HIS MATES** Daily Star Mon 19th Dec

* **Tue 20th Dec** Panorama are not backing down from their allegations on Terry Venables. As a result he is to carry on with his libel damage claim.

in the book

Referee: K Burge, Tonypandy
Rating: 6
Bookings:
Keane,
Giggs,
Lyttle,
Chettle,
Woan,
Stone,
Pearle

in the area

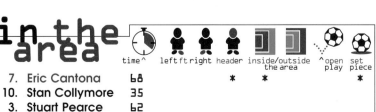

	time^	left ft	right	header	inside/outside the area	^open play	set piece
7. Eric Cantona	68			*	*		*
10. Stan Collymore	35						
3. Stuart Pearce	62						

✳ CHELSEA

v manchester united:
[Att: 31,161]
> Stamford Bridge

2-3

[Last season :1-0]

[Premier League match #20]

team lineups

home team

1.	Dmitri Kharine	
2.	Steve Clarke	
5.	Erland Johnsen	
6.	Frank Sinclair	
15.	Andy Myers	
12.	Craig Burley	
20.	Glenn Hoddle	54mins
17.	Nigel Spackman	
10.	Gavin Peacock	
7.	John Spencer	73mins
8.	Paul Furlong	

on the bench

9.	Mark Stein	
13.	Kevin Hitchcock	
18.	Eddie Newton	

visitors

rating

13.	Gary Walsh	8
16.	Roy Keane	7
6.	Gary Pallister	7
4.	Steve Bruce	7
3.	Denis Irwin	8
19.	Nicky Butt	8
9.	Brian McClair	9
8.	Paul Ince	7
11.	Ryan Giggs	7
10.	Mark Hughes	7
7.	Eric Cantona	7

45mins

76mins

on the bench

14.	Andrei Kanchelskis	6
25.	Kevin Pilkington	
27.	Gary Neville	7

Cantona confounds Spackman

John Peters

Giggs hands it to Choccy

stats

chelsea   united

shots/headers on target

| 2 | | 4 |

shots/headers off target

| 3 | | 2 |

free kicks

| 23 | | 23 |

| 5 | caught offside | 7 |

| 6 | corners | 7 |

| 17 | fouls | 15 |

bite ● this!

"Having squandered a two-goal lead, United found the reserve of energy needed to mount one last assault and snatch a winning goal and three points.
It was typically United, mixing the boldest approach of any team away from home in the Premiership, with the resilience often cited as the trademark of the ungifted." **THE SUN**
"Mark Hughes gave United the lead after 22 minutes and Chelsea looked set to be overwhelmed with the power coupled with the finesse of the champions' outstanding form." **TODAY**

"We got the winner from McClair and three points here are very valuable. Our last two games in London have each produced five goals, so you can't say people aren't getting their money's worth.
I'd describe this match as a bit of a cup-tie. Our passing in the first half was superb, but then we relaxed a little and got a bit careless. We had kept good possession, had good penetration and played superbly. So it almost turned into a disaster for us. I could not visualise that when we led 2-0. Their second goal was a real throw-away from our point of view, but maybe getting the penalty so early in the second half caused us to relax and get careless."

ALEX FERGUSON

> 84   [Premier League #20]
Chelsea   > 26-12-93   2-3
Stamford Bridge   away ✳ win

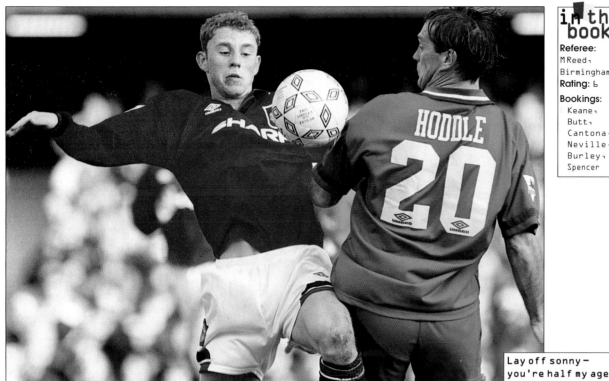

Lay off sonny — you're half my age

in the book

Referee:
M Reed, Birmingham
Rating: 6
Bookings:
Keane, Butt, Cantona, Neville, Burley, Spencer

>timeline

* **Wed 21st Dec** Leyton Orient are put up for sale by their Chairman. He even says he will except £5 for the club.

* Manchester City beat Newcastle United 2-0 in the Coca Cola Cup.

> **THE DEVASTATED PARENTS OF SCHOOLGIRL NIKKI LOCKLEY WEPT IN FURY LAST NIGHT AFTER JUDGES CHOSE NOT TO JAIL THE DRIVER WHO KILLED HER ON A ZEBRA CROSSING**
> The Sun Wed 21st Dec

* **Thu 22nd Dec** Peter Schmeichel will be out for Manchester United's next six games whilst he recovers from his back injury.

> **CRASH JET HAD OUTDATED RADAR - THE BOEING 737 THAT MISSED A HOUSING ESTATE BY FEET HAD OLD EQUIPMENT ONBOARD**
> The Independent Thu 22nd Dec

* **Fri 23rd Dec**

> **TWELVE STEPS TO JOY - ONE OF BEVERLY ALLITT'S VICTIMS TAKES TWELVE STEPS AFTER SHE WAS TOLD SHE WOULD NEVER WALK. PART OF HER RECOVERY IS DUE TO A UNIQUE THERAPY CENTRE IN AMERICA THAT ALLOWS PEOPLE TO SWIM WITH DOLPHINS**
> Today Fri 23rd Dec

* **Mon 26th Dec** Duncan Ferguson makes his debut for Everton.

> **BOY, 11 SEES MOTHER SHOT - A GUNMAN WAS ON THE LOOSE LAST NIGHT AFTER A MOTHER WAS SHOT DEAD IN FRONT OF HER YOUNG SON**
> Daily Express Mon 26th Dec

* **Tue 27th Dec**

> **JET HIJACKERS DIE AS 170 ARE FREED - GENDARMES STORMED AN AIR FRANCE AIRBUS AT MARSEILLE AIRPORT**
> The Independent

word up

A mid-day kick-off on Boxing day away at Chelsea proved very unpopular with United fans. For many it meant a 6am start, but the red performance on the Stamford Bridge pitch ensured that the early start was worth the effort.

With **Cantona** his usual brilliant self and **Giggs** showing signs of his old confidence, Chelsea were always going to be in trouble, **Giggs** should have given us the lead after 20 minutes, but he made amends shortly afterwards by providing a perfect cross for **Hughes**, who charged home his first goal since November. Chelsea looked neat and tidy without ever threatening the United goal.

Just 17 seconds into the second half, **Keane's** thrusting run into the box was brought to an end by a clumsy challenge from **Myers**. A penalty was awarded and **Cantona** put United 2-0 up.

Instead of consolidating their lead, United continued to attack, playing some exhibition football, and they very nearly paid the price for it. The home side equalised through **Spencer** following a dubious penalty.

Disaster struck when Newton,

Pally thwarts the threat from Peacock

who had only been on the pitch four minutes, levelled the scores to the delight of Chelsea's biggest crowd of the season. When all seemed lost **McClair** scored a killer winning goal to seal our second consecutive 3-2 away from home. Who said Chelsea were `carefree'?

in the area

		time^	leftft	right	header	inside/outside the area		^open play	set piece
10.	**Mark Hughes**	21		*		*		*	
	assist: RyanGiggs								
7.	**Eric Cantona**	46		*		*			*
9.	**Brian McClair**	78	*			*		*	
	assist: Eric Cantona								
8.	**Paul Furlong**	58							
18.	**Eddie Newton**	77							

manchester united v
LEICESTER CITY
1-1

>**Old Trafford**

>**Thursday 28 December 1994 / 8.00pm**

[Att: 43,789]

team lineups

home team

		rating
13.	Gary Walsh	6
27.	Gary Neville	6
6.	Gary Pallister	6
4.	Steve Bruce	6
3.	Denis Irwin	7
14.	Andrei Kanchelskis	6
9.	Brian McClair	8
16.	Roy Keane	7
11.	Ryan Giggs	8
10.	Mark Hughes	6
7.	Eric Cantona	7

69mins

on the bench

12.	David May
25.	Kevin Pilkington
24.	Paul Scholes 7

visitors

33.	Kevin Poole
4.	Jimmy Willis
2.	Simon Grayson
19.	Colin Hill
3.	Mike Whitlow
6.	Steve Agnew
17.	Steve Thompson
21.	Lee Philpott
10.	Mark Draper
20.	David Oldfield
9.	Iwan Roberts

73mins

on the bench

8.	Mark Blake
1.	Gavin Ward
18.	David Lowe

69mins

Simon Grayson bars Ryan's way

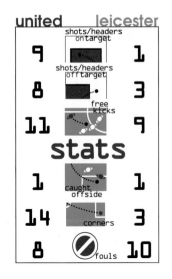

stats

united		leicester
9	shots/headers on target	1
8	shots/headers off target	3
11	free kicks	9
1	caught offside	1
14	corners	3
8	fouls	10

Cantona's header flies wide

John Peters

bite this!

"It was certainly a horrendous and costly mix-up for the reds in a game they dominated without being able to turn their command into goals."
MANCHESTER EVENING NEWS

"The quality of Leicester's play in the first half can only have encouraged their new manager. True, they made only one clear-cut chance, which Thompson drove narrowly past a post ten minutes before half-time, but their football was bright, unusually so for a team in their position - and at times United were distinctly second best."
THE TIMES

"United were missing Paul Ince, and although Roy Keane battled in midfield, the absence was clear for all to see." **DAILY STAR**

"I didn't think we got any more than we deserved. One point and one goal each was a fair result. We didn't create enough chances to win this match tonight, but we did have a fantastic amount of pressure to deal with in the second half.

The problem was that we didn't get enough quality crosses in and that stopped us getting the chances to hurt them. We didn't trouble their 'keeper too often but we were also quite unlucky at times. Roy Keane and Ryan Giggs might have been a bit luckier on a different night, but not this time."
ALEX FERGUSON

word up

A game most United fans will want to forget.

The reds attacked but lacked the firepower to put relegation certs Leicester in their place. **Chances came and went but the Foxes held out with some gutsy defending.**

By half-time there had been plenty of goal-mouth action at the Leicester end but no goals. Just when it looked like we were in for more of the same in the second half, up popped **Kanchelskis** with a ferocious drive to give us a much-needed goal. The relief on the pitch was mirrored by another capacity crowd in the stands.

Leicester didn't give up, though, and forced an equaliser a couple of minutes later. One-one, that is how the game ended, a bad result but one of those days when nothing seems to go your way.

Andrei milks the applause

Sportshot

in the book

Referee:
D J Gallagher, Banbury
Rating: 6

Bookings:
Hughes, Philpott,

John Peters

Spot the ball

>timeline

* **Wed 28th Dec**

> ANGRY MAN OF THEATRE DIES - PLAYWRIGHT JOHN OSBORNE DIES AT THE AGE OF 65
Daily Mail Wed 28th Dec

* **Thu 29th Dec** Ian Rush scores a hat-trick as Liverpool knock Blackburn Rovers out of the Coca-Cola Cup. Neil Ruddock and Alan Shearer receive a yellow card each for 'fisti-cuffs'.

* Shock results for Forest and West Ham as they are beaten by Milwall and Bolton respectively.

in the area

	time^	left ft	right	header	inside/outside the area	^open play	set piece
14. Andrei Kanchelskis 61		*			*	*	
assist: Mark Hughes							
3. Mike Whitlow 65							

✳ SOUTHAMPTON

> Saturday 31 December 1994 / 3.00pm

> The Dell

v manchester united:

[Att: 15,204]

2-2

[Last season] : 1-3

home team
1. Bruce Grobbelaar
2. Jeff Kenna
3. Francis Benali
4. Jim Magilton
6. Ken Monkou
7. Matthew Le Tissier
9. Iain Dowie
18. David Hughes
21. Tommy Widdrington
24. Ronnie Ekelund
15. Jason Dodd

66 mins

on the bench
8. Craig Maskell
13. Dave Beasant
12. Neil Heaney

visitors

		rating
13.	Gary Walsh	7
27.	Gary Neville	7
6.	Gary Pallister	9
4.	Steve Bruce	8
12.	David May	7
19.	Nicky Butt	7
9.	Brian McClair	7
16.	Roy Keane	8
11.	Ryan Giggs	7
10.	Mark Hughes	7
7.	Eric Cantona	8

79 mins

on the bench
24.	Paul Scholes	
25.	Kevin Pilkington	
31.	Keith Gillespie	8

Keano marks Pally's goal with a bear-hug

John Peters

Dowie (now with Palace) wrestles with Bruce for possession

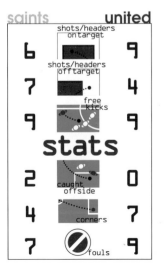

stats

saints		united
	shots/headers on target	
6		9
	shots/headers off target	
7		4
	free kicks	
9		9
	caught offside	
2		0
	corners	
4		7
	fouls	
7		9

▶88

[Premier League #22]
Southampton
> 31-12-94
The Dell

2-2
away draw ✳

word up

The Rolls Royce of efficiency that is Manchester United purred into Southampton following the long trek down from Manchester. **Donning the new blue and white third strip, the reds looked far from the classiest product on the market, more an unpredictable Cortina than a Roller, and that's how they played.**

Jim Magilton put the Saints one up just before half-time, but United stirred themselves enough to equalise through **Nicky Butt** seven minutes after the interval. **David Hughes**, the young Saints striker who has suffered a series of successive injuries, put the home side back in front when he struck home sweetly after 75 minutes

Gary Pallister, on a foray into the Southampton penalty area, headed a crucial equaliser soon after, to the mild satisfaction of manager Alex Ferguson who said bluntly: "We didn't deserve more than we got."

Pally beats Dowie to make it 2-2

Sir Nicky of Butt takes on Hughes of Southampton

Allsport

>timeline

* **Fri 30th Dec** Mike Marsh joins Coventry from West Ham for a fee of £450,000.

> WOMAN FORCED OFF MOTORWAY AFTER PURSUIT BY ANGRY DRIVER **The Times**

* **Sat 31st Dec** Manchester United is on John Major's New Years Honours list along with TV soccer pundit Jimmy Hill.

* Everton erase memories of their 4-1 defeat inflicted by Sheffield Wednesday on Boxing Day; they turn the score around to beat Ipswich Town 4-1.

> ABSOLUTELY FABULOUS! TELLY SWEETIE JOANNA (LUMLEY) GETS NEW YEAR GONG

Daily Star Sat 31st Dec

* **Sun 1st Jan** Sunderland's supporters sing "what a load of rubbish" after their 1-1 draw with Derby.

* Tottenham inflict a 4-0 defeat on Coventry City at Highfield Road. Coventry's Julian Darby started the scoring with an own goal in just the seventh minute.

in the area

		time^	left ft right	header	inside/outside the area	^open play	set piece
19.	Nicky Butt	51	*		*	*	
6.	Gary Pallister	78		*	*		*
assist: Eric Cantona							
4.	Jim Magilton	44					
18.	David Hughes	74					

in the book

Referee:
P Foulkes, Essex
Rating: 6
Bookings: Neville, Butt, McClair, Cantona, Benali, Dodd

*DAVID MAY
>defender

Allsport

personal file

born: Oldham, 24/06/70
height: 6'0" **weight:** 12st
international team: England
signed pro for United: 1/07/94
transfer fee: £1,200,000
United league debut: 20/08/94 v Queens Park Rangers

december 94

▾appearances/goals ➤

	Premier League	FA Cup	Coca Cola Cup	European Cup	Total	left ft	right	header	inside/outside the area	^open play	set piece	assists	scoring rate	performance rating average
Brian McClair	5 - 1	-	-	1 -	7 - 1	1			1	1		3	14%	8.1
Gary Pallister	5 - 1	-	-	1 -	7 - 1			1	1		1		14%	7.3
Gary Walsh	5	-	-	1	7								-%	7.3
Steve Bruce	4	-	-	-	6								-%	7.2
Eric Cantona	5 - 3	-	-	1 -	6 - 3		2	1	3	1	2	5	50%	7.8
Denis Irwin	4	-	-	-	6							1	-%	7.2
Roy Keane	4 - 1	-	-	1 - 1	6 - 2	2			2	2			33%	7.8
Mark Hughes	5	-	-	1	5 - 1			1	1	1			20%	7.0
Gary Neville	3 (2)	-	-	-	5 (2)								-%	6.0
Ryan Giggs	4	-	-	-	4							2	-%	7.3
Paul Ince	4	-	-	-	4								-%	7.5
Andrei Kanchelskis	3 (1) - 1	-	-	1	4 - 1		1		1	1			25%	6.6
Nicky Butt	2 (3) - 1	-	-	1	3 - 1			1	1	1			33%	7.4
Simon Davies	1	-	-	1 - 1	3 - 1	1			1	1			33%	7.7
David May	2	-	-	-	2								-%	7.0
David Beckham	-	-	-	1 - 1	1 - 1			1			1	1	100%	9.0
Paul Scholes	(1)	-	-	1 - 2	1 - 2	1	2			2	2	1	200%	8.0
Keith Gillespie	(2)	-	-	-	2								-%	7.3

season to december 94

▾appearances/goals ➤

	Premier League	FA Cup	Coca Cola Cup	European Cup	Total	left ft	right	header	inside/outside the area	^open play	set piece	assists	scoring rate	performance rating average
Gary Pallister	22 - 2	-	2	6	30 - 2			2	2		2		7%	7.3
Denis Irwin	21 - 1	-	2	5	28 - 1		1		1	1		2	4%	7.1
Steve Bruce	19 - 1	-	5 - 1	25 - 1	25 - 1			1	1	1			4%	7.4
Mark Hughes	20 - 4	-	5	2 - 2	24 - 6	5	1	4	2	6		3	25%	7.3
Paul Ince	18 - 1	-	5	-	24 - 1		1	-		1		3	4%	7.6
Andrei Kanchelskis	18 (1) - 11	-	5 - 1	23 - 12	23 - 12	3	8	1	11	11		4	48%	7.3
Brian McClair	17 - 3 - 4	3	2	22 - 5	22 - 5	1	2	4	4	4		3	20%	7.4
Eric Cantona	17 - 10	-	2	-	19 - 10	2	5	3	10	6	4	10	53%	7.6
Ryan Giggs	15 - 1	-	3	3 - 2	18 - 3	3			3	3		6	17%	7.1
David May	12 - 1	-	2	4	18 - 1	2		1	1		1		5%	6.6
Roy Keane	12	1	1	3 - 1	17 - 2	2			2	2		3	11%	7.4
Peter Schmeichel	13	-	3	-	16								-%	7.6
Gary Walsh	9	-	3	3	15								-%	7.1
Lee Sharpe	10 - 1	-	2	3 - 2	13 - 3	3	3		2		3	3	20%	7.0
Nicky Butt	4 (6)	-	5	1	12 - 1	1			1		1		6%	6.7
Gary Neville	6 (2)	-	2	1	9 (4)								-%	6.6
Simon Davies	2 - 1	-	3	2 - 1	7 - 1	1			1		1	2	11%	7.3
Keith Gillespie	2 (5) - 1	-	3	-	5 - 1	1			1		1		9%	7.3
Paul Scholes	1 (5) - 1	2	3 - 2	3	4 - 6	1	2	3	5	4	1		45%	8.1
David Beckham	-	-	3	1 - 1	4 - 1				1		1		25%	7.5
Paul Parker	1 - 1	-	-	2 - 1	3 - 2	1					1		-%	6.8
Chris Casper	-	-	1	-	1								-%	7.0
John O'Kane	-	-	1 - 1	-	1 - 1								-%	7.0
Kevin Pilkington	(2)	-	-	-	2								-%	7.5
Graeme Tomlinson	-	-	2	-	2								-%	7.0

league table

FA Carling Premiership 31 December 94	P	W	D	L	F	A	Pts
Blackburn Rovers	21	15	4	2	45	16	49
Manchester United	22	14	4	4	42	19	46
Liverpool	22	12	6	4	40	19	42
Newcastle Utd	22	11	6	4	40	24	39
Nottingham Forest	22	11	6	5	35	23	39
Tottenham Hotspur	22	9	6	7	38	34	33
Norwich City	22	9	6	7	21	19	33
Leeds United	21	9	5	7	29	27	32
Sheffield Wed	22	8	6	8	29	30	30
Chelsea	22	8	5	9	29	30	29
Manchester City	22	8	5	9	33	38	29
Wimbledon	22	8	5	9	29	36	29
Arsenal	22	7	7	8	26	25	28
Queens Park Rangers	22	7	6	9	34	38	27
Southampton	22	6	8	8	33	38	26
West Ham United	22	7	4	11	19	24	25
Coventry City	22	6	7	9	21	38	25
Crystal Palace	22	5	8	9	15	21	23
Everton	21	5	7	9	20	29	22
Aston Villa	22	4	9	9	27	33	21
Leicester City	22	3	6	13	21	37	15
Ipswich Town	22	3	4	15	21	46	13

time split

	0-10 mins	11-20 mins	21-30 mins	31-40 mins	41-50 mins	51-60 mins	61-70 mins	71-80 mins	81-90 mins
Andrei Kanchelskis			1		5	2	1	1	2
Eric Cantona		1	3	3		1	2		
Mark Hughes		1	1		3				
Brian McClair			1		1			1	
Paul Scholes			2		1		1		
Ryan Giggs					1				1
Lee Sharpe								2	1
Roy Keane					2				
Gary Pallister		1						1	
David Beckham			1						
Steve Bruce				1					
Nicky Butt									1
Simon Davies	1								
Keith Gillespie				1					
Paul Ince				1					
Denis Irwin	1								
David May									1
own goal									1
TOTAL SCORED	2	2	3	8	14		4	9	6
TOTAL CONCEDED	3	3	4	2	5	4	4	5	3

*player of the month
Brian McClair
performance rating average: 8.1

summary

	P	W	D	L	F	A
Premier League	22	14	4	4	42	19
Coca Cola Cup	3	2	-	1	4	3
European Cup	6	2	2	2	11	11
Total	31	18	6	7	57	33

notes

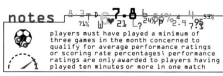

players must have played a minimum of three games in the month concerned to qualify for average performance ratings or scoring rate percentages; performance ratings are only awarded to players having played ten minutes or more in one match

manchester united v
COVENTRY CITY
[Att: 43,130]
2-0
> Tuesday 3 January 1995 / 7.45pm > Old Trafford

[Last season :0-0]

team lineups

home team | rating

13.	Gary Walsh	7
27.	Gary Neville	7
4.	Steve Bruce	7
6.	Gary Pallister	7
3.	Denis Irwin	7
31.	Keith Gillespie	8
16.	Roy Keane	7
19.	Nicky Butt	7
7.	Eric Cantona	7
24.	Paul Scholes	7
11.	Ryan Giggs	8

63mins

on the bench
9.	Brian McClair
25.	Kevin Pilkington
12.	David May

visitors

1.	Steve Ogrizovic
17.	Ally Pickering
6.	Steve Pressley
3.	Steve Morgan
16.	Paul Williams
7.	Sean Flynn
25.	Mike Marsh
15.	Paul Cook
14.	Leigh Jenkinson
8.	Roy Wegerle
19.	Dion Dublin

82mins

on the bench
53mins
24.	Cobi Jones
13.	Jonathan Gould
4.	Julian Darby

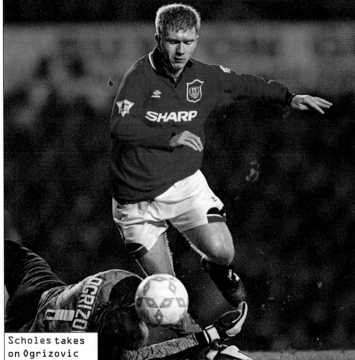

Scholes takes on Ogrizovic

Allsport

united   coventry

stats

	shots/headers on target	
5		1
	shots/headers off target	
9		4
	free kicks	
13		16
	caught offside	
7		4
	corners	
7		3
	fouls	
9		10

in the book
Referee:
G Willard, Worthing
Rating: 5
Bookings:
Neville, Bruce, Cook, Pressley,

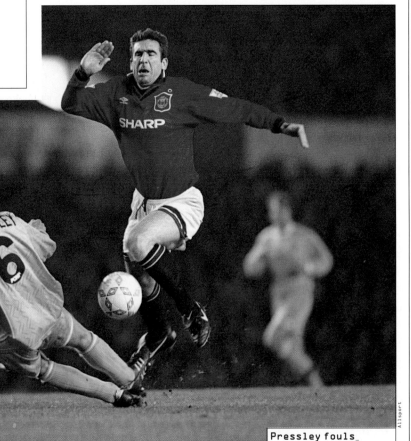

Pressley fouls Cantona — some people never learn!

Allsport

bite this!

"The exuberance of United's young stand-ins rolled United forward relentlessly, and the game was over within four minutes of the restart. Scholes robbed centre-back Pressley 25 yards out, and when the Coventry defender caught him in the box, referee Willard consulted his linesman before awarding the penalty... It could easily have been 4-0 by the final whistle."
DAILY EXPRESS

"Keith Gillespie took a fine Cantona pass and crossed low for Nicky Butt to flick it on and force Steve Ogrizovic into a tame punch out to the feet of the grateful Scholes."
DAILY STAR

"Coventry could have lost more heavily, some eccentric refereeing sparing their blushes as a blind eye was turned to two apparently blatant penalties." **THE TIMES**

"It was a great experience for the younger players. They all wanted to try things. They made mistakes, but they got on with it - they showed they have the right temperament and bottle. The kids know that they can do better than this. And they will.

Paul's run for the goal was brilliant. It was the kind Denis Law used to get for fun. It was as if to say to the keeper 'if you drop it I'm here.' It was a poacher's goal.

Coventry really didn't have a chance out there today. All my players were determined."
ALEX FERGUSON

word up

Paul Scholes put United a touch nearer Blackburn and alongside other youngsters, Gillespie, Butt and Gary Neville, showed the quality of the youth players Alex Ferguson has assembled at Old Trafford.

Hughes, McClair and May were all relegated to the subs bench for this match, as Fergie tried to "freshen things up" with the youngsters after United had dropped seven points in their last four games.

How right the manager was, because when Gillespie whipped in a delicious cross on 29 minutes, Butt unveiled a majestic back heel flick which keeper Steve Ogrizovic par-

ried into the path of the waiting Scholes, who gladly snapped up his chance of his first Premiership Old Trafford goal.

With Keane releasing Scholes into space all the time United were in rampant form. Indeed, it was Scholes who won United a penalty after 47 minutes, when he was pulled back by Pressley, which ended in the defenders sending off. When tempers had cooled, Cantona sent the 'keeper one way and the ball the other. Two-nil to the champions.

Action-packed stuff – on a night when United showed they are refusing to give up their treasured title without a fight.

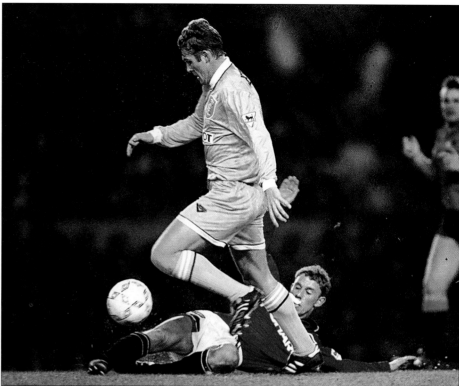

Nicky Butt perfects his sliding tackle

Coventry's defence is powerless to stop Scholes

>timeline

* Mon 2nd Jan Spurs win the big London derby by one goal to nil in a passionate affair which sees Schwarz of Arsenal sent off in England for the first time.

* Tue 3rd Jan

> KILLERS GO OVER JAIL WALL – TWO KILLERS AND A BOMB MANIAC BURST OUT OF A TOP SECURITY JAIL LAST NIGHT
Daily Star Tue 4th Jan

* Wed 4th Jan Anthony Yeboah of Eintracht Frankfurt is set to join Leeds United.

in the area

		time^	left ft right	header	inside/outside the area	^ open play	set piece
24.	Paul Scholes	29	*		*	*	
	assist: Steve Bruce						
7.	Eric Cantona	49	*		*	*	
	assist: Denis Irwin						

page 93

*SHEFFIELD UNITED

> **Monday 9 January 1995 / 7.45pm**

> **Bramall Lane**

[Att: 22,322]

v **manchester united:** 0-2

[Last season :0-3]

team lineups

home team
1. Alan Kelly
2. Kevin Gage
3. Brian Gayle
4. Roger Nilsen
5. Andy Scott
6. Paul Rogers
7. Charles Hartfield
8. Glynn Hodges
9. Dane Whitehouse — 75 mins
10. Carl Veart
11. Nathan Blake — 85 mins

on the bench
12. Philip Starbuck
13. William Mercer
14. Jostein Flo

visitors

		rating
1.	Peter Schmeichel	9
2.	John O'Kane	7
3.	Denis Irwin	7
4.	Steve Bruce	8
6.	Gary Pallister	7
7.	Eric Cantona	8
16.	Roy Keane	7
19.	Nicky Butt	7
9.	Brian McClair — 54 mins	7
10.	Mark Hughes	7
11.	Ryan Giggs	8

on the bench
5.	Lee Sharpe	7
25.	Kevin Pilkington	
24.	Paul Scholes	

John O'Kane **in only his second full game**

Empics

bite 🔴 this!

"United had to wait for their winner, missing a dozen chances before Hughes' goal came...that was decisive, but Cantona provided the final flourish with a beautiful chip over Kelly as United caught Sheffield on the break." **THE TIMES**

"United's superior number began to tell after the break, with Roy Keane shooting wide and Butt twice bringing excellent saves from Kelly." **THE INDEPENDENT**

"The wind tore relentlessly through the field, filling the Manchester United goal with pre-match balloons. In the sixth minute the ball nearly followed suit when Schmeichel, recalled because Walsh had flu and looking stiff after a ten-match absence with a slipped disc, allowed a shot from Blake to squirm from his grasp." **THE GUARDIAN**

"Cantona looked up, spotted keeper Alan Kelly a fraction off his line and casually chipped in off the underside of the bar from 15 yards." **TODAY**

"I was beginning to think that our goal was never going to come. Mark broke the deadlock with the first. And when the second goal came it was worth waiting for. That really was tremendous skill and vision.
At the other end there was a penalty appeal. Steve Bruce is adamant that he got a touch on the ball and I believe he did.
It was a hard match but I am happy because it was a typical cup-tie." **ALEX FERGUSON**

> "I thought it was going to be one of those nights when we would never score."
>
> ▶ ALEX FERGUSON

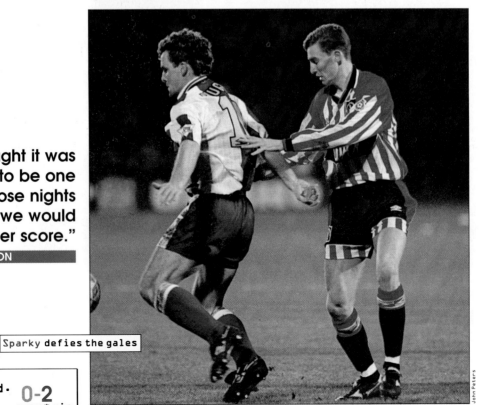

Sparky defies the gales

John Peters

▶94

[FA Cup R#3]
Sheffield Utd.
>9-1-95·
Bramall Lane

0-2
away * win

Cantona's **killer goal** earns the praise

sheffield united

shots/headers on target	
6	12
shots/headers off target	
5	8
free kicks	
14	9

stats

5	5
caught offside	
4	6
corners	
4	9
fouls	

On a cold, wet and windy night in Sheffield, **Hughes** knocked the Blades out of the FA Cup on home soil for the second time in as many years.

The Blades were a man down after just 13 minutes when **Charlie Hartfield** was given his marching orders. United attacked from then on and **Butt**, **Cantona**, **Hughes** and **Giggs** all missed openings against manager Dave Bassett's side.

As Alex Ferguson later said, "I thought it was going to be one of those nights when we would never score." Fortunately **Hughes** made amends for the missed chances, but it took him till the 79th minute, when he met a **Giggs** cross and headed home.

With the home side pressing for an equaliser, **Cantona** and **Giggs** counter-attacked and the genius **Cantona** chipped 'keeper **Kelly** from twenty yards.

It was a magnificent goal and sealed our passage to the 4th round, much to the delight of the 5,000 reds who had crossed the Pennines.

John Peters

in the area

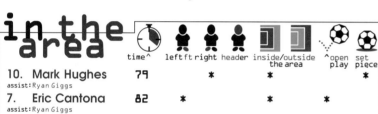

	time^	left ft	right	header	inside/outside the area	^open play	set piece
10. Mark Hughes	79		*		*		*
assist: Ryan Giggs							
7. Eric Cantona	82	*			*	*	
assist: Ryan Giggs							

John Peters

Cantona **goes close** with a header

in the book

Referee:
R Hart, Darlington
Rating: 7
Bookings:
Irwin,
Bruce,
▌Hartfield

>timeline

* **Tue 10th Jan**
> **PETER COOK, FATHER OF SIXTIES SATIRE, DIES - AGED 57**
The Daily Telegraph Tue 10th Jan

* **Wed 11th Jan** Manchester United sign Andy Cole for £6 million. Keith Gillespie departs Old Trafford as part of the deal for £1 million.

* Kevin Keegan says he's ready to take the flak concerning Andy Cole's departure.

> **PARKHURST PRISON GOVERNOR SACKED - HE'S SACKED FOLLOWING THE ESCAPE OF THREE IN-MATES**
The Daily Telegraph Wed 11th Jan

* **Thu 12th Jan**
> **OP YOURS - DOC ORDERS NURSE TO TAKE OUT APPENDIX**
Daily Mirror Thu 12th Jan

* **Fri 13th Jan**
> **WITCH HUNT OF THE INNOCENTS - FOUR COUPLES FREED AFTER CHILDREN FALSELY ACCUSE THEM OF SEXUAL ABUSE**

manchester united v
"NEWCASTLE UNITED

> Sunday 15 January 1995 / 4.00pm

[Att: 34,471]

> St. James' Park

1-1

[Last season : 1-1]

team lineups

home team

1.	Pavel Srnicek
12.	Marc Hottiger
15.	Darren Peacock
6.	Steve Howey
3.	John Beresford
2.	Barry Venison
5.	Ruel Fox
10.	Lee Clark
7.	Robert Lee
26.	Robbie Elliot
28.	Paul Kitson

on the bench

14.	Alex Mathie
30.	Mike Hooper
19.	Steve Watson

visitors

rating

1.	Peter Schmeichel	8
3.	Denis Irwin	7
4.	Steve Bruce	7
6.	Gary Pallister	7
5.	Lee Sharpe	7
19.	Nicky Butt	8
16.	Roy Keane	9
9.	Brian McClair	7
11.	Ryan Giggs	7
10.	Mark Hughes	7
7.	Eric Cantona	7

45mins

13mins

on the bench

12.	David May	6
13.	Gary Walsh	7
24.	Paul Scholes	

Giggs **fends off Lee**

Ryan **and Robert meet again**

bite this!

"In the last exhausting minutes of the game Eric Cantona, of all people, squandered two chances to secure a victory United hardly deserved. Whatever the gut feeling of Newcastle's fanatical fans about the loss of Andy Cole - and some have shown less bereavement for the dearly beloved of their own families - they refused to turn their grief on Kevin Keegan."
DAILY EXPRESS

"Hughes' injury had an unsettling effect on both teams, and the first half was a mess of misplaced passes and players straying offside."
THE INDEPENDENT

"You did not need to have played the game as daringly or successfully as Hughes to fear that his pain and the collision had cost him this match and maybe many more. He was taken off on a stretcher, knees bound together."
THE OBSERVER

"We didn't deserve a point and we were lucky to come away with a draw. It was always going to be hard for us and I think it was a predictable outcome after the events of the last week.

We came out of it without Mark Hughes and Nicky Butt.

I knew Mark's was a serious injury the moment he went down, because he never stays on the ground unless there is a problem. He got his goal with some cost. He just didn't pull away from his challenge, but then Mark doesn't. It's even worse because he's hardly ever injured.

Nicky Butt was suffering with double vision, so I couldn't even take off Steve Bruce who was suffering with flu."
ALEX FERGUSON

newcastle united

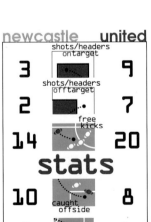

stats

shots/headers on target
3 | 9

shots/headers off target
2 | 7

free kicks
14 | 20

10 | 8
caught offside

0 | 6
corners

11 | 11
fouls

first aid box

> Mark Hughes gashed knee
Nicky Butt sustained a head injury

word up

The **shock signing of Andy Cole** three days before this match gave the game an **added edge** and this was reflected by the excellent atmosphere in a capacity crowd at St James' Park

Just 880 tickets were allocated to United fans but the small following were in fine voice when **Hughes** gave us the lead after ten minutes. However, **Hughes** wasn't in any state to celebrate his goal as he lay motionless on the turf after colliding with Srnicek.

The Welshman, was stretchered off the pitch to a standing ovation because some thought it would be his last game for United.

Despite losing **Hughes**, United (the real United) still held their grip on the game in the first half.

Things were different after the break when the Geordies came out to a revitalised outfit hurrying and scurrying at the champions at every opportunity.

Recent signing **Kitson** levelled the score following a period of Newcastle pressure and the home crowd tried to roar their team onto victory in front of the watching nation.

Neither side could add to their goal tally although **Manchester's finest came close on no less than three occasions in the dying minutes** .

A point earned rather than lost.

Srnicek clashes with Hughes

John Peters

in the area

	time^	left ft	right	header	inside/outside the area	^open play	set piece
10. Mark Hughes	13		*		*		*
assist: Roy Keane							
28. Kitson	67						

>timeline

* **Sun 15th Jan** John Deehan is the target of what-seems-like every Norwich supporter's anger.

* Hughes scores what is feared to be his last goal for Manchester United. He is strechered off with a knee injury which occurred as a result of his commitment to scoring United's goal against Newcastle in the 1-1 draw.>

> **RUSSIANS CLOSE IN ON PALACE - GROZNY'S PRESIDENTIAL PALACE IS BURNING UNDER FIERCE RUSSIAN ARTILLERY BOMBARDMENT**
The Observer

* **Mon 16th Jan** Jürgen Klinsmann is signed up by the BBC as football analyst. He will join Gary Lineker, who is already the presenter of *Grandstand's Football Focus*.

* Paul Merson begins to train with his Arsenal team-mates once again.

* Gordon Strachan has to pay £100 to Bryan Robson. The two had a bet in 1989 as to who would continue playing the longest, and Gordon Strachan has now decided to hang up his boots.

> **BLAIR PUTS BOOT INTO MONEY-MAD FOOTBALL**
The Daily Telegraph Mon 16th Jan

* **Tue 17th Jan** Bryan Robson's Middlesbrough are knocked out of the FA cup by second division Swansea.

* Jack Walker, having already spent £54.1 million, is ready to give Rovers more money when they require it.

> **GERE WE GO AGAIN - HE'S BACK WITH LAURA**
The Sun Tue 17th Jan

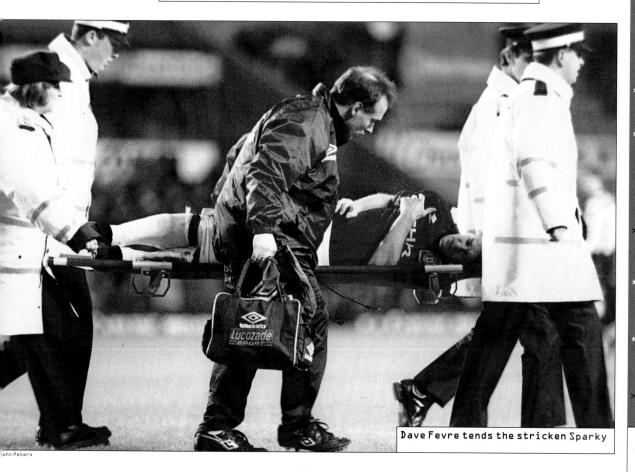

Dave Fevre tends the stricken Sparky

John Peters

✱GARY WALSH
>goalkeeper

personal file

born: Wigan, 21/03/68
height: 6'3" **weight:** 15st 10lb
international team: England
signed pro for United: 21/03/86
United league debut: 13/12/89 v Aston Villa (h)

Sportshot

[Player Portrait #12]

Gary Walsh
goalkeeper

*ANREI KANCHELSKIS

>manchester united & russia

14

>forward

[Squad number: 14]

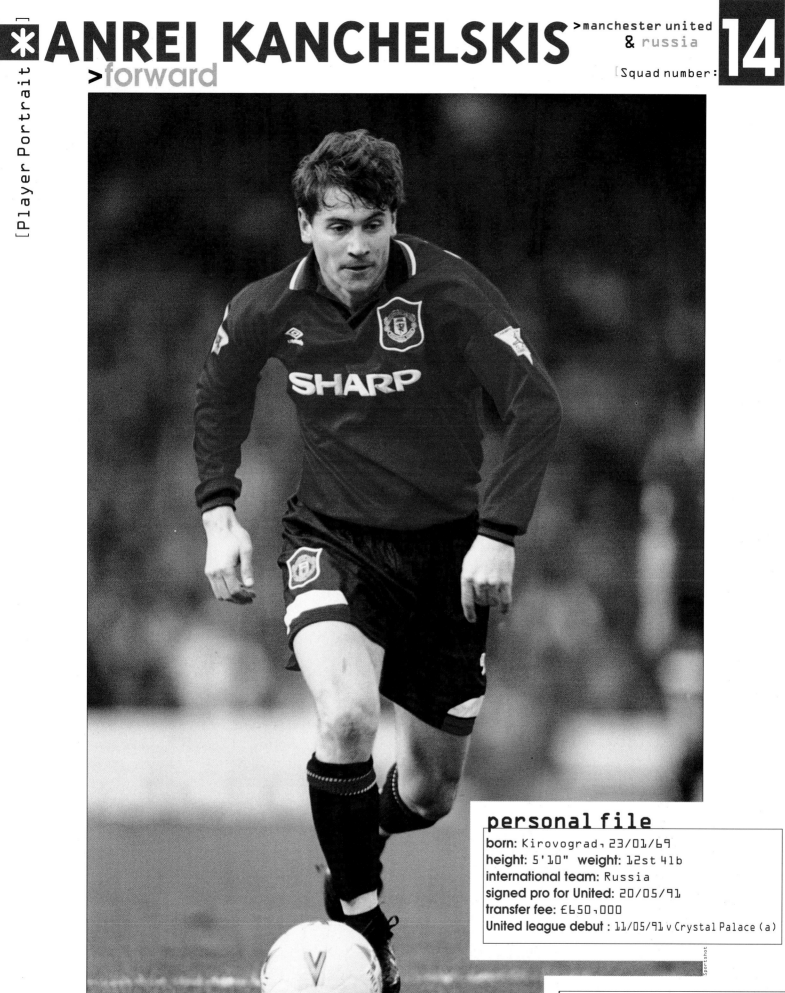

Sportsshot

personal file

born: Kirovograd, 23/01/69
height: 5'10" **weight:** 12st 4lb
international team: Russia
signed pro for United: 20/05/91
transfer fee: £650,000
United league debut: 11/05/91 v Crystal Palace (a)

manchester united v
BLACKBURN ROVERS

>Sunday 22 January 1995 / 4.00pm   >Old Trafford

[Att: 43,742]

1-0

[Last season : 1-1]

team lineups

home team
		rating
1.	Peter Schmeichel	7
3.	Denis Irwin	8
4.	Steve Bruce	8
6.	Gary Pallister	8
16.	Roy Keane	8
8.	Paul Ince	9
9.	Brian McClair	7
5.	Lee Sharpe	7
7.	Eric Cantona	8
17.	Andy Cole	7
11.	Ryan Giggs	9

77 mins

on the bench
12.	David May
25.	Kevin Pilkington
14.	Andrei Kanchelskis

visitors
1.	Tim Flowers
20.	Henning Berg
24.	Paul Warhurst
5.	Colin Hendry
6.	Graham Le Saux
11.	Jason Wilcox
4.	Tim Sherwood
22.	Mark Atkins
3.	Alan Wright
9.	Alan Shearer
16.	Chris Sutton

90 mins

on the bench
10.	Mike Newell
13.	Bobby Mimms
25.	Ian Pearce

Congratulations for Eric from the debutant

bite this!

"Britain's most expensive player (Cole) never really settled, and will need time to become acquainted with United's approach, which demands that the front-runner holds up play as midfielders dart through." THE DAILY TELEGRAPH

"Let's face it… Alan Shearer had been pushing and shoving right through the match. So it was hardly surprising when the Blackburn striker gave Roy Keane a nudge in the back, which enabled him to head the ball into the goal mouth.
But referee Paul Durkin spotted him, and disallowed Tim Sherwood's brave effort into the back of the net to leave Manchester United 1-0 victors and starting to breathe down the leaders' necks, just two points behind." MANCHESTER EVENING NEWS

"We played some excellent football out there. The lads played with a marvellous imagination. There was no doubting we played the better football, and we made a lot more chances. We should have had two or three goals by half-time.
We got the three points and it would have been an absolute travesty if we hadn't won.
Rovers had a goal disallowed but Roy (Keane) says he was shoved in the back and that's what happened.
Credit to the referee, some wouldn't have seen that. If you're seeking to gain the advantage by a push then you can't complain if you're penalised for it." ALEX FERGUSON

Pallister and Shearer

in the book
Referee: P Durkin, Dorset
Rating: 7
Bookings:
Bruce, Cantona, Le Saux, Wright, Sutton

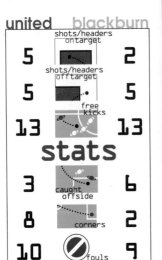

stats
united   blackburn

united		blackburn
	shots/headers on target	
5		2
	shots/headers off target	
5		5
	free kicks	
13		13
	caught offside	
3		6
	corners	
8		2
	fouls	
10		9

Professional Sport

The big one. First against second and a real six-pointer if there ever was one. A Blackburn victory at Old Trafford would have spelt disaster for United in the championship race and it was imperative they didn't lose.

Cole, making his red-shirted debut, nearly got off to a dream start when his first touch of the ball was a shot that scurried just wide of the post. A minute into your debut against top of the league is not the time to get a chance like that, and you had to feel for him.

Chances came and went but Rovers justified their position with some fluent football. **Shearer** went close for the visitors in the second half, but then so did **Cantona** for us.

Both teams seemed destined to share the points.

Back-to-form **Giggs** crossed a perfect high ball over to **Eric the King**, who headed into the roof of the net. Cue ecstasy around Old Trafford, and the most pleasing points of the season.

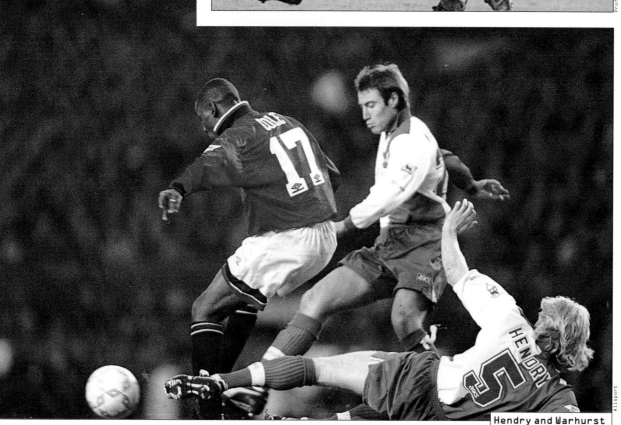

Hendry and Warhurst shut out Cole

Professional Sport

Allsport

> time*line*

* **Wed 18th Jan**

DESPERATE DIANA BACK IN CARE OF BULIMIA DOC
The Sun Wed 18th Jan

* **Thu 19th Jan** Ian Wright gains his twelfth yellow card for this season in Arsenal's third round replay against Milwall. The Gunners are beaten 2-0 at Highbury.

> LIKE A LAMB TO SLAUGHTER - RIOT POLICE WERE LAST NIGHT ACCUSED OF ACTING LIKE "RENT-A-THUGS" TO END A PEACEFUL ANIMAL RIGHT PROTEST
Today Thu 19th Jan

* **Fri 20th Jan** George Graham is handed a cheque book and told to spend as much money as he likes in the transfer market.

* Kenny Dalglish pleads to the referee not to go with the crowd at Old Trafford this Sunday when Rovers take on United.

* **Sat 21st Jan** Howard Kendall's Notts County beat Sunderland 2-1. County's newest players Jason Kearton (goalkeeper on loan from Everton) and Steve Nicol (free transfer from Liverpool) gave the most spectacular performances of the evening.

* **Sun 22nd Jan** Manchester United's Andy Cole makes his debut in their 1-0 victory over league-leaders Blackburn Rovers. Blackburn have a goal disallowed and Dalglish says that "could have cost us the title."

in the area

	time^	left ft	right	header	inside/outside the area	^open play	set piece

7. Eric Cantona   80   *   *   *
assist: Ryan Giggs

*CRYSTAL PALACE

>Sunday 25 January 1995 / 7.30pm [Att: 18,224]

>Selhurst Park   v manchester united: **1-1**

team lineups

home team

1.	Nigel Martyn	
3.	Dean Gordon	
4.	Gareth Southgate	
6.	Chris Coleman	
8.	Iain Dowie	75mins
9.	Chris Armstrong	
11.	John Salako	
14.	Richard Shaw	
16.	Darren Pitcher	
22.	Darren Patterson	
23.	Ricky Newman	

on the bench

18.	Andy Preece	
15.	Bobby Bowry	
19.	Rhys Wilmot	

visitors

		rating
1.	Peter Schmeichel	8
3.	Denis Irwin	7
12.	David May	7
6.	Gary Pallister	7
16.	Roy Keane	7
8.	Paul Ince	7
9.	Brian McClair	7
5.	Lee Sharpe	7
7.	Eric Cantona	7
17.	Andy Cole	7
11.	Ryan Giggs	8

63mins

on the bench

14.	Andrei Kanchelskis	
25.	Kevin Pilkington	
24.	Paul Scholes	

Giggs shields from Gordon

Sportshot

stats

palace / united

	shots/headers on target	
3		2
	shots/headers off target	
6		3
	free kicks	
12		15
	caught offside	
8		6
	corners	
2		1
	fouls	
7		6

bite this!

"Cantona's dismissal and subsequent lunge at a spectator in the front row of the stands left an image no-one will ever forget… That the champions managed to retain what was left of their composure and sneak away from the ground with a point spoke more for the resolve of the players, rather than any level of ability." **DAILY MAIL**

"The ten United men left behind after the Cantona red card showed admirable qualities. In the mayhem that followed Cantona's exit, David May opened the scoring. But the goal seemed almost insignificant." **DAILY STAR**

"Eric Cantona, the heartbeat of Manchester United for the last two seasons, last night did the club he loves his greatest disservice by taking the law into his own hands. The borderline between genius and insanity has always been fragile and for Cantona it shattered at Selhurst Park in a flurry of flying fists and feet. A pitch carving up badly after days of rain did not suit the silken passes and balletic movement of the finely balanced Frenchman, but nothing suggested what might happen in the 48th minute. Football has had enough off-the-field disruption without one of its highest profile players behaving like the hooligans we felt had been driven from the sport." **DAILY EXPRESS**

"It is a deficiency of Selhurst park that a player sent off is likely to have to take a lengthy walk past spectators, and Cantona was flooded with verbal abuse and gestures as he proceeded along the touch line." **THE TIMES**

In a match largely overshadowed by Eric Cantona's sending off and the consequent events, United's players channelled their emotions into one cause. The match itself will be virtually unmentioned in tomorrow's press due to Eric Cantona's extra curricular activities. Andy Cole failing in his attempt to put the ball into the net summed up a frustrating night for the reds.

Cole, again through on goal, missed the target; a bumpy pitch creating the block rather than Palace's defence. With ten men on the pitch United rallied to grab a one-goal lead. It was an error at the other end involving the goalscorer that eventually let the lead slip. The fact United had ten men was the only consolation for a disappointing night at Selhurst Park." **OUR VERDICT**

May's first Premiership goal for the reds brings relief to all

Ince leaves Pitcher behind

Allsport

The events on the pitch at Selhurst Park tonight will be forever overshadowed by what happened off it. **A million words and probably more have been written about the incident in the media**

The match itself was a scrappy affair, with niggling tackles frequently going unpunished. **The Shaw tackle on Cantona was one such tackle. Eric reacted to it and was sent off.**

A United side with ten men at last looked to have some conviction and took the lead through **May**, to the delight of the 5,000-strong red army.

The eagles managed to level the score, but the points were shared in a game best forgotten on a night that never will be.

Eric is sent off for an early shower but ends up in confrontation with a Palace fan

>timeline

* **Tue 24th Jan** The Merseyside Derby ends with no goals, but Leeds more than compensate for the lack of goals at Anfield by putting four past QPR keeper Tony Roberts.

* **Wed 25th Jan** As managers request a "red-card court", Eric Cantona reacts dramatically after his red card. The French footballer hit-out at a supporter hurling verbal abuse at the him.

* **Thu 26th Jan**
> CANTONA ATTACKS FAN AFTER BEING SENT OFF
The Daily Telegraph

Frank Spooner

in the book

Referee:
A Wilkie, Chester-Le-Street
Rating: 5

Bookings:
Keane,
■Cantona,
Coleman

in the area

	time^	left ft right	header	inside/outside the area	^open play	set piece
12. David May	56	*		*		*
assist: Lee Sharpe						
4. Gareth Southgate	79					

manchester united v
WREXHAM

>Saturday 28 January 1995 / 3.00pm

[Att: 43,222]

>Old Trafford

5-2

[Last season : 1-2]

team lineups

home team

		rating
1.	Peter Schmeichel	7
23.	Phil Neville	7
12.	David May	7
6.	Gary Pallister	7
3.	Denis Irwin	7
8.	Paul Ince	6
16.	Roy Keane	7
9.	Brian McClair	7
5.	Lee Sharpe	7
24.	Paul Scholes	7
11.	Ryan Giggs	8

on the bench
14.	Andrei Kanchelskis
13.	Gary Walsh
28.	David Beckham

visitors

1.	Andrew Marriot
2.	Barry Jones
3.	Barry Hunter
4.	Tony Humes
5.	Phil Hardy
6.	Kieron Durkan
7.	Bryan Hughes
8.	Gareth Owen
9.	Karl Connolly
10.	Gary Bennett
11.	Steve Watkin

on the bench
12.	Wayne Philips
13.	Mark Cartwright
14.	Jonathan Cross

Ince breaks into his familiar stride

Sportshot

in the book
Referee:
M Bodenham, Cornwall
Rating: 8
Bookings:
Hughes

Keano auditions for *Give us a Clue*

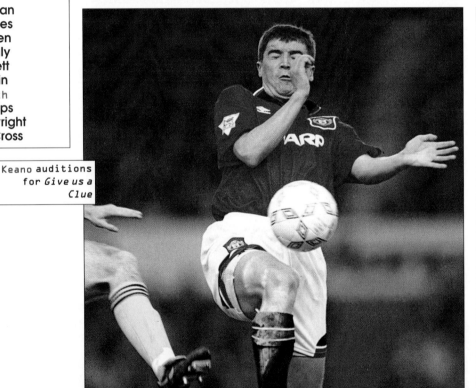

Allsport

bite this!

"The early stages indicated the dangers as the Welsh club raced into the lead after only ten minutes. The reds were caught coming out of defence to put the opposition offside, but the plan misfired when they lost the ball and Keiron Durkin was left in possession on his own.
A quick exchange with Gareth Owen and he was through to score... But the response was first class. It was the quiet man of the team who raced to the rescue seven minutes later, after a Ryan Giggs corner had been scrambled away."
MANCHESTER EVENING NEWS

"Having gone from Zenith to Nadir in four days, when sweet success against Blackburn was followed by Cantona's sour disgrace, a club in turmoil were very grateful for the sanctuary of a straightforward win."
THE SUNDAY TIMES

"It was a terrific cup-tie, I really enjoyed it. Wrexham fully deserved their early lead, and I thought it added a wee bit of spice to the game. We had to work really hard to get into the match.
We looked sharp and created a lot of chances. On the other hand, so did Wrexham. They gave us a few embarrassing moments.
All in all, 5-2 was a true reflection on the game - although we could have let a few more in." **ALEX FERGUSON**

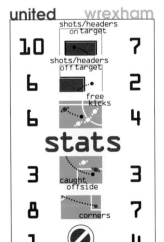

stats

united   wrexham

united		wrexham
10	shots/headers on target	7
6	shots/headers off target	2
6	free kicks	4
3	caught offside	3
8	corners	7
1	fouls	4

word up

6,000 patriotic Welshmen travelled to Old Trafford in the hope of an FA Cup shock against the holders.

When **Durkan** gave Wrexham the lead after six minutes, their fans were ecstatic, and probably shocked too.

Irwin cracked home a shot from distance soon after to level the score, and from then on it was straightforward for United, **as Eric Cantona's name echoed around Old Trafford** (who said United's fans wanted **Eric** to leave?). **Giggs** put the reds in front to silence the Wrexham hoards.

Brian Flynn's side continued to attack but paid the price as United created further openings, for **McClair**, an **Irwin** penalty, and an own goal to put the game well out of their reach.

Wrexham grabbed a late consolation goal to cap a game in which the fans sang more about somebody who wasn't even playing; their hero **Eric Cantona**.

John Peters

McClair swoops to conquer

Phil Neville (centre) decides to mingle after his debut

in the area

		time^	left ft right	header	inside/outside the area	^open play	set piece
3.	Denis Irwin	17	*		*		*
		73	*		*		*
11.	Ryan Giggs	26	*		*	*	
	assist: Phil Neville						
9.	Brian McClair	67	*		*	*	
6.	Kieron Durkan	9					
4.	Tony Humes	80	OG				

> **timeline**

* **Fri 27th Jan**
> HURD'S BRIEF ON EUROPE IS REJECTED
The Times Fri 27th Jan

* **Sat 28th Jan** Gordon Taylor is to defend Cantona in his FA hearing. It is apparent that comments about Eric's Mother sparks the incident.

* Manchester United shelve all feelings of loss over Cantona and overcome Wrexham 5-2 to succeed to the next round of the FA Cup.

* Joe Kinnear and Vinny Jones are given cautions by the police. Kinnear's is for verbal and physical abuse of referee, Mike Reed; Vinny Jones' for a verbal attack on Kevin Keegan.

> SCHOOL STABBING BOY, 15, FIGHTS FOR LIFE
Daily Star Sat 29th Jan

* **Sun 29th Jan** Milan's match in Genoa is abandoned at half-time following the news that a fan stabbed before kick-off had died.

> RAIL SALE STUMBLES AT FIRST HURDLE - RED STAR PRIVATISATION SHELVED AT THE 11TH HOUR
Independent on Sunday Sun 29th Jan

* **Mon 30th Jan** Ian Wright is banned for four games and concedes a £1,000 ban as he exceeds the FA's maximum 41 disciplinary points.

> JANUARY RAINS HEAD FOR RECORD
The Times Mon 30th Jan

* **Tue 31st Jan** Notts County enter their second successive Anglo-Italian Cup final as Stoke City score only two of their penalty attempts in a tense shoot-out.

*ROY KEANE
>midfielder

personal file

born: Cork, 10/08/71
height: 5'10" weight: 11st 1b
international team: Republic of Ireland
signed pro for United: 19/07/93
transfer fee: £3,750,000
United league debut : 15/08/93 v Norwich City (a)

▽ appearances/goals

appearances / apps as sub / goals	Premier League			FA Cup			Coca Cola Cup			European Cup			Total		left ft	right	header	inside	outside	open play	set piece	assists	scoring rate	performance rating average
Ryan Giggs	4	-	-	2	-	1	-	-	-	-	-	-	6	1	1	-	-	1	-	1	-	3	17%	8.0
Denis Irwin	4	-	-	2	-	2	-	-	-	-	-	-	6	2	-	2	-	2	-	-	2	-	33%	7.2
Roy Keane	4	-	-	2	-	-	-	-	-	-	-	-	6	-	-	-	-	-	-	-	-	-	-%	7.5
Gary Pallister	4	-	-	2	-	-	-	-	-	-	-	-	6	-	-	-	-	-	-	-	-	-	-%	7.2
Eric Cantona	4	-	2	1	-	1	-	-	-	-	-	-	5	3	2	-	1	3	-	2	1	-	60%	7.4
Brian McClair	3	1	-	2	-	1	-	-	-	-	-	-	5	1	1	-	1	1	-	1	-	-	20%	7.0
Peter Schmeichel	3	-	-	2	-	-	-	-	-	-	-	-	5	-	-	-	-	-	-	-	-	-	-%	7.8
Steve Bruce	3	-	-	1	-	-	-	-	-	-	-	-	4	-	-	-	-	-	-	-	-	-	-%	7.5
Lee Sharpe	3	-	-	1	1	-	-	-	-	-	-	-	4	1	1	-	-	-	-	-	-	1	-%	7.0
Nicky Butt	2	-	-	-	-	-	-	-	-	-	-	-	3	-	-	-	-	-	-	-	-	-	-%	7.3
Paul Ince	2	-	-	-	-	-	-	-	-	-	-	-	3	-	-	-	-	-	-	-	-	-	-%	7.3
Andy Cole	2	-	-	-	-	-	-	-	-	-	-	-	2	-	-	-	-	-	-	-	-	-	-%	7.0
Mark Hughes	1	-	1	1	-	1	-	-	-	-	-	-	2	2	-	2	-	2	-	1	-	-	100%	7.0
David May	1	1	-	1	-	-	-	-	-	-	-	-	2	1	1	1	-	1	-	1	-	-	33%	6.7
Paul Scholes	1	1	1	-	1	-	-	-	-	-	-	-	1	2	1	-	1	1	-	1	-	-	33%	7.0
Keith Gillespie	1	-	-	-	-	-	-	-	-	-	-	-	1	-	-	-	-	-	-	-	-	-	-%	8.0
Gary Neville	1	-	-	-	-	-	-	-	-	-	-	-	1	-	-	-	-	-	-	-	-	-	-%	7.0
Phil Neville	-	-	-	1	-	-	-	-	-	-	-	-	1	-	-	-	-	-	-	-	-	1	-%	7.0
John O'Kane	-	-	-	1	-	-	-	-	-	-	-	-	1	-	-	-	-	-	-	-	-	-	-%	7.0
Gary Walsh	1	-	-	-	-	-	-	-	-	-	-	-	1	-	-	-	-	-	-	-	-	-	-%	7.0
David Beckham	-	-	-	1	-	-	-	-	-	-	-	-	1	-	-	-	-	-	-	-	-	-	-%	0.0
Andrei Kanchelskis	-	2	-	1	-	-	-	-	-	-	-	-	3	-	-	-	-	-	-	-	-	-	-%	0.0

season to january 95 — cumulative statistics ∗

▽ appearances/goals

appearances / apps as sub / goals	Premier League			FA Cup			Coca Cola Cup			European Cup			Total		left ft	right	header	inside	outside	open play	set piece	assists	scoring rate	performance rating average
Gary Pallister	25	-	-	3	-	-	2	-	-	6	-	-	36	-	-	-	2	2	-	-	-	2	6%	7.3
Denis Irwin	24	-	1	3	-	2	2	-	-	5	-	-	34	-	3	-	3	-	3	-	1	-	2	9%	7.3
Steve Bruce	21	-	1	2	-	-	1	-	-	5	1	-	29	1	1	-	-	1	1	-	-	1	3%	7.4
Paul Ince	20	-	1	2	-	-	-	-	-	5	-	-	27	-	1	-	-	-	1	-	1	3	4%	7.6
Brian McClair	19	4	4	3	-	1	3	-	1	2	-	-	27	4	6	1	3	2	5	1	5	1	3	24%	7.3
Mark Hughes	20	-	5	1	-	1	-	-	-	5	-	2	26	-	8	-	7	1	6	2	7	1	3	31%	7.2
Eric Cantona	21	-	12	1	-	1	-	-	-	2	-	-	24	-	13	4	5	4	13	-	9	4	10	54%	7.6
Ryan Giggs	19	1	-	2	-	1	-	-	-	5	-	-	24	-	4	4	-	-	4	-	4	-	9	17%	7.3
Andrei Kanchelskis	18	3	11	1	-	-	3	-	1	2	1	-	24	4	12	3	8	1	11	-	11	1	4	50%	6.5
Roy Keane	15	1	-	3	-	1	1	-	-	4	-	-	23	1	-	2	-	-	2	-	2	-	4	8%	7.4
Peter Schmeichel	16	-	-	2	-	-	-	-	-	3	-	-	21	-	-	-	-	-	-	-	-	-	-	-%	7.6
David May	13	3	1	1	-	-	2	-	1	-	-	-	20	3	2	-	-	2	2	-	2	-	-	10%	6.6
Lee Sharpe	13	1	1	1	-	-	-	-	-	3	2	3	17	3	3	1	2	-	3	-	3	-	4	15%	7.0
Gary Walsh	9	-	-	1	-	-	3	-	-	3	-	-	16	-	-	-	-	-	-	-	-	-	-	-%	7.1
Nicky Butt	6	5	1	1	-	-	3	-	-	5	1	-	15	6	1	-	-	1	1	-	1	-	-	6%	6.8
Gary Neville	6	2	-	1	-	-	1	-	-	2	1	-	10	4	-	-	-	-	-	-	-	-	-	-%	6.6
Simon Davies	2	1	-	-	-	-	3	-	-	2	-	1	8	1	1	1	-	-	1	-	1	-	2	11%	7.3
Paul Scholes	2	6	2	2	-	2	3	-	2	-	1	-	7	7	6	-	3	3	6	-	4	2	-	84%	7.9
Keith Gillespie	3	5	1	-	1	-	3	-	-	-	-	-	6	6	1	-	6	1	1	-	1	-	-	15%	7.3
David Beckham	-	-	-	-	1	-	3	-	1	1	-	-	4	1	1	1	-	-	1	-	1	-	1	25%	6.0
Paul Parker	1	-	-	-	-	-	-	-	-	2	1	-	3	2	-	-	-	-	-	-	-	-	-	-%	6.8
Andy Cole	2	-	-	-	-	-	-	-	-	-	-	-	2	-	-	-	-	-	-	-	-	-	-%	7.0
Chris Casper	-	-	-	-	-	-	1	-	-	-	-	-	1	-	-	-	-	-	-	-	-	-	-%	7.0
Phil Neville	-	-	-	1	-	-	-	-	-	-	-	-	1	-	-	-	-	-	-	-	-	-	-%	7.0
Kevin Pilkington	-	2	-	-	-	-	-	-	-	-	-	-	2	-	-	-	-	-	-	-	-	-	-%	7.0
Graeme Tomlinson	-	-	-	-	-	-	2	-	-	-	-	-	2	-	-	-	-	-	-	-	-	-	-%	7.5

league table

FA Carling Premiership 25 January 95

Team	P	W	D	L	F	A	Pts
Blackburn Rovers	24	17	4	3	52	19	55
Manchester United	26	16	6	4	47	21	54
Liverpool	25	13	7	5	44	20	46
Newcastle United	25	12	9	4	43	26	45
Nottingham Forest	26	13	6	7	37	28	45
Tottenham Hotspur	25	11	6	8	41	36	39
Leeds United	24	10	7	7	33	27	37
Sheffield Wed	26	9	9	8	33	32	36
Wimbledon	25	10	5	10	31	40	35
Norwich City	25	9	9	7	24	27	34
Arsenal	26	8	9	9	29	28	33
Chelsea	26	8	7	10	32	35	31
Aston Villa	26	7	10	9	32	35	31
Manchester City	25	8	7	10	29	48	31
Southampton	25	6	11	8	35	40	29
Crystal Palace	26	6	10	11	19	26	27
Everton	26	6	9	10	25	32	27
QPR	24	7	6	11	35	34	27
Coventry City	26	6	9	11	23	43	27
West Ham United	25	7	4	14	22	32	25
Ipswich Town	25	4	6	15	23	43	18
Leicester City	25	4	6	15	23	43	18

time split

	0-10 mins	11-20 mins	21-30 mins	31-40 mins	41-50 mins	51-60 mins	61-70 mins	71-80 mins	81-90 mins
Eric Cantona	-	-	1	3	4	-	1	3	1
Andrei Kanchelskis	-	-	1	-	5	2	1	1	2
Mark Hughes	-	2	1	-	-	-	3	1	-
Paul Scholes	-	-	1	2	1	-	-	-	-
Brian McClair	-	-	-	1	-	2	1	-	-
Ryan Giggs	-	-	-	1	-	-	-	-	1
Denis Irwin	1	-	-	-	-	-	-	1	-
Lee Sharpe	-	-	-	-	-	-	-	2	1
Roy Keane	-	-	-	-	2	-	-	-	-
David May	-	-	-	-	-	-	-	-	-
Gary Pallister	-	-	-	-	-	-	-	-	-
David Beckham	-	-	-	-	-	-	-	-	-
Steve Bruce	-	-	-	-	-	-	-	-	-
Nicky Butt	-	-	-	-	-	-	-	-	-
Simon Davies	-	-	-	-	-	-	-	-	-
Keith Gillespie	-	-	-	-	-	-	-	-	-
Paul Ince	-	-	-	-	-	-	-	-	-
own goal	-	-	-	-	-	-	-	-	-
TOTAL SCORED	2	4	5	8	15	6	9	13	7
TOTAL CONCEDED	4	3	4	2	5	4	5	6	4

∗ player of the month

Eric Cantona

performance rating average: **8.5**

summary

	P	W	D	L	F	A
Premier League	26	16	6	4	47	21
FA Cup	2	2	-	-	7	2
Coca Cola Cup	3	2	-	1	4	3
European Cup	6	2	2	2	11	11
Total	37	22	8	7	69	37

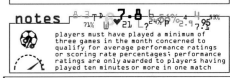

notes

players must have played a minimum of three games in the month concerned to qualify for average performance ratings or scoring rate percentages; performance ratings are only awarded to players having played ten minutes or more in one match

manchester united v
ASTON VILLA
>Saturday 4 February 1995/3.00pm

[Att: 43,795]

>Old Trafford

1-0

[Last season :3-1]

[Premier League match #27] team lineups

home team	rating
1. Peter Schmeichel	8
3. Denis Irwin	7
4. Steve Bruce	8
6. Gary Pallister	8
27. Gary Neville	6
8. Paul Ince	7
5. Lee Sharpe	6
9. Brian McClair	7
24. Paul Scholes	8
17. Andy Cole	8
11. Ryan Giggs	7

44 mins

on the bench

12. David May	7
13. Gary Walsh	
14. Andrei Kanchelskis	7

44 mins

visitors

13. Mark Bosnich	
22. Gary Charles	
5. Paul McGrath	
4. Shaun Teale	
20. Bryan Small	
18. Dwight Yorke	
11. Andy Townsend	
17. Ian Taylor	
3. Steve Staunton	
8. John Fashanu	
9. Dean Saunders	

51 mins

on the bench

7. Ray Houghton	
1. Nigel Spink	
25. Tommy Johnson	

45 mins

Giggs and ex-United man McGrath

Cole gets the better of Small

stats

united		villa
3	shots/headers on target	3
7	shots/headers off target	9
8	free kicks	14
6	caught offside	4
9	corners	9
8	fouls	4

"It was nice for Andy Cole to get off the mark today. We were always confident that Andy would score goals.

The match itself was one which we just had to churn out. We got the victory, which was the most important thing, and it is a good sign to come away with three points when you've not played to your best standard.

We did play well some of the time, and it was penetration which got us the goal.

One thing I have learnt is that if we don't keep possession then our opponents will give us a rough time."
ALEX FERGUSON

United inflicted Villa's first defeat in eight games with a single goal from **Andy Cole**, his first in a red shirt since his £6 million transfer from Newcastle.

Overall though, it was an unconvincing United performance. Both **Sharpe** and **Irwin** came close early in the first half, but Bosnich stood firm with a couple of outstanding saves in the Villa goal.

On 17 minutes **Pallister** headed down a **Giggs** corner for **Cole**, who hooked the ball in. As expected, the celebrations were long and loud and **Cole** immediately began to play with more confidence.

Saunders, Townsend and Fashanu troubled **Schmeichel**, but the Dane wasn't letting his record of not letting in a single league goal at Old Trafford this season slip. Despite further Villa pressure in the second half, the reds hung on for another valuable three points.

Ince **sails** past Townsend

first aid box

> **Fashanu** sustained a knee injury

>timeline

* **Wed 1st Feb** Blackburn Rovers' security is under the spotlight after a 40-year-old man was able to run on to the Ewood Park pitch on Wednesday night and attack the referee.

* **Thu 2nd Feb** The FA announce the date of Eric Cantona's hearing as 24th February

> LORRY KILLS VEAL DEMO MUM – YOUNG MOTHER JILL PHIPPS CRUSHED TO DEATH TRYING TO STOP A TRUCK TRANSPORTING VEAL

Today Thu 2nd Feb

* **Fri 3rd Feb**

> HILLSBOROUGH POLICE MAY GET £250,000 FOR TRAUMA – 14 POLICE OFFICERS SAY THAT THEY WERE TRAUMATISED BY THE HILLSBOROUGH SOCCER INCIDENT

The Daily Telegraph Fri 3rd Feb

* **Sat 4th Feb** Paul Gascoigne is set a comeback target from one of Lazio's directors. April 15 is when Lazio take on Juventus in the second leg of their semi-final of the Italian equivalent of the FA Cup.

> EXECUTION OF THE BEST BOSS IN THE WORLD – SUPERMARKET MANAGER SHOT DEAD IN OFFICE, WEST DIDSBURY

The Sun Sat 4th Feb

in the area

	time^	left ft right	header	inside/outside the area	^open play	set piece
17. Andy Cole assist: Gary Pallister	18	*		*		*

Sportshot

MANCHESTER CITY
>Maine Road

v manchester united: **0-3**

[Att: 26,368]

[Last season :2-3]

[Premier League match #28]

team lineups

home team
25.	Andy Dibble	
16.	Nicky Summerbee	
18.	David Brightwell	
4.	Maurizio Gaudino	
5.	Keith Curle	
15.	Alan Kernaghan	
12.	Ian Brightwell	
8.	Paul Walsh	
28.	Uwe Rösler	
10.	Garry Flitcroft	
11.	Peter Beagrie	63 mins

on the bench
2.	Andy Hill	
33.	John Burridge	
9.	Niall Quinn	

visitors
		rating
1.	Peter Schmeichel	8
3.	Denis Irwin	8
4.	Steve Bruce	8
6.	Gary Pallister	8
23.	Philip Neville	7
8.	Paul Ince	8
5.	Lee Sharpe	7
9.	Brian McClair	7
14.	Andrei Kanchelskis	7 — 53 mins
17.	Andy Cole	7
11.	Ryan Giggs	7 — 82 mins

on the bench
12.	David May	
24.	Paul Scholes	7
13.	Gary Walsh	

King Cole **salutes the fans**

stats

city		united
	shots/headers on target	
3		8
	shots/headers off target	
4		5
	free kicks	
8		12
	caught offside	
3		2
	corners	
7		9
	fouls	
9		6

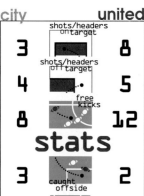
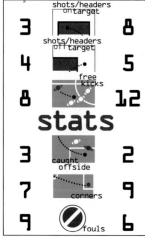

John Peters

It's never boring beating City...

bite this!

"Local Derbies, by tradition, are a law unto themselves, owing more to the conflicting passions of the day than to form and league position... Here Derby days have become bi-seasonal victory parades put on to remind any lingering doubter who is in charge." **DAILY TELEGRAPH**

"United weathered a first-half storm, but once they got into their stride they turned on the style, following November's 5-0 thrashing of City at Old Trafford with another masterful display." **SUNDAY MIRROR**

"Brian Horton's men, without a win in their previous nine League games, produced an attacking style that demanded complete vigilance from United defenders and goalkeeper Peter Schmeichel." **THE MAIL ON SUNDAY**

Our second-half performance was outstanding. Our football was excellent and our composure was also good.

We didn't use Andy Cole well in the first half, but when we did in the second, you saw what happened. He's only played a couple of games, but I am very pleased with him. His movement is such a problem for defenders, and he's got great vision.

Overall that was a great result for the club. We've done our job and that's all anyone can expect of us. We are top of the Premiership and that's the only place to be. **ALEX FERGUSON**

Tens of thousands of United fans would have loved to witness the follow-up Derby to that great five-nil trouncing in November. In reality, many reds were lucky to get tickets for the Old Trafford big screen beaming pictures live from Maine Road, let alone one of the prized tickets for stadium itself. The couple of thousand reds inside a re-developing Maine Road were in for a treat as United bagged three second-half goals. Under-pressure City manager Horton later quipped, "If only these Derby matches finished at half-time."

The introduction of **Paul Scholes** in the 53rd minute allowed **Cole** to wander and cause havoc amongst the City defence. It was **Cole** who set up United's first when he turned Kernaghan brilliantly and left Ince to shoot past Dibble. With the United defence and midfield solid the front men began to punish City further.

Kanchelskis beat Dibble at the near post on 75 minutes, and a simple **Cole** side-foot three minutes later to **McClair**, let him release **Giggs** to score United's third and seal the lid on a fine victory. We beat the City 8-0 (that's eight-nil on aggregate in the two games we played this season).

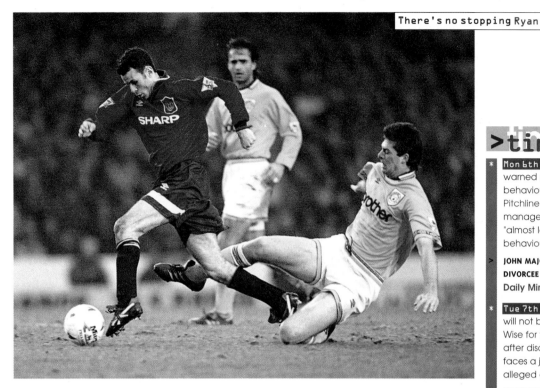

There's no stopping Ryan

Andrei keeps ahead of Wetherall

John Peters

>timeline

* **Mon 6th Feb** Managers are warned about their behaviour by police. Pitchline protests by managers have been said to "almost legitimise such behaviour."

> JOHN MAJOR'S AFFAIR WITH A DIVORCEE
> **Daily Mirror** Mon 6th Feb

* **Tue 7th Feb** Terry Venables will not be selecting Denis Wise for the England team after discovering that Wise faces a jail sentence for alleged common assault.

> NEW ROW OVER POWER CHIEF'S PROFITS ON SHARE OPTIONS
> **The Daily Telegraph** Tue 7th Feb

* **Wed 8th Feb** Chelsea are eliminated from the FA Cup. They lost their tie with Milwall on a night when violence broke out around Stamford Bridge.

* **Thu 9th Feb** Graham Kelly promises football supporters that fences will not be re-introduced as a measure to curb violence.

> WHERE AAH OOH CANTONA - SCOTLAND YARD CHIEFS DECLARED CANTONA A WANTED MAN YESTERDAY
> **Daily Star** Thu 9th Feb

* **Fri 10th Feb**

> SICK JOKE - NURSES ARE BEING PALMED OFF WITH A MISERLY RISE OF £3 A WEEK
> **Daily Star** Fri 10th Feb

* **Sat 11th Feb** Aston Villa score a massive seven goals against Wimbledon's one.

* Derby day in Manchester, as United beat City 3-0 at Maine Road.

* **Sun 12th Feb**

> BABY LYDIA SAFE AFTER PARENTS' 24 HOURS OF AGONY - BABY WAS RETURNED AFTER SHE HAD BEEN SNATCHED FROM HOSPITAL
> **The Sunday Telegraph** Sun 12th Feb

in the area

		time^	left ft	right	header	inside/outside the area		^open play	set piece
8.	Paul Ince	58	*				*	*	
14.	Andrei Kanchelskis	74		*		*		*	
17.	Andy Cole	77		*		*		*	

LEEDS UNITED

v manchester united:

> Old Trafford

3-1

[Att: 42,744]

[FA CUP R5]

team lineups

home team

		rating
1.	Peter Schmeichel	7
16.	Roy Keane	8
3.	Denis Irwin	7
4.	Steve Bruce	8
5.	Lee Sharpe	7
6.	Gary Pallister	8
14.	Andrei Kanchelskis	7
8.	Paul Ince	7
9.	Brian McClair	9
10.	Mark Hughes	8
11.	Ryan Giggs	8

54mins — 73mins

on the bench
19.	Nicky Butt
13.	Gary Walsh
24.	Paul Scholes

visitors

1.	John Lukic
2.	Gary Kelly
3.	Tony Dorigo
19.	Noel Whelan
12.	Joh Pemberton
6.	David Wetherall
14.	David White
8.	Rod Wallace
26.	Phil Masinga
10.	Gary McAllister
11.	Gary Speed

45mins — 45mins

on the bench
21.	Anthony Yeboah
13.	Mark Beeney
15.	Nigel Worthington

Kelly and Giggs jostle for the ball

stats

united		leeds
	shots/headers on target	
10		3
	shots/headers off target	
4		5
	free kicks	
13		13
	caught offside	
4		2
	corners	
8		9
	fouls	
9		11

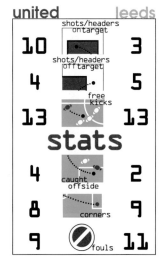

"My friend Brian has just scored against Leeds!"

bite this!

"No Cole, no Cantona, no problem. Despite the absence of two of their finest attacking forces, Manchester United tightened their grip on the FA Cup... Hughes and Co. began as they finished – in style."
DAILY TELEGRAPH

"Some of the football they produced sent the sort of shivers down the spine all right-minded football fans love to feel." **TODAY**

"I think that must be two of the fastest goals that have been scored here whilst I've been manager. Two goals in four minutes isn't bad.

When Leeds scored after half-time I felt a bit nervous. You automatically start to wonder what is going to happen. After all this was a cup-tie and if you are leading by one goal in the last ten minutes you await the other team's onslaught. That's why I think Mark Hughes' goal was so important. It killed them off just at the right time.

We played some excellent football today and I can't let this occasion pass without mentioning the help having a really good pitch gives us."
ALEX FERGUSON

Sportshot

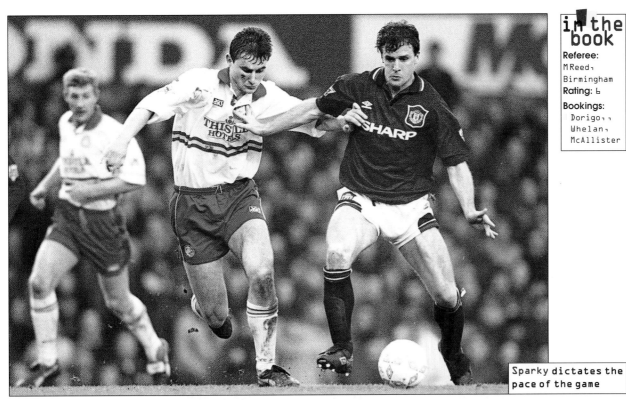

Sparky dictates the pace of the game

Allsport

word up

The chant which echoed around Old Trafford after just four minutes, when United had gone two goals up said it all.

"Two-nil without **Cantona**," they roared, as stunned themselves as the travelling 6,000 Leeds fans. **Eric** is no doubt a star but it's teamwork and team spirit which has made United so successful and today they proved it.

Just 63 seconds were on the clock when **Bruce** rose, unmarked, to power the ball into the net with his head. A couple of minutes on and **Pallister** flicked a **Giggs** ball onto **McClair**, who headed the ball into the net.

Could the match have started any better? Cup ties always have a special atmosphere of their own, let alone when we play Leeds. Two early goals nearly set three sides of the great stadium alight with noise.

With **Ince**, **Keane** and **McClair** faultless in midfield United dominated. A double substitution by the visitors at half time gave them new impetus. New £3m signing Yeboah prodded home a goal and then missed a sitter when he had a chance to level the score.

It was left to the stalwart **Hughes**, fresh back from injury and a newly-signed contract to confirm the champions dominance when he headed a lofted ball from **Kanchelskis** past Lukic.

Dorigo and Keano indulge in the Eskimo ritual of nose-rubbing

>timeline

* **Wed 15th March** English Football is in crisis again as three Premier League Football stars are arrested by police investigating bribery claims – John Fashanu, Bruce Grobbelaar and Hans Segers.
* One of the best ever 0-0 draws takes place at Old Trafford, with United and Tottenham failing to convert their chances.
* Barcelona are knocked out of the Champions' cup by Paris St Germain who are now in the semi-finals.
> **SOCCER'S NEW BRIBE CRISIS** Daily Express Wed 15th March

* **Thu 16th March** The FA tells Bruce Grobbelaar he is free to carry on playing.
> **TORY ALARM AT FEEL GOOD FACTOR - IT MIGHT TAKE ANOTHER TWO YEARS TO CLOSE THE NEXT GENERAL ELECTION SAYS KENNETH CLARKE.** The Daily Telegraph Thu 16th March

* **Fri 17th March**
> **ADAMS GETS CLINTON HAND-SHAKE - BUT MAYHEW WARNS THAT PEACE CANNOT LAST WHILE TERRORISTS HAVE GUNS.** The Independent Fri 17th March

* **Sat 18th March**
> **REDS CLINCH DEAL FOR £28M STAND - 3 TIER GIANT WILL HELP BOOST OLD TRAFFORD CAPACITY TO 55,300.** Manchester Evening News Sat 18th March

* **Sun 19th March** Liverpool repeat their punishment of three years ago as they beat United 2-0 at Anfield, piling increasing doubt onto their championship hopes.

in the area

		time^	left ft right	header	inside/outside the area	^open play	set piece
4.	Steve Bruce	1		*	*		*
	assist: Ryan Giggs						
9.	Brian McClair	4	*		*		*
	assist: Gary Pallister						
10.	Mark Hughes	72		*	*	*	
	assist: Andrei Kanchelskis						
21.	Anthony Yeboah	52					

NORWICH CITY
[Att: 21,824]

>Carrow Road v manchester united:

0-2
[Last season :0-2]

in the book
Referee:
T J Holbrook, Walsall
Rating: 6
Bookings:
◻ Polston

[Premier League match #29]

team lineups

home team
		rating
24.	Andy Marshall	
16.	Carl Bradshaw	
5.	Jon Newsome	
10.	John Polston	
2.	Mark Bowen	
6.	Neil Adams	
19.	Andy Johnson	
8.	Mike Milligan	
20.	Darren Eadie	
22.	Mike Sheron	
7.	Ashley Ward	

on the bench
3.	Rob Newman	
34.	Simon Tracy	
15.	Darryl Sutch	

visitors
		rating
1.	Peter Schmeichel	8
16.	Roy Keane	8
4.	Steve Bruce	9
6.	Gary Pallister	7
5.	Lee Sharpe	8
8.	Paul Ince	8
14.	Andrei Kanchelskis	8
9.	Brian McClair	8
17.	Andy Cole	8
10.	Mark Hughes	8
11.	Ryan Giggs	7

on the bench
3.	Denis Irwin	
13.	Gary Walsh	
19.	Nicky Butt	

Ince takes on Mark Bowen

stats
norwich **united**

norwich		united
3	shots/headers on target	5
5	shots/headers off target	7
10	free kicks	13
2	caught offside	4
9	corners	8
11	fouls	6

Jon Newsome says hello to Sparky

bite this!

"Manchester United played with the arrogance of men who know they are on course for more medals as they ran Norwich ragged in a torrential downpour.... On this type of surface few teams in the country can pass the ball with more accuracy and pace than the champions."
DAILY MAIL

"Driving rain, howling wind, thick mud - it did not matter to magnificent Manchester United. It could have been a spring evening such was the skill, pace and dominance of Alex Ferguson's side. They began like a Porsche, to win the game in the first half, when the conditions were at their best. They turned into a tractor to make sure they ploughed their way towards an incredible third Premiership championship."
THE SUN

"Their fifth successive victory was assured even before the first quarter of the game had passed."
THE INDEPENDENT

"We have reached that ticklish stage of the season when we can't make mistakes and have to go on winning. The title will be won by the side with the most ability, determination, concentration and luck. It was a good win tonight although nothing like as good as our recent performances. Our performance tonight was economical. There was a safety element, keeping the ball in midfield when we might have got it forward. We hardly got the ball to the front pair. I think Peter Schmeichel got more passes from midfield than they did."
ALEX FERGUSON

John Peters

word up

The long journey to Norwich used to result in a United defeat, and what seemed like an even longer journey back to Manchester. Since the turn of the decade, however, Carrow Road has been our most successful away ground and arguably the scene of United's best performance in recent years, the 3-1 victory in 1993.

United settled straight away on the lush surface and went ahead, with **Ince** scoring in the second minute after a **Giggs** corner was headed into his path by a defender. On 16 minutes United struck again, a classic break following a Norwich attack featured **McClair**, **Giggs** and then **Kanchelskis**, who firmly placed his 14th goal of the season past Gunn.

Home or away, these early goals certainly get United fans going. **The two thousand-strong travelling army were in fine voice, a 15-minute rendition of "Ferguson's red & white army," must go down as one of the best atmospheres of the season.**

A rout could have been on the cards, but Norwich battled hard and came close in the first half through Bowen and then ex-blue Sheron.

In the second half United contained Norwich, although they should have gone further ahead in the 70th minute when **Hughes** was brought down by Newsome for what looked a clear penalty. Ref Terry Holbrook decided otherwise, but the reds were more than happy with the three points gained.

Another tumble for Mark Hughes

in the area

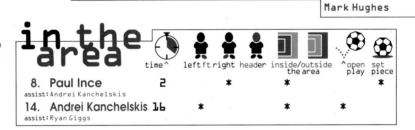

	time^	left ft	right	header	inside/outside the area	^open play	set piece
8. Paul Ince	2		*		*		*
assist: Andrei Kanchelskis							
14. Andrei Kanchelskis	16	*			*	*	
assist: Ryan Giggs							

Giggsy leaves Johnson flailing in his wake

>timeline

* **Fri 17th Feb** Mark Hughes makes his return to Manchester United in the fifth round of the FA Cup.

> **WARNING OF SOCCER RIOT IGNORED - IRISH POLICE FAILED TO PASS ON DETAILS OF ENGLAND THUGS**
The Daily Telegraph Fri 17th Feb

* **Sat 18th Feb**

> **REAL FANS SHOP THUGS - HOOLIGAN HOTLINE IS SWAMPED BY HUNDREDS OF CALLS**
Daily Express Sat 18th Feb

* **Sun 21st Feb** Arsenal manage to beat Nottingham Forest by one goal amidst the frantic news of George Graham's dismissal today.

* **Mon 22nd Feb** Both Coca-Cola Cup semi-final matches are postponed due to flooded pitches.

* Both Coca-Cola Cup semi-final matches are postponed due to flooded pitches.

> **OUT ON HIS ARSENAL - GEORGE GRAHAM IS SACKED**
Daily Star Mon 22nd Feb

* **Tue 23rd Feb**

> **FEARS AS FRY GOES MISSING - STEPHEN FRY DISAPPEARS**
The Daily Mirror Tue 23rd Feb

* **Wed 24th Feb** Ex-Arsenal Boss says he will do all he can to help an FA inquiry should there be one.

EVERTON

v **manchester united:**
> Goodison Park

[Att: 40,011]

1-0

[Last season : 0-1]

team lineups

home team

1.	Neville Southall	
4.	Earl Barrett	
5.	Dave Watson	
26.	David Unsworth	
3.	Andy Hinchcliffe	
13.	John Ebbrell	
17.	Joe Parkinson	
10.	Barry Horne	
18.	Stuart Barlow	
16.	Anders Limpar	
9.	Duncan Ferguson	

on the bench

31.	Stephen Reeves	
17.	Daniel Amokachi	
7.	Vinny Samways	

visitors

rating

1.	Peter Schmeichel	7
3.	Denis Irwin	6
4.	Steve Bruce	6
6.	Gary Pallister	7
5.	Lee Sharpe	6
8.	Paul Ince	8
16.	Roy Keane	6
9.	Brian McClair	6
17.	Andy Cole	6
10.	Mark Hughes	6
11.	Ryan Giggs	6

on the bench

14.	Andrei Kanchelskis	7
13.	Gary Walsh	
19.	Nicky Butt	

Pally tries his luck

John Peters

in the book

Referee:
J Worrall,
Warrington
Rating: 6
Bookings:
Ince,
Ebbrell

bite e this!

"Joe Royle elevated Duncan Ferguson into the galaxy of great Everton No 9s after the young Scottish giant headed the goal in a deserved 1-0 win over a Manchester United side chasing an historic second Double." **DAILY MAIL**

"Duncan Ferguson, like Eric Cantona, is a footballing firebrand with that Gaelic flair for attracting trouble." **DAILY STAR**

"It was heady stuff - but so was Ferguson's display as Everton stood toe-to-toe with the Double winners in a thrilling, if not exactly elegant, collision that swept away the stench of corruption hanging over the Premier League.... Ferguson was the focal point, but it was unsung duo Dave Watson and Barry Horne who were the heroes in the heat of battle, with United duo Mark Hughes and the outstanding Paul Ince." **TODAY**

"Everton hungered for survival in the FA Carling Premiership more than Manchester United aspired to a third consecutive title."

"A lot of teams will come to Everton and lose. Duncan Ferguson is a real big handful, and will give most defenders problems. We coped as well as I expected us to. He was up against the two best centre-backs in the country. We had five really good chances in the match and if we had taken one of them I believe we would have won. I was reasonably happy and thought we were a little unlucky. I felt if we had got through the first hour and then brought Andrei on when we weren't losing, we would have a chance. But in the end we never quite made it." **ALEX FERGUSON**

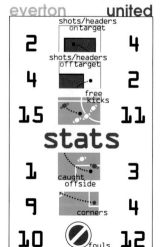

stats

everton **united**

2	shots/headers on target	4
4	shots/headers off target	2
15	free kicks	11
1	caught offside	3
9	corners	4
10	fouls	12

Everton have caught the imagination of their fans this season; over 40,000 crammed into Goodison for the visit of United.

United's sense of style deserted them on a bumpy pitch and the run of five wins post-Cantona was halted. The reds did have the better of a first half delayed by twenty minutes due to traffic congestion on the M62; **Hughes** shot against Southall's legs then sliced a volley from a **Giggs** cross. **Cole** also had chances either side of the break but it was the home team who took the lead when £4 million signing Ferguson headed past **Schmeichel** from a corner.

Amidst scenes of celebrations (had Everton won the European Cup or something?), United were left to pick up the pieces but were a pale imitation of their recent selves. The midfield dominance so evident in our last few games wasn't there and Watson in the Toffees' defence handled the United attack almost single-handedly as they held out for a win.

Any loss is a bad one, but at least Blackburn could only draw at home to Norwich.

Incey lays on another tireless performance

in the area
time^

9. Duncan Ferguson 58

No way through for Giggsy

>timeline

* **Sat 25th Feb** George Graham claims that Arsenal had promised him £750,000 to resign at the end of the season. Meanwhile, ex-Manchester United player Stewart Houston gets his second win as Arsenal manager in five days.

* Everton inflict Manchester United's first league defeat since Nottingham Forest's back in November.

> **I'M A SILLY OLD FOOL - STEPHEN FRY BREAKS HIS SILENCE ON DISAPPEARANCE**
Today Sat 25th Feb

* **Sun 26th Feb**

> **ERIC THE RED NOT FOR SALE VOWS FERGIE**
Manchester Evening News
Sun 26th Feb

* **Mon 27th Feb**

> **BARINGS BANK GOES BUST**
The Guardian Mon 27th Feb

* **Tue 28th Feb**

> **COME BACK YOU LITTLE BANKER**
Daily Star Tue 28th Feb

*ANDY COLE
>forward

Sportshot

personal file

born: Nottingham, 15/10/71
height: 5'11" **weight:** 10st 6lb
international team: England
signed pro for United: 12/01/95
transfer fee: £6,000,000
United league debut: 22/01/95 v Blackburn (h)

appearances/goals

appearances / apps as sub / goals	Premier League			FA Cup			Coca Cola Cup			European Cup			Total			left ft	right	header	inside the area	outside the area	open play	set piece	assists	scoring rate	performance rating average
Steve Bruce	4	-	-	1	-	1	-	-	-	-	-	-	5	-	1			1	1					20%	7.8
Ryan Giggs	4	-	-	1	-	-							5	-	-								2	-%	7.0
Paul Ince	4	-	2	1	-	-							5	-	2				2		2			40%	8.0
Brian McClair	4	-	-	1	-	1							5	-	1			1	1					20%	7.4
Gary Pallister	4	-	-	1	-	-							5	-	-								1	-%	7.6
Peter Schmeichel	4	-	-	1	-	-							5	-	-									-%	7.6
Lee Sharpe	4	-	-	1	-	-							5	-	-										6.8
Andy Cole	4	-	2	-	-	-							4	-	2				2		2		1	50%	7.3
Denis Irwin	3	-	-	1	-	-							4	-	-									-%	7.0
Mark Hughes	2	-	-	1	-	1							3	-	1			1	1			1		33%	7.3
Andrei Kanchelskis	2	2	2	1	-	-							3	2	2				2		2			66%	7.2
Roy Keane	2	-	-	1	-	-							3	-	-										7.3
Gary Neville	1	-	-										1	-	-										6.0
Phil Neville	1	-	-										1	-	-										7.0
Paul Scholes	1	1	-										1	1	-										7.5
David May	-	2	-										-	2	-										3.5

appearances/goals

appearances / apps as sub / goals	Premier League			FA Cup			Coca Cola Cup			European Cup			Total			left ft	right	header	inside the area	outside the area	open play	set piece	assists	scoring rate	performance rating average
Gary Pallister	30	-	2	3	-	-	2	-	-	6	-	-	41	-	2			2	2			2*	1	5%	7.3
Denis Irwin	28	-	1	3	-	2	2	-	-	5	-	-	38	-	3			3	3		1	2	2	8%	7.1
Steve Bruce	26	-	1	3	-	1	1	-	-	5	1	-	34	1	2			2	2				2	6%	7.5
Paul Ince	25	-	3	2	-	-	2	-	-				32	-	3	1	2			3	3		3	9%	7.6
Brian McClair	24	5	4	3	-	2	3	-	1	2	-	-	32	5	7	1	3	3	6	1	5	2	3	22%	7.3
Ryan Giggs	23	-	1	3	-	-	1	-	-	3	-	2	29	-	4	4			4		4		11	14%	7.2
Mark Hughes	22	-	5	2	-	2	2	-	-	3	-	2	29	-	9		7	2	7	2	8	1	3	31%	7.2
Andrei Kanchelskis	21	5	13	1	1	-	1	-	-	4	-	1	27	6	14	3	10	1	13	1	13	1	4	52%	6.6
Roy Keane	18	2	-	3	-	1	1	-	-	4	-	1	26	2	2	2			2		2		4	8%	7.4
Peter Schmeichel	20			3						3			26											-%	7.6
Eric Cantona	21	-	12	1	-	-				2	-	1	24	-	13	4	5	4	13		9	4	10	54%	7.6
Lee Sharpe	17	1	1	2	-	-	1	-	-	2	-	1	22	1	4		3		3		3	1	4	14%	7.0
David May	13	4	1	2	-	-	2	-	1	3	-	-	20	4	2			2	2			2	-1	10%	6.3
Gary Walsh	10			3						3			16											-%	7.1
Nicky Butt	6	7	1	1	-	-	3	-	-				15	8	1			1	1		1			6%	6.8
Gary Neville	8	2	-	1	-	-	2	-	-				11	4	-									-%	6.6
Simon Davies	3	3	-	1	-	-				2	1	-	8	11	1	1			1		1		2	11%	7.3
Paul Scholes	4	7	4	1	1	1	-	2	-	-	2	2	8	10	6		3	3	6		4	2		75%	7.8
Andy Cole	6	-	2										6	-	2				2		2		1	12%	7.2
Keith Gillespie	3	6	1	3	-	-							6	6	1				1		1			15%	7.3
David Beckham	1	-	-	1	-	1	3	-	-				4	1	1				1		1	1	1	25%	6.0
Paul Parker	1	-	-				2	1	-				3	2	-									-%	6.8
Phil Neville	1	-	-										2	-	-										7.0
John O'Kane	1	1	-				1	1	-				2	-	-										7.0
Chris Casper							2	-	-				2	-	-										7.0
Kevin Pilkington	1	-	-										1	-	-									-%	7.5
Graeme Tomlinson							-	2	-				-	2	-									-%	7.0

league table

FA Carling Premiership 25 February 95

	P	W	D	L	F	A	Pts
Blackburn Rovers	30	20	6	4	63	26	66
Manchester United	30	19	6	5	53	22	63
Newcastle United	29	15	9	5	50	31	54
Liverpool	28	14	9	5	48	23	51
Nottingham Forest	30	13	8	9	42	33	47
Leeds United	28	11	10	7	35	28	43
Tottenham Hotspur	28	12	7	9	46	40	43
Arsenal	30	10	10	10	35	32	40
Sheffield Wed	30	10	9	11	39	40	39
Wimbledon	29	11	6	12	35	50	39
Aston Villa	31	9	11	11	46	45	38
Coventry City	30	9	10	11	33	47	37
Chelsea	28	9	9	10	37	39	36
Norwich City	29	9	9	11	27	33	36
Manchester City	29	9	9	11	37	44	36
Everton	30	8	10	12	30	39	34
QPR	27	8	11	12	40	46	32
Southampton	28	6	13	9	40	46	31
Crystal Palace	29	7	9	13	21	31	30
West Ham United	29	8	5	16	27	29	29

time split

	0-10 mins	11-20 mins	21-30 mins	31-40 mins	41-50 mins	51-60 mins	61-70 mins	71-80 mins	81-90 mins
Andrei Kanchelskis	-	1	1	-	5	2	1	2	2
Eric Cantona	-	-	3	4	-	1	3	1	
Mark Hughes	-	2	1	-	1		3	2	1
Brian McClair	1	-	1	-	1	2	1	1	
Paul Scholes			1		1	1			
Ryan Giggs									
Paul Ince	1			1	1	-	1		
Denis Irwin	1	1		-		1			
Lee Sharpe							2		1
Andy Cole		1							
Roy Keane				2					
Steve Bruce	1								
David May					1		1		
Gary Pallister			1						
David Beckham								1	
Nicky Butt								1	
Simon Davies	1								
Keith Gillespie									
own goal					1			1	
TOTAL SCORED	5	6	8	5	8	6	10	16	7
TOTAL CONCEDED	4	3	4	2	5	6	5	6	4

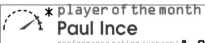

* player of the month
Paul Ince
performance rating average: 8.0

summary

	P	W	D	L	F	A
Premier League	30	19	6	5	53	22
FA Cup	3	3	-	-	10	3
Coca Cola Cup	3	2	-	1	4	3
European Cup	6	2	2	2	11	11
Total	42	26	8	8	78	39

notes

players must have played a minimum of three games in the month concerned to qualify for average performance ratings or scoring rate percentages; performance ratings are only awarded to players having played ten minutes or more in one match

manchester united v
IPSWICH TOWN

[Att: 43,804]

9-0

>Saturday 4 March 1995/3.00pm

>Old Trafford

[Last season
:0-0]

team lineups

home team

		rating
1.	Peter Schmeichel	7
16.	Roy Keane	8
4.	Steve Bruce	8
6.	Gary Pallister	8
3.	Denis Irwin	8
14.	Andrei Kanchelskis	9
8.	Paul Ince	9
9.	Brian McClair	9
11.	Ryan Giggs	9
17.	Andy Cole	10
10.	Mark Hughes	9

79mins · 45mins

on the bench

5.	Lee Sharpe	8
13.	Gary Walsh	
19.	Nicky Butt	8

visitors

1.	Craig Forrest	
19.	Frank Yallop	
5.	John Wark	
6.	David Linighan	
3.	Neil Thompson	
18.	Steve Palmer	
7.	Geraint Williams	
14.	Steve Sedgeley	
21.	Stuart Slater	
33.	Alex Mathie	
11.	Lee Chapman	

63mins

on the bench

10.	Ian Marshall	
4.	Paul Mason	
23.	Philip Morgan	

Seven down, two to go

Sportshot

bite e this!

"Andy Cole claimed five of the nine goals that devastated Premiership strugglers Ipswich at Old Trafford yesterday. Manchester United's record-breaking £7 million striker insisted the fourth, which some observers had attributed to Ipswich defender Frank Yallop, was his in the 9-0 demolition."
THE MAIL ON SUNDAY

"Amazingly, it looked in the seventh minute as if it wasn't going to be Cole's day. When Paul Ince put the striker clean through with a dream pass, Cole lost control.
But he didn't put a foot wrong for the rest of an amazing afternoon."
SUNDAY MIRROR

"Magnificent, mesmerising, magical and merciless United ripped the record book to shreds in sensational style. Cole the Goal and Hughes the Fuse exploded into spectacular action as the mighty Reds went one over the eight in a heady display of destructive football."
THE PEOPLE

"Poor Ipswich goalkeeper Craig Forrest was simply engulfed by a red tide of United forwards and, believe me, the lad really did not have such a bad game."
NEWS OF THE WORLD

"This is the kind of performance that you always dream about but only happens once in a lifetime.
We haven't trained a lot recently, in fact we've been indoors quite a bit because of the weather. Perhaps that is the recipe for success.
The goal difference is a significant factor, but I hope the league doesn't come down to that. The most important aspect of today's match was the passion, the passing and the movement – it was magnificent.
I have never seen us score more than five goals at Old Trafford. Five of ours today came from Cole. Even though he got a knock when he scored his second, I'm glad he carried on." **ALEX FERGUSON**

John Peters

Ipswich at sixes and sevens (or should that be...)

[Premier League #31]
Ipswich
>4-3-95   9-0
Old Trafford   home * win

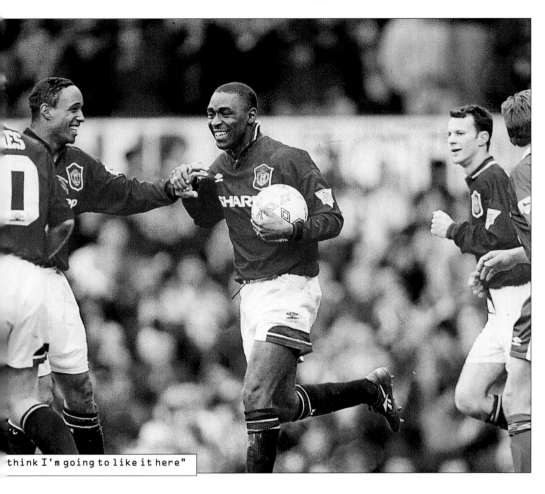

"...think I'm going to like it here"

Chapman duels with Pally

word up

n recent years United
e frequently threat-
d but never carried out
ut. Five goals against
six against Arsenal
Oldham, but never
. **Andy Cole**, however,
ged all that. Five
s he struck, as perenni-
ugglers Ipswich were
olished 9-0 in what was
ed's biggest win for 103
s.

On a day that went
for United, **Keane** put
eds ahead after only
nutes. **Cole** made his

first impression on the
scoresheet when he slid in
for our second goal on 19
minutes, before adding a
third just before half-time.
In the second half United
began to destroy the East
Anglians. Three goals in six
minutes, two from **Hughes**
and another from **Cole**,
made it 6-0 with 30 minutes
still to play. **When Cole
scored his fourth, and
United's seventh the crowd
began to chant "what a
waste of money." The new
signing appreciated the**

humour. The banter continued when **Ince** chipped
home our eighth goal after
72 minutes, and a "we
want ten" cry went up from
cheeky United fans. The
dismayed Ipswich fans
replied: "we want one!"

With three minutes left
on the clock, that man
Cole concluded United's
nine-goal rout. An unbe-
lievable performance on a
once-in-a-lifetime
occasion.

in the book

Referee:
G Poll,
Tilehurst
Rating: 7

Bookings:
Forrest,
Linighan

united Ipswich

shots/headers on target

| 14 | | 1 |

shots/headers off target

| 7 | | 5 |

free kicks

| 8 | | 10 |

stats

caught offside

| 3 | | 2 |

corners

| 8 | | 4 |

fouls

| 7 | | 6 |

in the area

	time^	left ft	right	header	inside/outside the area		^open play	set piece
. Roy Keane	15		*			*	*	
st: Mark Hughes								
. Andy Cole	19		*		*		*	
st: Ryan Giggs								
st: Mark Hughes	37		*		*		*	
st: Andrei Kanchelskis	53		*		*		*	
	65	*			*		*	
	87			*	*		*	
. Paul Ince	72		*			*		*
st: Mark Hughes								

>timeline

* **Weds 1st Mar** Premier
League chief executive Rick
Parry says the game needs
"time to cool".

* FIFA prolong Eric Cantona's
ban to 30 September.

> **THE £800M STING — WHIZ KID
TRADER AND HIS PAL HAVE TAKEN
US FOR A RIDE, SAYS BARINGS
BOSS**
The Sun Weds 1st Mar

* **Thurs 2nd Mar** Arsenal draw
1-1 with Auxerre.

> **MAJOR ESCAPES TRAP ON EUROPE
— LAMONT SUPPORTS LABOUR AS
TORIES WIN BY FIVE VOTES**
The Guardian Thurs 2nd Mar

* **Fri 3rd Mar**
> **I'LL TAKE THEM ALL WITH ME —
RUNAWAY WHIZ-KID NICK LEESON
WAS ARRESTED YESTERDAY, AFTER
VOWING TO DRAG HIS COL-
LEAGUES DOWN WITH HIM OVER
THE BARINGS BANK CRASH**

* Referee Mike Reed saves
Blackburn's Tim Sherwood
from a four-match ban by
awarding only two points for
a recent booking

WIMBLEDON
>Selhurst Park
v manchester united:

[Att:18,224]

0-1

[Last season
:0-1]

team lineups

home team
rating

1.	Hans Segers	
2.	Warren Barton	
4.	Vinnie Jones	
10.	Dean Holdsworth	
12.	Gary Elkins	
15.	Alan Reeves	
16.	Alan Kimble	
20.	Marcus Gayle	
21.	Chris Perry	
36.	Jon Goodman	
37.	Kenny Cunningham	

65 mins

on the bench

25.	Mick Harford	
23.	Neil Sullivan	
26.	Neil Ardley	

visitors

1.	Peter Schmeichel	7
27.	Gary Neville	7
3.	Denis Irwin	7
4.	Steve Bruce	7
5.	Lee Sharpe	7
6.	Gary Pallister	8
8.	Paul Ince	7
9.	Brian McClair	7
17.	Andy Cole	7
10.	Mark Hughes	7
11.	Ryan Giggs	7

on the bench

18.	Simon Davies	
13.	Gary Walsh	
26.	Chris Casper	

Alan Reeves finds out what an irresistable force *and* an immovable object looks like

stats

wimbledon **united**

wimbledon		united
5	shots/headers on target	7
3	shots/headers off target	4
9	free kicks	12
3	caught offside	2
3	corners	8
9	fouls	7

word up

Selhurst Park has been a controversial place for United this season. Tonight was no different, but thankfully it wasn't United employees who were making the headlines for the wrong reasons. The team were too busy earning the much-needed points which they will take back to Manchester.

The game was a scrappy one, with the home side seemingly content to frustrate United in the hope of picking up something. If a point was what they were after, Wimbledon nearly achieved their objective but **Steve Bruce** had other ideas. **Bruce** took advantage when the ball stuck in the mud, to beat keeper **Segers** six minutes from time.

The relief was evident all over the stadium as upwards of twelve thousand reds celebrated wildly.

The goal and prior sending-off of Dons' defender **Alan Kimble** was too much for manager **Roy Kinnear** to take, as he was sent off for complaining. **Kinnear** later said "I'm bitterly disappointed with the result. I thought we deserved to win, but I realise I shouldn't have reacted like I did."

Even **Alex Ferguson** admitted: "We were lucky, but you need luck; it was a really disappointing performance but I'm pleased about being top again."

Alan Kimble is dismissed by Robbie Hart in an incident that incensed the Wimbledon bench

bite this!

"It was all so unexpected. With 11 minutes to go, the match seemed destined to end as a sterile goalless draw. Then Hart dismissed Kimble for encroaching at a corner - his second bookable offence - and the game exploded. Five minutes later, Brian McClair's hopeful long ball stuck in the mud as Hans Segers went to collect it. Bruce roared in, poked the ball away as the hapless goalkeeper tried to gather, and scored."

THE DAILY TELEGRAPH

"Alex Ferguson had pushed his skipper forward in a last-ditch effort to break the brave resistance of Wimbledon's defence, already depleted by the sending-off of Alan Kimble for two bookable offences. After the ballet at Old Trafford last Saturday this was more of a clog dance through a muddy pitch passed fit only after three inspections."

DAILY MIRROR

"Forget the nine against Ipswich on Saturday, the one which caused such consternation on the Wimbledon bench may well turn out to be the most significant of the season as the destiny of the Premiership title bounces back and forth between the champions and Blackburn, their arch-challengers."

THE INDEPENDENT

"People might say we were lucky and I would have to agree with them. Sometimes, though, you need that bit of luck to get you through, and Segers dropping the ball gave that to us.

Overall this was a disappointing performance, but I'm glad we're top. We didn't really create that much and Wimbledon could easily have had a draw. After all, they had the best efforts in the first half."

ALEX FERGUSON

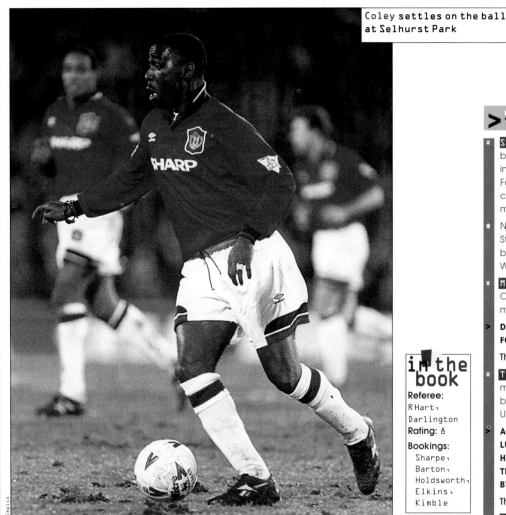

Coley settles on the ball at Selhurst Park

Emplcs

in the book

Referee:
R Hart, Darlington
Rating: 8

Bookings:
Sharpe, Barton, Holdsworth, Elkins, Kimble

in the area

4. Steve Bruce	time^	left ft	right	header	inside/outside the area	^open play	set piece
	84	*			*		

A salute from the match-winner

Like puppets on a string

>timeline

* **Sun 5th Mar** New Soccer bribery sensation – Police are investigating another bid by Far-Eastern betting syndicates to fix top Premiership matches.

* New Arsenal manager Stewart Houston sees his side beaten for the first time by West Ham

* **Mon 6th Mar** Aston Villa 0 Coventry City 0. A confusing match for Ron Atkinson!

> **DUTCH GROUP WINS BATTLE FOR BARINGS**

   The Times Mon 6th Mar

* **Tues 7th Mar** Stick in the mud. Steve Bruce steals the ball from Segers to give United three points

> **ANOTHER ONE BITES THE LUST-MINISTER ROBERT HUGHES BECAME THE THIRTEENTH TORY TO BE TAINTED BY SLEAZE**

   The Daily Mirror Tues 7th Mar

* **Weds 8th Mar** Bolton earn their place at Wembley by beating Swindon Town 4-3 on aggregate in the semifinal of the Coca-Cola Cup

> **WHO DESERVES THE SYMPATHY-CONTROVERSY GROWS OVER POLICEMAN FACING THE SACK FOR PUNCHING THE TEENAGER WHO THREATENED HIS BABY'S LIFE**

   The Daily Mail Weds 8th Mar

* **Fri 10th Mar** Celtic proceed to the semis of the Scottish Cup, beating Kilmarnock by one goal. The match had a 25-minute break due to Hampden Park's floodlights failing to work

> **GIVE UP HOLS FOR A PAY RISE-BRITISH GAS BOSSES HAVE TOLD STAFF THEY MUST GIVE UP HOLIDAYS AND WORK EXTRA HOURS TO EARN A PAY RISE THIS YEAR**

   The Daily Mirror Fri 10th

manchester united v
TOTTENHAM HOTSPUR 0-0

> Wednesday 15 March 1995 / 8.00pm > Old Trafford

[Att: 43,802]

[Last season :2-1]

team lineups

home team | rating

No.	Player	Rating
1.	Peter Schmeichel	7
3.	Denis Irwin	8
4.	Steve Bruce	7
6.	Gary Pallister	7
5.	Lee Sharpe	6
14.	Andrei Kanchelskis	7
8.	Paul Ince	6
9.	Brian McClair	6
17.	Andy Cole	6
10.	Mark Hughes	7
11.	Ryan Giggs	7

76mins

on the bench

19.	Nicky Butt	7
13.	Gary Walsh	
27.	Gary Neville	

visitors

13.	Ian Walker
2.	Dean Austin
5.	Colin Calderwood
6.	Gary Mabbutt
3.	Justin Edinburgh
11.	Ronny Rosenthal
9.	Darren Anderton
15.	David Howells
7.	Nick Barmby
18.	Jürgen Klinsmann
10.	Teddy Sheringham

on the bench

14.	Stuart Nethercott
1.	Erik Thorstvedt
20.	Darren Caskey

Ince moves away from Barmby

word up

Tottenham arrived at Old Trafford in a buoyant mood after their 2-1 victory over Liverpool four days earlier ensured their passage to the FA Cup semi-finals.

Their confidence was evident in a game which provided many examples of the quality of the English Premiership, although United fans may argue the touch of French spice in the form of **Eric Cantona** could perhaps have added to their enjoyment of the night's proceedings.

The champions did, however, tear into Spurs from the kick-off, with the crossbar denying **Mark Hughes** after only 30 seconds and **Andy Cole** emulating his striking partner's misfortune by firing against the woodwork twice when it seemed scoring would have been easier.

Tottenham rallied strongly after the break despite being outplayed in the first 45 minutes. As one would expect, **Klinsmann** was at the heart of the visitors' moves, first setting up **Rosenthal** and then **Barmby**, whose ambitious chip just failed to hit the target. United hit back, however, with **Cole** powering a drive into keeper **Ian Walker's** chest and with three minutes remaining **Rosenthal** had to clear off the line to maintain parity in the scoreline.

The game ended goalless – on what was the first time this season that United had failed to score at Old Trafford. **The quality of the football on display was only a small comfort to the home crowd, who knew that three points could have been priceless in the push for a third consecutive championship crown.**

Cole just misses out

stats

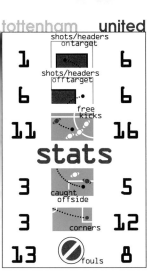

shots/headers on target	
1	6
shots/headers off target	
6	6
free kicks	
11	16
caught offside	
3	5
corners	
3	12
fouls	
13	8

---

bite ⚫ this!

"Andy Cole, who scores goals or is nothing, missed all his opportunities to win the match, hitting the post and bar, and thumping another shot into Walker's chest. There was more fluid, thrilling football in the opening 15 minutes than most matches manage in 90. The pace of Kanchelskis and Giggs was stunning."

THE GUARDIAN

"The notion that goalless draws cannot be exciting was put to rest last night as Manchester United and Tottenham served up a spectacle that would have graced any stadium."

DAILY TELEGRAPH

"Tottenham star Jürgen Klinnsmann helped man the defences in Manchester United's full-scale first-half assault, then set up wave after wave of attacks to threaten the Double-chasers."

DAILY MIRROR

You would never have thought a game like that would end 0-0. It was a disappointing result, but not a disappointing performance. We defended well - clean sheets are always a good thing. We created plenty of chances in the first half, but we frittered them away by hitting the woodwork, and their goalkeeper made an excellent save from Paul Ince's strike.

When Spurs started asserting themselves we got a little nervous at the back. They showed they're a very capable side now, with much more discipline in defence.

You are always concerned when you have a chance to make up some ground while Blackburn are not playing, but if you look at the history of the club, you'll notice that we have always done things the hard way. Our supporters are kept hanging on until the last goal, and it will probably be the same story this season.

ALEX FERGUSON

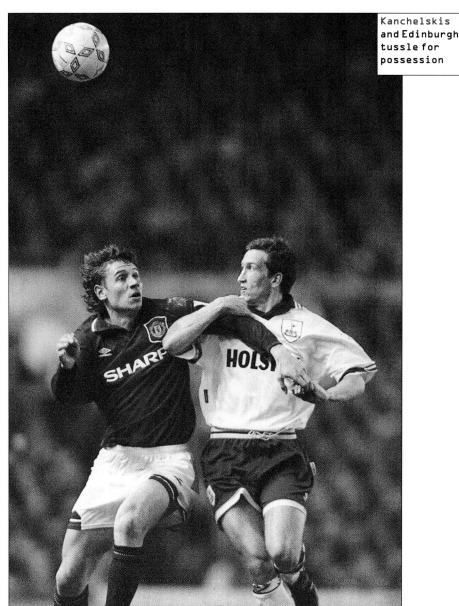

Kanchelskis and Edinburgh tussle for possession

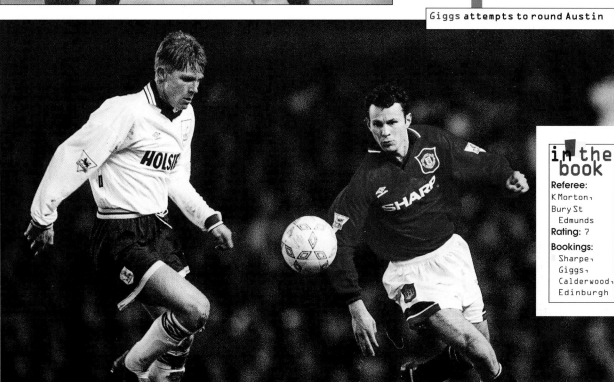

Giggs attempts to round Austin

>timeline

* **Tues 14th Mar** Chelsea beat Brugge 2-0 to win a place in the semis of the European Cup Winners' Cup

> **£132,000 TO SAVE MAN, 79-DOCTORS SPEND £132,000 IN TWO DAYS SAVING THE LIFE OF A 79-YEAR-OLD MAN**
The Daily Express Tues 14th Mar

* **Weds 15th Mar** One of the best ever 0-0 draws takes place at Old Trafford, with United and Tottenham failing to convert their chances

* Barcelona are knocked out of the Champions' Cup by Paris St Germain, who are now in the semi-finals

> **SOCCER'S NEW BRIBE CRISIS-ENGLISH FOOTBALL IS IN CRISIS AGAIN AS 3 PREMIER LEAGUE FOOTBALL STARS ARE ARRESTED BY POLICE INVESTIGATING BRIBERY CLAIMS. JOHN FASHANU, BRUCE GROBBELAAR AND HANS SEGERS.**
THE DAILY EXPRESS Wed 15th Mar

* **Thurs 16th Mar** The FA tells Bruce Grobbelaar he is free to carry on playing

> **TORY ALARM AT FEEL GOOD FACTOR-IT MIGHT TAKE ANOTHER TWO YEARS TO CLOSE THE NEXT GENERAL ELECTION, SAYS KENNETH CLARKE**
The Daily Telegraph Thu 16th Mar

---

in the book

Referee: K Morton, Bury St Edmunds
Rating: 7
Bookings: Sharpe, Giggs, Calderwood, Edinburgh

Sportsshot

manchester united v
QUEENS PARK RANGERS 2-0
>Sunday 12 March 1995 / 1.00pm >Old Trafford
[Att: 42,830]

team lineups

home team
		rating
1.	Peter Schmeichel	7
27.	Gary Neville	7
3.	Denis Irwin	7
4.	Steve Bruce	7
5.	Lee Sharpe	9
6.	Gary Pallister	8
14.	Andrei Kanchelskis	7
8.	Paul Ince	7
9.	Brian McClair	7
10.	Mark Hughes	7
11.	Ryan Giggs	7

45mins

on the bench
16.	Roy Keane	7
13.	Gary Walsh	
23.	Philip Neville	

visitors
1.	Tony Roberts	
16.	Danny Maddix	
3.	Clive Wilson	
14.	Simon Barker	
2.	David Bardsley	
15.	Rufus Brevett	
20.	Kevin Gallen	
6.	Alan McDonald	
7.	Andrew Impey	
8.	Ian Holloway	
9.	Les Ferdinand	

62mins

on the bench
12.	Gary Prentice	
13.	Sieb Dykstra	
5.	Karl Ready	

Choccy closes in

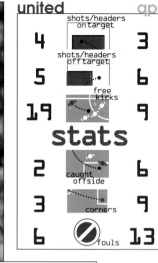

united — stats — qpr
united		qpr
4	shots/headers on target	3
5	shots/headers off target	6
19	free kicks	9
2	caught offside	6
3	corners	9
6	fouls	13

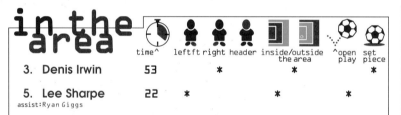

in the area
		time^	leftft	right	header	inside/outside the area	^open play	set piece
3.	Denis Irwin	53		*		*		*
5.	Lee Sharpe	22	*			*	*	

assist: Ryan Giggs

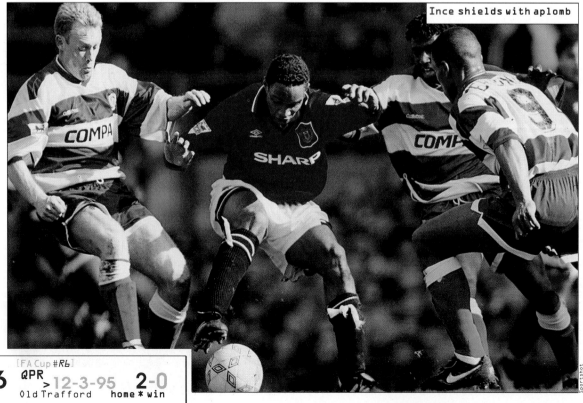

Ince shields with aplomb

bite this!

"Rangers' mugging of Mark Hughes at Old Trafford yesterday was an open invitation for United to call in their own terminator in the stocky shape of Denis Irwin.
When Hughes was grounded by Danny Maddix on the edge of the penalty area, they seized their opportunity. Irwin's clubbing free-kick round the wall to make it 2-0 in the 53rd minute finally killed off Rangers' challenge."
DAILY EXPRESS

"The last of the Sunday roast was going down yesterday when Manchester United were prodded into enough life to keep the prospect of a historic football success."
DAILY MAIL

"It was the all important breakthrough and a huge relief for Sharpe who a couple of minutes earlier had been put through by Hughes only to shoot straight at the keeper."
MANCHESTER EVENING NEWS

"We're very pleased to have got through to the semi-final. We have to give the team a lot of credit for their performance. They defended well, and at the other end, Peter Schmeichel made a superb save from Les Ferdinand.

It was a tough game as Mark Hughes will tell you. I made a change at half-time by bringing Ryan Giggs off because he had a calf strain, but he's okay now."
ALEX FERGUSON

Sportshot

Sharpie
finds the net

> timeline

* **Sat 11th Mar** The FA Cup quarter-finals get under way. Spurs beat Liverpool at Anfield 2-1, whilst Wolves and Palace will require a replay, after sharing two goals

> **GIRL DYING OF CANCER LOSES COURT FIGHT FOR 'LAST CHANCE' TREATMENT. ("CHILD B" IS REFUSED TREATMENT FROM THE NATIONAL HEALTH.)**
> The Daily Telegraph Sat 11th Mar

* **Sun 12th Mar** FA Cup weekend continues. Everton knock out near-favourites Newcastle in an un-inspiring 1-0 victory. Then QPR are knocked out by United at Old Trafford

> **I'VE LOST THE LOVE OF MY LIFE- COMIC ACTOR DAVID JASON TOLD OF HIS GREAT SADNESS AFTER HIS BELOVED GIRLFRIEND LOST HER BATTLE AGAINST BREAST CANCER**
> The Sunday Express Sun 12th Mar

* **Mon 13th Mar** SHE MUST HAVE THE OP DAD-LITTLE B'S FATHER OPENS HIS HEART TO THE DAILY MIRROR
> The Daily Mirror Mon 13th Mar

word up

Denis gets there first

eague aspirations
e forgotten for a
as QPR and their
n thousand sup-
ers converged on
Old Trafford sun for
mportant cup tie.

harpe gave
d the lead in the
minute. The goal
e with a brilliant
bined build-up
ving **Hughes** and
s, who left
pe free to shoot
keeper **Roberts**
15 yards - the first
Rangers had con-
d in this season's
up.
e lads from
herds Bush had
 disappointing in
rst half, but a
ng from manager
ins saw them
e out more deter-
d after the break.
 timing was all
g though,
ause United

gained a crucial two-
goal cushion on 52
minutes. Unsung hero
Denis Irwin bent a
free-kick round the line
of defenders and past
the diving goalkeeper.
 Rangers' spirited
play came too late
and lacked the confi-
dence of United's
dominance. **Brevett**,
McDonald and
Ferdinand had
chances, but failed to
take them and the
score stayed at 2-0.
 Talk in the press
room after the match
centred on United's
chances of achieving
a unique back-to-back
Double. "It's a distinct
possibility" said Rangers
manager and ex-red
hero **Wilkins**. As fans,
we can only dream
and hope.

in the book

Referee:
D Gallagher,
Banbury
Rating: 7

Bookings:
Hughes,
Brevett,
Holloway,
Ferdinand

LIVERPOOL
>Sunday 19 March 1995 / 4.00pm

v **manchester united:**
> **Anfield** [Att:38,906]

2-0
[Last season :3-3]

team lineups

home team
1.	David James	
5.	Mark Wright	
6.	Phil Babb	
12.	John Scales	
15.	Jamie Redknapp	
17.	Steve McManaman	
10.	John Barnes	
20.	Stig Bjornbye	
23.	Robbie Fowler	81mins
9.	Ian Rush	
25.	Neil Ruddock	

on the bench
16.	Michael Thomas	86mins
30.	Tony Warner	
11.	Mark Walters	

visitors
		rating
1.	Peter Schmeichel	7
3.	Denis Irwin	7
4.	Steve Bruce	6
5.	Lee Sharpe	6
6.	Gary Pallister	6
8.	Paul Ince	7
9.	Brian McClair	6
14.	Andrei Kanchelskis	6
16.	Roy Keane	8 75mins
10.	Mark Hughes	7
11.	Ryan Giggs	7 75mins

on the bench
17.	Andy Cole	6
25.	Kevin Pilkington	
19.	Nicky Butt	6

stats

liverpool — united

liverpool		united
5	shots/headers on target	2
3	shots/headers off target	3
9	free kicks	9
2	caught offside	3
7	corners	4
7	fouls	6

Ryan on the run

Sparky gets the Wright treatment

bite this!

"Certainly the **Reds** are now underdogs, with Blackburn six points ahead and only eight games to go.
But there are still 24 points to play for, and though Blackburn have their destiny in their own hands, who is to say they will win the lot?"
MANCHESTER EVENING NEWS.

"**Steve Bruce** saw Liverpool shred his side's title hopes on a passionate afternoon where United simply failed to function at their true level."
TODAY.

"Jamie Redknapp, the game's outstanding performer, put Liverpool ahead after 23 minutes.
When the dust settled yesterday United found themselves still six points behind Blackburn Rovers. Both sides have eight games left."
THE INDEPENDENT.

"John Barnes, despite being floored, still managed to swivel round and somehow put the ball into Redknapp's path for him to fire home his fifth goal of the campaign."
DAILY STAR.

"A superb save from **Peter Schmeichel** prevented Fowler from making it 2-0 on the half-hour.
Too often United's shooting was wayward."
DAILY MIRROR.

"This is a very disappointing result. In the past we've won big games when they matter, but we only drew with Spurs and now lost to Liverpool. There's no question about it - we are in a very difficult position now.

I don't think we deserved anything from the match; we didn't play anywhere near to our true form.

I put Andy Cole on as substitute, but looking back, maybe I should have risked him from the start. I took Keane off due to his injury. We need him now that Steve Bruce is suspended for the semi-final and David May won't be back for at least a month."
ALEX FERGUSON

in the area

time^ leftft right header inside/outside the area ^open play set piece

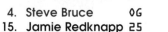
4.	Steve Bruce	OG
15.	Jamie Redknapp	25

Charming Mr Ruddock comforts Hughsie following a clash

word up

For the second time in four years, Anfield echoed with the **"You've lost the league on Merseyside"** chant directed at United players and fans alike.

The not-so-witty Scousers were right last time and after today's 2-0 defeat I've got a gut feeling they will be right again. It's sad, though, that a team we once considered to be our greatest rivals now measure their success in our failure. For once they had something to celebrate, as Liverpool were worthy of their victory.

Just as United seemed the more settled side, Liverpool took the lead. Jamie Redknapp, the game's outstanding performer, put them ahead after 23 min-

utes with a perfect finish. **Schmeichel** had to earn his wages for the rest of the first half, but United came back strongly in the second period, with David James forced to make fine saves from **Giggs** and **Hughes**.

Any possibility of the Reds from Manchester salvaging anything from the game was thwarted when a Michael Thomas cross from the right was struck by **McManaman** at the edge of the 18 yard box on to the head of Bruce, who helplessly deflected the ball into the back of his own net.

"Always Look On The Bright Side Of Life" sang Anfield in unison, and with two months of the season still to go and a back-to-back Double still a possibility, there may well be a very bright side to life as a United fan.

Captain Steve clears his lines

>timeline

* **Sat 18th Mar**

> **REDS CLINCH DEAL FOR £28M STAND** – 3 tier giant will help boost Old Trafford capacity to 55,300
Manchester Evening News
Sat 18th Mar

* **Sun 19th Mar** Liverpool repeat their punishment of three years ago, as they beat United 2-0 at Anfield, piling increasing doubt onto their championship hopes

* **Mon 20th Mar** The Anglian Derby is won by Norwich, who beat Ipswich by three goals

> **£1M FOR PRISON SOCCER PITCHES** – Britain's toughest jails have spent nearly £1m installing Premier League quality soccer pitches
Daily Express Mon 20th Mar

manchester united v
ARSENAL

>Wednesday 22 March 1995 / 8.00pm

[Att: 43,623]

>Old Trafford

3-0

[Last season] :1-0.

team lineups

home team

		rating
1.	Peter Schmeichel	7
16.	Roy Keane	7
4.	Steve Bruce	7
6.	Gary Pallister	8
3.	Denis Irwin	7
14.	Andrei Kanchelskis	7
8.	Paul Ince	8
5.	Lee Sharpe	7
10.	Mark Hughes	7
17.	Andy Cole	7
11.	Ryan Giggs	7

on the bench

9.	Brian McClair
25.	Kevin Pilkington
19.	Nicky Butt

visitors

13.	Vince Bartram
2.	Lee Dixon
6.	Tony Adams
12.	Steve Bould
3.	Nigel Winterburn
23.	Ray Parlour
14.	Martin Keown
21.	Steve Morrow
10.	Paul Merson
31.	Chris Kiwomya
8.	Ian Wright

57 mins

on the bench

32.	Glenn Helder
26.	Lee Harper
11.	Eddie McGoldrick

Classy Kan-Kan celebrates scoring number three

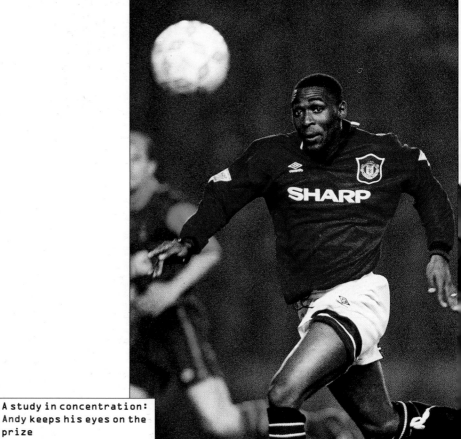

word up

After the disappointment of the 2-0 defeat at Anfield it was vital **Alex Ferguson** rallied his troops and restored confidence to a team which had been far from its best in recent weeks.

A resounding win over Arsenal would surely be just the tonic the manager was looking for. The game was only four minutes old when **Lee Sharpe** flashed a 20-yard shot narrowly wide, but it wasn't until the 26th minute when the home crowd were rewarded, with a goal which came in the form of a **Mark Hughes** strike from six yards out. Five minutes later **Cole** and **Hughes** combined to find **Kanchelskis** flying down the right flank. The Russian in turn laid on a cross for **Sharpe** to power a low drive into the bottom corner of the Stretford End goal.

After the break United began to play some exhilarating football, safe in the knowledge that they had a two-goal cushion with **Giggs**, **Sharpe** and **Hughes** causing mayhem in the Gunners defence. The inevitable third goal came after 78 minutes, when **Kanchelskis** was first to react to a **Giggs** shot palmed away by Arsenal 'keeper Bartram.

This was a pleasing performance from United which keeps the championship race as tight as it has been in recent years. One disappointing aspect, however, was the booking of **Bruce**, which keeps him out of the forthcoming FA Cup semi-final against Palace.

A study in concentration: Andy keeps his eyes on the prize

bite this!

"For the first 27 minutes last night, it appeared that Alex Ferguson's fears were well-founded, as Arsenal dealt efficiently with what few questions they were asked. Then Vince Bartram failed to hold a routine Giggs cross and, after Sharpe had seen a shot blocked, Hughes rammed the ball through a cluster of defenders. The anxiety disappeared from the United ranks...."

THE DAILY TELEGRAPH

"An inspirational display by midfield dynamo Ince, who today faces an assault charge alongside Eric Cantona, and goals from Mark Hughes, Lee Sharpe and Andrei Kanchelskis ensured the jury stays out on their tussle with Blackburn."

DAILY EXPRESS

"Mark Hughes was the tough man who got going for Manchester United last night, responding superbly to his manager's questions to offer a glimmer of title hope." **TODAY**

"The champions underlined their desire in glowing red last night. Nobody is throwing in the towel at Old Trafford."

DAILY STAR

"That was a good result for us. Arsenal are one of the biggest names in British football, but we came through even after a nervy start.

A question that I am asking at the moment is why we don't come back anymore in the last fifteen minutes of a match. We showed that old kind of spirit again tonight and every game now until the end of the season will be the same. The players have a responsibility to bring out a performance from themselves and each other.

The crowd were excellent tonight. They got behind us and gave us a boost."

ALEX FERGUSON

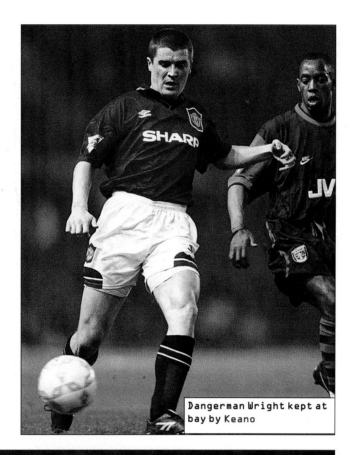

Dangerman Wright kept at bay by Keano

united   arsenal

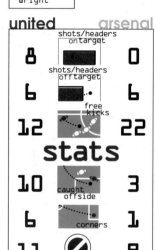

stats

united		arsenal
8	shots/headers on target	0
6	shots/headers off target	6
12	free kicks	22
10	caught offside	3
6	corners	1
11	fouls	9

>timeline

Salivatastic: Hughesie tastes success

in the area

		time^	left ft	right	header	inside/outside the area		^open play	set piece
10.	Mark Hughes	26		*		*		*	
5.	Lee Sharpe	31		*		*		*	
	assist: Mark Hughes								
14.	Andrei Kanchelskis	80		*		*		*	
	assist: Ryan Giggs								

✳MARK HUGHES
>forward

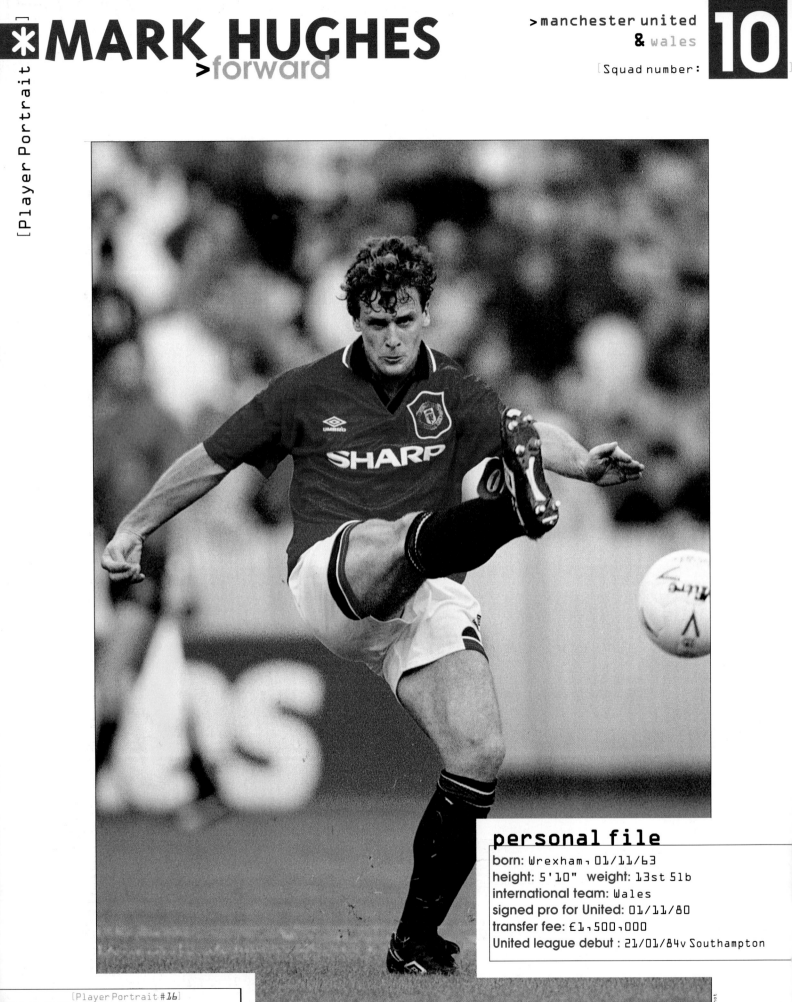

personal file

born: Wrexham, 01/11/63
height: 5'10" weight: 13st 5lb
international team: Wales
signed pro for United: 01/11/80
transfer fee: £1,500,000
United league debut: 21/01/84v Southampton

Sportshot

appearances/goals

Player	PL apps	sub	goals	FA Cup apps	sub	goals	Coca Cola apps	sub	goals	European apps	sub	goals	Total apps	sub	goals	left ft	right	header	inside/outside area	open play	set piece	assists	scoring rate	performance rating average
Steve Bruce	5	-	1	1	-	-							6	-	1			1		1			17%	7.0
Ryan Giggs	5	-	-	1	-	-							6	-	-							4	-%	7.3
Mark Hughes	5	-	3	1	-	-							6	-	3		2	1	3	3		4	50%	7.3
Paul Ince	5	-	1	1	-	-							6	-	1			1	1	1			17%	7.3
Denis Irwin	5	-	1	1	-	1							6	-	1			1			1	1	17%	7.3
Gary Pallister	5	-	-	1	-	-							6	-	-								-%	7.5
Peter Schmeichel	5			1									6										-%	7.0
Andrei Kanchelskis	4	-	-	1	-	-							5	-	1		1		1	1			20%	7.2
Brian McClair	4			1									5										-%	7.0
Lee Sharpe	4	1	1	1	-	-							5	1	2	1		1	2	2			33%	7.2
Andy Cole	4	1	5										4	1	5	1	3	1	5	5		5	125%	7.2
Roy Keane	3	-	1				1						3	1	1		1		1				25%	7.5
Gary Neville	1	1											2										-%	7.0
Nicky Butt	-	3											-	3									-%	7.0

appearances/goals

Player	PL apps	sub	goals	FA Cup apps	sub	goals	Coca Cola apps	sub	goals	European apps	sub	goals	Total apps	sub	goals	left ft	right	header	inside/outside area	open play	set piece	assists	scoring rate	performance rating average
Gary Pallister	34	-	2	4	-	-	2	-	-	6	-	-	47	-	2			2	2		2	1	4%	7.3
Denis Irwin	32	-	1	4	-	3	2	-	-	5	-	-	44	-	4		4		3	1	3	2	9%	7.2
Steve Bruce	30	-	2	3	-	1	1	-	-	5	1	-	40	1	3	1		2	3	1	2	-	7%	7.4
Paul Ince	29	-	4	3	-	-				5	-	-	38	-	4	1	3			4	3	3	11%	7.6
Brian McClair	27	5	4	4	-	2	2	-	1	5	-	-	37	5	7				6	5	2	3	19%	7.3
Ryan Giggs	28	-	1	4	-	1				3	-	2	35	-	4	4			4	4		15	11%	7.3
Mark Hughes	27	-	8	3	-	2				5	-	2	35	-	12		9	3	10	2	11	1	7	34%	7.3
Andrei Kanchelskis	24	5	14	2	-	1				5	1		32	6	15	3	11	1	14	1	14	1	5	48%	6.7
Peter Schmeichel	25			4						3			32										-%	7.5
Roy Keane	20	2	1	3	1	1				1	-	1	29	3	3	2	1		2	1	3	4	10%	7.4
Lee Sharpe	21	2	2	3	1	1	-	2		3	-	2	27	5	5	2	3		5	5		4	16%	7.0
Eric Cantona	21	-	12							3	-	1	24	-	13		4	4	13	9	4	10	54%	7.6
David May	13	5	1	1	-	-	2	-	-	4	-	-	20	5	2				2	2	1		10%	6.3
Gary Walsh	9						3	-	-	3	-	-	16										-%	7.1
Nicky Butt	6	8	1	1	-	-				3	-	-	15	9	1		1			1		1	6%	6.8
Gary Neville	8	2	-	1	-	-	2	1	-	1	1	-	13	4	-								-%	6.6
Andy Cole	10	1	7										10	1	7	1	5	1	7	6	1		70%	7.2
Simon Davies	3	1	-				3	-	-	1	-	-	8	1	1							2	12%	7.3
Paul Scholes	4	7	2	1	-	1	2	-	1	1	-	1	8	10	6			3	6	4	2		38%	7.8
Keith Gillespie	3	6	1				3						6	6	1	1				1			15%	7.3
David Beckham				1	-	1	3	-	-				4	1	1		1				1	1	25%	6.0
Paul Parker	1	-	-				2	1	-				3	2	-								-%	6.8
Phil Neville	1	-	-	1	-	-							2	-	-							1	-%	7.0
John O'Kane				1	-	-	1	1	-				2	1	-								-%	7.0
Chris Casper				1	-	-							1	-	-								-%	7.0
Kevin Pilkington	1	-	-										1	-	-								-%	7.5
Graeme Tomlinson							2	-	-				2	-	-								-%	7.0

league table

FA Carling Premiership 31 March 95

Team	P	W	D	L	F	A	Pts
Blackburn Rovers	34	23	7	4	70	29	76
Manchester United	35	22	7	6	66	24	73
Newcastle United	34	18	9	7	56	36	63
Nottingham Forest	35	17	9	9	56	38	60
Liverpool	32	16	10	6	54	26	58
Leeds United	33	14	10	9	44	35	57
Tottenham Hotspur	33	14	10	9	52	42	52
Wimbledon	34	14	6	14	41	54	48
QPR	32	12	8	12	50	50	44
Sheffield Wed	35	11	10	14	43	46	43
Coventry City	35	10	13	12	37	53	43
Norwich City	34	10	15	12	37	38	42
Manchester City	34	10	11	13	43	52	41
Arsenal	34	10	10	14	36	40	40
Chelsea	33	10	10	13	40	46	40
Aston Villa	34	9	12	13	46	48	39
Everton	34	9	12	13	37	36	39
West Ham United	34	10	7	17	33	54	37
Southampton	32	7	15	10	44	51	36
Crystal Palace	32	8	10	14	23	34	34
Ipswich Town	33	6	5	22	31	75	23
Leicester City	34	4	9	21	36	64	21

time split

Player	0-10	11-20	21-30	31-40	41-50	51-60	61-70	71-80	81-90
Andrei Kanchelskis	-	1	1	-	5	2	1	3	2
Eric Cantona	-	-	1	3	4	-	1	3	1
Mark Hughes	-	2	1	-	1	2	3	2	-
Andy Cole	-	2	-	1	1	1	1	-	-
Brian McClair	1	-	-	-	1	1	2	1	-
Paul Scholes	-	-	2	-	2	1	1	-	-
Lee Sharpe	-	-	-	-	-	-	2	-	-
Ryan Giggs	-	-	1	-	1	-	1	-	-
Paul Ince	1	-	-	-	1	-	-	-	-
Denis Irwin	1	-	-	1	-	-	1	-	-
Steve Bruce	1	-	-	-	-	1	-	1	-
Roy Keane	-	-	-	-	2	-	-	-	-
David May	-	-	-	1	-	-	-	-	-
Gary Pallister	-	-	-	-	-	-	1	-	-
David Beckham	-	-	-	-	1	-	-	-	-
Nicky Butt	-	-	-	-	-	1	-	-	-
Simon Davies	1	-	-	-	-	-	-	-	-
Keith Gillespie	-	-	-	-	-	1	-	-	-
own goal	-	-	1	1	-	1	-	1	-
TOTAL SCORED	5	8	7	10	15	11	10	18	8
TOTAL CONCEDED	4	3	4	2	5	6	5	6	6

* player of the month
Gary Pallister
performance rating average: **7.5**

summary

	P	W	D	L	F	A
Premier League	35	22	7	6	66	24
FA Cup	4	4	0	0	12	3
Coca Cola Cup	3	2	-	1	4	3
European Cup	6	2	2	2	11	11
Total	48	30	9	9	93	41

notes

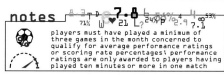

players must have played a minimum of three games in the month concerned to qualify for average performance ratings or scoring rate percentages; performance ratings are only awarded to players having played ten minutes or more in one match

manchester united v
LEEDS UNITED

[Att: 43,712]

> Monday 2 April 1995 / 2.00pm

> Old Trafford

0-0

[Last season :0-0]

team lineups

home team

		rating
1.	Peter Schmeichel	8
2.	Gary Neville	9
16.	Roy Keane	8
6.	Gary Pallister	8
3.	Denis Irwin	7
8.	Paul Ince	7
14.	David Beckham	7
9.	Brian McClair	7
17.	Andy Cole	7
10.	Mark Hughes	7
11.	Ryan Giggs	8

on the bench

24.	Paul Scholes
13.	Gary Walsh
19.	Nicky Butt

visitors

1.	John Lukic
2.	Gary Kelly
6.	David Wetherall
4.	Carlton Palmer
12.	John Pemberton
10.	Gary McAllister
3.	Tony Dorigo
23.	Andrew Couzens
21.	Anthony Yeboah
9.	Brian Deane
8.	Rod Wallace

on the bench

82 mins 88 mins

15.	Nigel Worthington
13.	Mark Beeney
19.	Noel Whelan

word up

Manchester United needed three points from this fixture, anything less would leave Blackburn clear favourites to snatch our coveted title.

Leeds were always going to be a difficult side to break down and from the first minute they seemed content to play for a draw. United failed to win the all-important battle in midfield. **Ince** needed assistance against the effective thrusts of **McAllister** and **Speed**. Whilst West Yorkshire's finest held the midfield, they offered little up front and once again United's defence stood firm.

Cole and **Hughes** did have chances for the Reds, but as the game went on it always seemed that Leeds would achieve their objective of snatching an away point. United's frustration on the pitch was mirrored in the stands, and **the crowd became subdued as they sensed our chances, not only of three points, but of the league title were slipping away.**

Higher and higher: Choccy jumps to it

in the book

Referee:
R Gifford,
Mid Glamorgan
Rating: 6
Bookings:
Kelly,
McAllister,
Wallace

bite this!

"The last team to deny Manchester United the honour of being champions of England played a massive part in ensuring that this season's Premiership crown will be snatched away from Old Trafford and handed to Blackburn."
THE MAIL ON SUNDAY

"As Paul Ince, shoulders sagging and the truth dawning by the second, trudged away down the tunnel, the Guv'nor of this United team gave the impression he almost agreed with the intimidating army of Elland Road fans who sneered their contempt: 'You're not the Champions any more'"
THE SUN

"Peter Schmeichel's clearance struck Carlton Palmer and rebounded towards the goal but the Dane scrambled back to save.
Cole should have put the home side ahead a minute later, following a centre by Ryan Giggs, but his effort was blocked.
Brian McClair went close on the hour with a low shot after good work by Gary Neville and Cole. Giggs had a shot blocked and Mark Hughes put the rebound wide. Paul Ince saw a goal-bound shot deflected for a corner."
THE DAILY TELEGRAPH

"I have a feeling about this result and that feeling tells me this match is decisive. The omens are with Blackburn and the only way we can win the league now is by them throwing it away.

We will never give in. Manchester United is a club that's been built on stamina and we will not give up, no matter what the odds are.

I thought we were really unlucky not to win today but we did really well and our performance was excellent."
ALEX FERGUSON

> 134

[Premier League #36]
Leeds United
>2-4-95
Old Trafford   0-0
home * draw

Paul the Guv'nor and Tony the Tiger tussle for supremacy

Tightly-marked Ryan lays off a pass

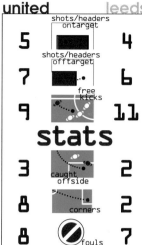

	shots/headers on target	
5		4
	shots/headers off target	
7		6
	free kicks	
9		11
stats		
3	caught offside	2
8	corners	2
8	fouls	7

>timeline

* **Sat 1st April**
> **APRIL FOOL** – Fishy philosopher Eric Cantona left his fans floundering yesterday by welcoming his jail reprieve with a dotty ditty on the sea, "When the seagulls follow the trawler it is because they think that sardines will be thrown into the sea"
Daily Star Sat 1st April

* **Sun 2nd April** Brave Bolton Wanderers are beaten at Wembley by Liverpool who are now the proud holders of the Coca-Cola Cup

> **TRAWLER WAR DRUG ARMADA** – Cocaine from Spanish boats reaching our cities
Sunday Express Sun 2nd April

* **Mon 3rd April** The FA announce their drug-testing schemes for the future. There are reports that players as young as nine could face the tests

> **ABBIE SNATCH GIRL IS OUT** – after just 6 weeks in clinic
The Sun Mon 3rd April

* **Tue 4th April** Blackburn leap eight points clear at the top of the table. Chris Sutton scored the Rovers' goal in a one-nil defeat over QPR

* "I'm back on track and I can't explain how good my life is." Paul Merson announces his new-found happiness to the FA

> **JUDGES BAN MAJOR'S TV INTER-VIEW** – Major's televised interview banned in Scotland
The Times Tue 4th April

manchester united v
CRYSTAL PALACE

[Att: 38,256]

2-2

>Sunday 9th April 1995 /4.00pm

>Villa Park

team lineups

home team
		rating
1.	Nigel Martyn	
22.	Darren Patterson	
5.	Eric Young	
14.	Richard Shaw	
12.	Chris Coleman	
20.	Ray Houghton	
4.	Gareth Southgate	
16.	Darren Pitcher	
11.	John Salako	45mins
9.	Chris Armstrong	
8.	Iain Dowie	

on the bench
3.	Dean Gordon	
19.	Rhys Wilmot	
21.	Ian Cox	

visitors
1.	Peter Schmeichel	6
27.	Gary Neville	7
16.	Roy Keane	6
6.	Gary Pallister	6
3.	Denis Irwin	6
28.	David Beckham	6
8.	Paul Ince	6
9.	Brian McClair	5
5.	Lee Sharpe	5	75mins
10.	Mark Hughes	6
11.	Ryan Giggs	6

on the bench
19.	Nicky Butt	8
13.	Gary Walsh	
24.	Paul Scholes	

Sportshot

Schmikes' ball: Peter plucks the ball out of the sky

stats
palace		united
4	shots/headers on target	6
5	shots/headers off target	4
11	free kicks	11
3	caught offside	4
11	corners	14
8	fouls	7

word up

Almost 40,000 football supporters converged on Villa park for the big FA Cup semi-final between United and Crystal Palace. However, the travelling red hordes were shocked into silence when Ian Dowie put the Eagles ahead after 33 minutes.

Schmeichel had palmed away Salako's cross into the path of Armstrong who crossed for the blond striker to head home.

A period of United pressure in the second half ensured a much-needed equaliser. Southgate brought Ince down just outside the box and Irwin curled home the resulting free kick. With the score level after 90 mins, referee David Elleray blew for extra time.

Disaster struck for United when the quicksilver Armstrong broke through the middle to neatly chip over the head of Schmeichel. Palace must have had visions of a repeat of the 1990 semi-final victory over Liverpool, but Gary Pallister had other ideas. He performed the ultimate rescue act when he casually headed in a long throw from Gary Neville six mintues into extra time. Two-a-piece was how the game finished, and a replay that nobody wanted would be needed to separate the two sides three days later.

in the book
Referee:
D Elleray, Harrow
Rating: 7
Bookings:
Keane, Pallister, Pitcher

bite this!

"Wembley may not be getting the dream final most had wanted, but this breathtaking FA Cup semi-final, coming in the wake of the other classic tie at Leeds, is proof that football is not necessarily the sport of sleaze many perceive it to be." THE DAILY TELEGRAPH

"Gary Pallister's glancing header six minutes into extra time forced a replay back at Villa Park on Wednesday night. Up to that point, Alan Smith's band of Palace underdogs must have believed they were on course to join Joe Royle's self-proclaimed dogs of war in the Wembley showpiece the purists patently didn't want." DAILY MAIL

"Palace deserved at least a draw yesterday, relying on their resilience rather than any superior skills to get a second chance. With Dowie battling fiercely and the pacey Armstrong always threatening to expose United's shaky defence, Palace held their own. Like Oldham Athletic last year, however, they may find that their best chance has gone." THE TIMES

"Palace had a very good first half. Overall though, I felt that we deserved the draw because we upped the pace in the second half. The key to our defending tonight was set-pieces. Palace are very good at them and tonight we defended them very poorly. It looked like an excellent game from the spectator's point of view.

I'll never get any peace that's for sure. This club always take you to the edge." ALEX FERGUSON

in the area

		time^	left ft	right	header	inside/outside the area	^open play	set piece
3.	Denis Irwin	69		*		*		*
6.	Gary Pallister	96			*	*		*
	assist: Gary Neville							
9.	Chris Armstrong	91						
8.	Iain Dowie	33						

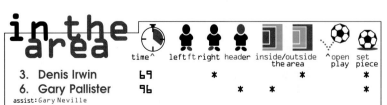

[Premier League #6]
Norwich City 0-2
>15-8-93
Old Trafford **home * loss**

The Equaliser: Pally is triumphant

Incey and Dowie go for the special gurning prize

* `Thurs 6th Apr` The European Cup Winners' Cup semi (first leg) takes place and Arsenal beat Sampdoria 3-2. Two away goals could mean bad news for Arsenal

> Even worse news for Chelsea as they concede three goals from Real Zaragoza and they don't manage to score any away goals

> **BOUND TO DIE -DEATH ROW BRITON NICK INGRAM STANDS GAUNT IN AN AMERICAN COURT YESTERDAY**
Daily Express Thurs 6th Apr

* `Fri 7th Apr` In the Tennents Scottish Cup Final, Hibernian and Celtic draw without producing any goals for the 40,000 plus spectators

> **SPARED - BRIT ESCAPES ELECTRIC CHAIR BY 55 MINUTES**
The Sun Fri 7th Apr

* `Sat 8th Apr` Ray Houghton is confident Palace will over-turn United in tomorrow's FA Cup tie at Villa Park

* Andy Impey and Trevor Sinclair are said to be in with a chance to join the England squad soon, as Terry Venables looks to improve his wing power

* Liverpool are beaten by Leeds at Anfield. The only goal of the match came from a penalty

> **INGRAM DIES IN ELECTRIC CHAIR**
The Independent Sat 8th Apr

* `Sun 9th Apr` John Aldridge creates bad feeling on the terraces. After scoring a controversial penalty against Bristol City, he apparently raised his fist in celebration and then exchanged words with the crowd. Spectators were later giving statements to the police

* An exclusive report by the Daily Mail reveals that another young professional footballer has been tested as having given a positive sample for a drugs test

CRYSTAL PALACE
v manchester united:
>Villa Park

0-2

[Att: 17,987]

team lineups

home team

19. Rhys Wilmot
22. Darren Patterson
14. Richard Shaw
5. Eric Young
3. Dean Gordon
20. Ray Houghton
16. Darren Pitcher
4. Gareth Southgate
11. John Salako
9. Chris Armstrong
8. Iain Dowie

81mins

on the bench
21. Ian Cox
25. Jimmy Glass
23. Ricky Newman

81mins

visitors

		rating
1.	Peter Schmeichel	8
27.	Gary Neville	8
4.	Steve Bruce	7
6.	Gary Pallister	7
3.	Denis Irwin	7
19.	Nicky Butt	7
8.	Paul Ince	7
16.	Roy Keane	8
5.	Lee Sharpe	7
10.	Mark Hughes	7
11.	Ryan Giggs	7

58 mins

on the bench
9.	Brian McClair	7
13.	Gary Walsh	
24.	Paul Scholes	

word up

There were less than 18,000 inside Villa Park to see the replay to Sunday's match, the lowest attendance for an FA Cup semi-final for 50 years. Palace fans had been urged to boycott the game following the death of a supporter three days before and the boycott seemed to work, as less than 3,000 fans made the trip north.

In an unusual atmosphere United settled quickly, looking much sharper than in the first game. **Butt** tested stand-in 'keeper Wilmot in the second minute; **Ince** and **Giggs** did likewise.

United took the lead for the first time in the tie on 29 minutes, when a **Sharpe** cross was met by **Bruce**, who headed powerfully into the net. 11 minutes later United were two up; again **Sharpe** hit a pacey outswinger to the far post, and this time it was **Pallister** who met the cross to score.

The game seemed over, but there was more drama to follow after the break, when **Keane** was sent off after reacting to a tackle by defender **Southgate**. Within seconds there were a dozen players involved, some acting as peace-makers, others seeking retribution.

It wasn't the incident that the game needed on a day when football should have been the winner. Still, United reached their 13th FA Cup final – though sometimes it didn't feel like it.

in the area

		time^	left ft	right	header	inside/outside the area	^open play	set piece
4.	Steve Bruce	30			*	*		*
	assist: Lee Sharpe							
6.	Gary Pallister	41		*	*		*	
	assist: Lee Sharpe							

Sharpey shuffles inside Patterson

Allsport

bite this!

Allsport

Alex and Alan's pre-match peace pact

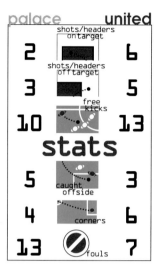

stats

palace		united
shots/headers on target		
2		6
shots/headers off target		
3		5
free kicks		
10		13
caught offside		
5		3
corners		
4		6
fouls		
13		7

first aid box

> **Roy Keane** needed 7 stitches to the ankle

in the book

Referee:
D Elleray, Harrow
Rating: 6
Bookings:
Keane, Patterson, Young, Pitcher

Pitchers sliding tackle fells Paul

>timeline

LEICESTER CITY

v manchester united: **0-4**

[Att: 21,281]

> **Filbert Street**

team lineups

home team

		rating
33.	Kevin Poole	
2.	Simon Grayson	
3.	Michael Whitlow	
4.	Jim Willis	
19.	Colin Hill	
10.	Mark Draper	
18.	Garry Parker	55 mins
22.	Jamie Lawrence	
9.	Iwan Roberts	
6.	Mark Robins	
25.	David Lowe	

on the bench

15.	Brian Carey	
1.	Gavin Ward	
8.	Mark Blake	

visitors

		rating
1.	Peter Schmeichel	7
3.	Denis Irwin	7
4.	Steve Bruce	8
5.	Lee Sharpe	7
6.	Gary Pallister	7
8.	Paul Ince	7
9.	Brian McClair	7
10.	Mark Hughes	7
17.	Andy Cole	7
19.	Nicky Butt	7
27.	Gary Neville	7

on the bench

24.	Paul Scholes	7
13.	Gary Walsh	
28.	David Beckham	

Superkid Scholes shoots for goal

in the book

Referee:
M Boedenham,
Cornwall
Rating: 7

Vaulting ambition:
Cole flies in to score

in the area

	time^	left ft right	header	inside/outside the area	^open play	set piece
5. Lee Sharpe	33	*		*		
assist: Gary Pallister						
17. Andy Cole	45	*		*	*	
assist: Lee Sharpe						
	52	*		*		*
8. Paul Ince	90	* *		*	*	

bite this!

Sportshot

AbFab: Paul puts the finishing touch to a fabulous display

stats

leicester		united
4	shots/headers on target	13
0	shots/headers off target	5
3	free kicks	6
1	caught offside	1
5	corners	7
5	fouls	5

How d'ya like me now: Steve congrats Andy

United travelled to relegated Leicester City knowing that anything other than a victory would end our glimmering title hopes. Fortunately, United were always a class above the Foxes, and **Sharpe** put us on our way to victory with a goal on the half-hour. It came when **Gary Neville** launched a speciality long throw to **Pallister**, who headed across goal for sharpe to shoot low past 'keeper **Poole**.

Cole added a second goal for the Reds before the break when in-form, **Sharpe** had a shot saved only for **Cole** to slide the ball into the back of the net when the 'keeper couldn't control it.

Backed by a strong, united contingent in full-voice, a youthful red side set about exploiting Leicester further in the second half.

Beckham, who had replaced the injured **Sharpe**, hit a great corner for **Bruce** to get in a header, defender **Lowe** blocked the ball but **Cole** once again knocked the ball home from a distance of inches.

With the youngsters showing many attractive touches and playing their way out of defence in neat triangles, United were never in danger.

One such youngster, **Scholes**, missed a great chance for the Reds when he blazed the ball over the bar, but Ince made it 4-0 for United when he scored from a **Beckham** cross seconds before the whistle.

"We were totally outclassed" said Leicester manager **Mark McGhee** in the after-match press conference.

McGhee's complimentary comments and the news that Blackburn had only picked up a point at Elland Road, provided some good news on what had been another turbulent week for United.

>timeline

* **Thurs 13th Apr** United once again are the subject of the back pages. Roy Keane's 'stamp' has attracted all the bad publicity

> **FURY AS LIVE EXPORTS BAN IS LIFTED**

The Independent **Thurs 13th Apr**

* **Fri 14th Apr** Fear as a Keane final ban is threatened

* **Sat 15th Apr** David Batty announces his comeback. He is due to play against old club Leeds today

> Manchester City gain three essential points by beating Liverpool at Maine Road. Meanwhile, Tottenham hold Palace to a 1-1 draw, giving City more room to move up the table

> **CLINTON FACES RUSSIA CRISIS**

The Guardian **Sat 15th Apr**

manchester united v
CHELSEA
> Monday 17 April 1995/3.00pm   > Old Trafford

[Att: 43,728]

0-0

[Last season :0-1]

team lineups

home team
		rating
1.	Peter Schmeichel	7
27.	Gary Neville	7
4.	Steve Bruce	7
6.	Gary Pallister	7
3.	Denis Irwin	7
28.	David Beckham	7
8.	Paul Ince	7
9.	Brian McClair	7
17.	Andy Cole	7
10.	Mark Hughes	7
19.	Nicky Butt	7

45 mins

on the bench
18.	Simon Davies	7
13.	Gary Walsh	7
24.	Paul Scholes	7

67 mins

visitors
13.	Kevin Hitchcock	
2.	Steve Clarke	
27.	Gareth Hall	
5.	Erland Johnsen	
6.	Frank Sinclair	
21.	David Rocastle	
25.	David Lee	
17.	Nigel Spackman	
10.	Gavin Peacock	
9.	Mark Stein	
8.	Paul Furlong	

60 mins

on the bench
12.	Craig Burley	
23.	Nick Colgan	
7.	John Spencer	

67 mins

chelsea — united

stats

chelsea		united
6	shots/headers on target	1
6	shots/headers off target	3
14	free kicks	18
9	caught offside	1
7	corners	0
10	fouls	13

word up

The misery of the Mancunian rain only added to a tense and frustrating atmosphere for this Easter Monday's clash against Kings Road's finest.

Time after time United had chances to score but the lady luck who had an executive seat for the Ipswich game was obviously stood outside ticketless today.

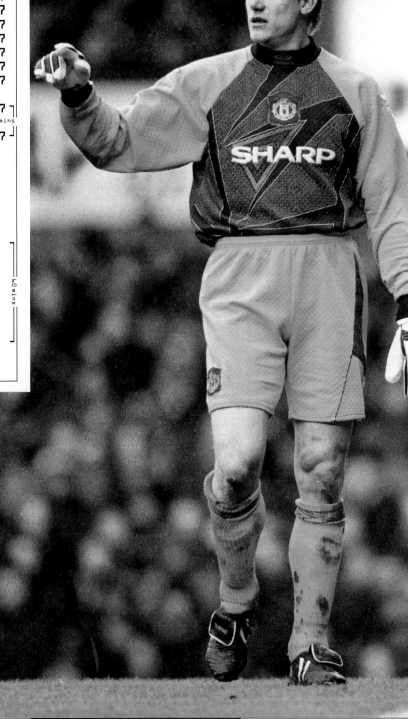

Big Peter points out the way to beat Chelsea, but no one seems to listen

bite this!

"Victory was imperative in the chase of Blackburn, but Cole has yet to find his feet at Old Trafford since his arrival from Newcastle and he could not provide a goal.
Indeed, as the match drifted to its goalless conclusion and the title faded into the distance, it was defender Steve Bruce who came closest to salvaging United's fading hopes after being thrown into the attack."
TODAY

"He thought it was all over. Suddenly now it might not be. Alex Ferguson solemnly raised his hands in acknowledgement of Championship surrender 16 days ago.
But nobody quite believed Manchester United's boss when he forecast that Blackburn could only rescue him by committing football suicide."
THE SUN

"Manchester City have breathed new life into the Championship to leave their neighbours kicking themselves all the way to Old Trafford."
MANCHESTER EVENING NEWS

"If God is a United supporter he has to act now. We are now looking for miracles. There's no doubt about that.
We have lost our width with Andrei, Giggs and Sharpe all out. All our play was coming through the middle, making it really easy for Chelsea to play for offside. We did have a few chances in the first half, but never took them then it became desperate.
I could go on about the penalty that we never got, but there's no point."
ALEX FERGUSON

Beckham gets a short, sharp shock from Rocastle

in the book
Referee:
S Lodge,
Barnsley
Rating: 7

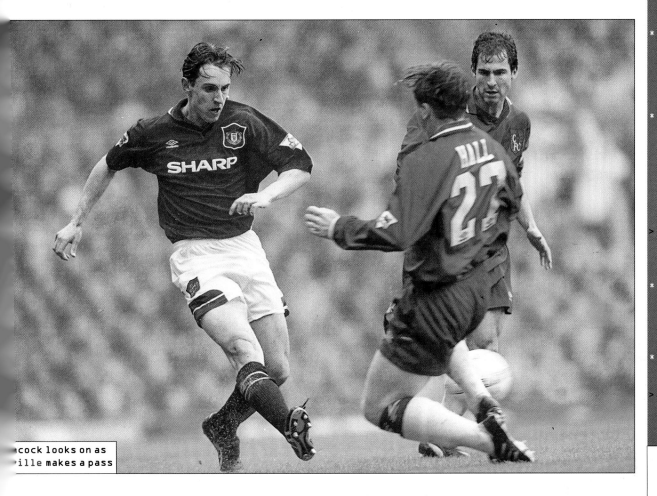

cock looks on as
ille makes a pass

>timeline

Sun 16th Apr

> **AT LAST! – BRITONS FEAR REVENGE AS NAVY GRABS SPANISH BOAT**

The Sunday Express Sun 16th Apr

Mon 17th Apr David Platt suffers a knee injury during Sampdoria's 0-0 draw with Torino. The injury puts a cloud over England's approaching summer tournament

Gordon Strachan announces he will pay Bryan Robson £100. He owes Robbo due to a bet from their days at Old Trafford, when Robbo said he would be playing longer than him. Strachan, on his move to Coventry, has hung up his boots!

> **SNOOKER STARS IN BETS PROBE – WHITE AND FRANCISCO ARE TO BE QUIZZED**

Today Mon 17th Apr

Tues 18th Apr Man City beat Blackburn Rovers in their best performance of the season. The result gives hope to United's league campaign

Dave Bassett labels Fjortoft and Fuchs 'a disgracer' were the men accused

> **PARALYSED – TEACHER WHO WAS BEATEN UP BY PUPIL AGED 10**

Today Tues 18th Apr

> Monday 1 May 1995 / 8.00pm

COVENTRY CITY
v manchester united:

> Highfield Road [Att: 21,885]

2-3

[Last season :0-1]

team lineups

home team
13.	Jonathan Gould
25.	Marcus Hall
5.	David Rennie
6.	Steven Pressley
2.	Brian Borrows
28.	Kevin Richardson
31.	Gordon Strachan
8.	Roy Wegerle
15.	Paul Cook
9.	Peter Ndlovu
19.	Dion Dublin

on the bench
17.	Alan Pickering
27.	Mike Marsh
30.	John Filan

visitors
		rating
1.	Peter Schmeichel	8
27.	Gary Neville	8
6.	Gary Pallister	9
12.	David May	8
3.	Denis Irwin	8
9.	Brian McClair	8
19.	Nicky Butt	9
24.	Paul Scholes	8
17.	Andy Cole	8
10.	Mark Hughes	8
5.	Lee Sharpe	8	76mins

on the bench
28.	David Beckham
13.	Gary Walsh
29.	Pat McGibbon

Andy Cole proves his worth

On a warm Coventry night, United prised open the championship door which had been left ajar by Blackburn following their defeat at West Ham.

The Sky Blues, under **Ron Atkinson**, look a sharper and more determined side than the perennial strugglers you usually associate them with being. With United needing a victory, the game was played at a hectic pace from kick-off.

Scholes broke the deadlock in our favour when he fired home from fifteen yards out on thirty-two minutes. United continued to attack against a background cascade of noise from the visiting fans, pressuring Coventry all the time. However, it was the home side who grabbed a surprise equaliser seven minutes later when ex-red Dublin had his shot flicked in by **Ndlovu**.

After the break the intense action continued, **Neville** touched the cross bar with a shot from a distance, then **Cole** went one better when he fired past **Gould** into the Coventry net.

The home side refused to lie down and managed yet another equaliser on seventy-two minutes. A **Pressley** header glided past **Schmeichel**.

Backed by a passionate following of four thousand fans, **the reds pushed forward once again for a winner and three points**. It was that man **Cole** who answered our prayers with ten minutes to play when he picked up a stray backpass, flicked the ball up and lobbed it over keeper **Gould** and under the bar

A new wave of optimism has swept through the red legions and we can only hope that Blackburn's nerves get the better of them and they slip up as we did three years sago.

Our championship dream hasn't finished yet.

stats

	coventry		united
shots/headers on target	4		6
shots/headers off target	5		3
free kicks	18		12
caught offside	3		2
corners	5		6
fouls	10		17

in the book
Referee:
P Don,
Manworth Park
Rating: 6
Bookings:
Neville,
Cole,
Sharpe,
Hall,
Borrows

in the area

		time^	left ft	right	header	inside/outside the area		^open play	set piece
24.	Paul Scholes assist: Andy Cole	32		*		*		*	
17.	Andy Cole assist: Nicky Butt	55	*			*		*	
		79	*			*		*	
6.	Stephen Pressley	72							
9.	Peter Ndlovu	39							

bite this!

"Since United's last game, Eric Cantona had signed to stay for a further three years, Blackburn had lost two out of three and, if not exactly granted a new lease of life, a glimmer had appeared at the end of the prize-giving tunnel. Makeshift they may have been, but United had the quality to respond to the potentially-sapping experience of seeing the home side twice strike back with opportunist goals."

DAILY MAIL

"Butt was outstanding and each time he wears the United shirt he looks more and more an international in the making. Scholes, too, is a little terrier. This was a new role for him in midfield yet he was the man who set United on the road to this success."

DAILY EXPRESS

"Youngster Paul Scholes - asked to play in an unnatural midfield - and Nicky Butt were quite outstanding in giving United the drive they needed to overcome Coventry's experienced engine room." **TODAY**

"Andy Cole's famous feet last night gave manager Alex Ferguson the chance to grab the Premiership trophy with one hand. And the Manchester United boss can slap the other hand around the 2ft-high piece of silverware if his £7 million man carries on in this explosive mood."

DAILY MIRROR

"It's possible the title could go to the last day of the season. Blackburn have given us a chance by losing at West Ham, but we can't afford to let another opportunity slip. Winning is the name of the game now. With a goal difference of six in our favour compared with Blackburn's, the door is slightly ajar. We need to kick it wide open if we can. We have the scent of blood. The hunt is on. We are on fire and so are our fans."

ALEX FERGUSON

Young man Scholes scores a goal

Mark Hughes gets in a tangle with Marcus Hall

>time*line*

* **Fri 28th April** Manchester United and Eric Cantona sign a new three year deal ending all rumours of his transfer to another club.

* Cantona is warned that this is his last chance in this country.

> **NURSES SEEK TO LIFT BAN ON STRIKING – FURY AT 'MEAN AND SHABBY' PAY DEAL.**
The Times Fri 28th April

* **Sat 29th April** Bryan Robson announces he is fit and ready to take part in Middlesbrough's match against Luton tommorrow.

> **COURT FREES DRUG DOCTOR – A DOCTOR RECEIVED A SUSPENDED 12 MONTH PRISON SENTENCE YESTERDAY FOR FALSIFYING PRESCRIPTIONS TO FEED HIS SEVERE HEROIN ADDICTION.**
The Guardian Sat 29th April

* **Sun 30th April** West Ham surprise Blackburn with a two-nil defeat leaving the championship door ajar for United to crack open.

> **BLAIR BURIES SOCIALISM BY CLAUSE 4 WIN**
The Sunday Telegraph Sun 30th April

* **Mon 1st May**
I LOVE HUGH SO MUCH – LIZ HURLEY
Daily Star Mon 1st May

* **Tue 2nd May** Gary Neville is told that he may not be banned for the Cup Final. His 41 points accumulated over the season takes him over the FA's limit.

* **Wed 3rd May** John Burridge, Manchester City's 43 year old goalkeeper will start the match tonight against Aston Villa after taking over as sub when Tony Coton got injured against Newcastle on Saturday.

> **TORY'S FORCED INTO TAX REBATE**
The Guardian

*GARY NEVILLE
>defender

Sportshot

personal file

born: Bury, 18/02/75
height: 5'11" weight: 11st 10lb
international team: England under 21
signed pro for United: 23/01/93
United league debut : 8/05/94 v Coventry City (h)

▼ appearances/goals

appearances / apps as sub / goals	Premier League			FA Cup			Coca Cola Cup			European Cup			Total			left ft	right	header	inside/outside the area		^open play	set piece	assists	scoring rate	performance rating average
Gary Pallister	3	-	-	2	-	2	-	-	-	-	-	-	5	-	2	-	-	2	2	-	1	1	1	40%	7.6
Peter Schmeichel	3	-	-	2	-	-	-	-	-	-	-	-	5	-	-	-	-	-	-	-	-	-	-	-	7.3
Mark Hughes	3	-	3	2	-	-	-	-	-	-	-	-	5	-	3	-	2	1	3	-	3	-	4	-	7.0
Paul Ince	3	-	1	2	-	-	-	-	-	-	-	-	5	-	1	-	1	-	1	-	1	-	1	20%	7.0
Denis Irwin	3	-	-	2	-	1	-	-	-	-	-	-	5	-	1	-	1	-	-	1	-	1	-	20%	7.0
Gary Neville	3	-	-	2	-	-	-	-	-	-	-	-	5	-	-	-	-	-	-	-	-	-	1	-	7.6
Nicky Butt	3	-	-	1	1	-	-	-	-	-	-	-	4	1	-	-	-	-	-	-	-	-	-	-	7.0
Brian McClair	3	-	-	1	1	-	-	-	-	-	-	-	4	1	-	-	-	-	-	-	-	-	-	-	7.0
Andy Cole	3	1	2	-	-	-	-	-	-	-	-	-	3	1	2	1	1	-	2	-	1	-	-	66%	7.0
Roy Keane	1	-	1	2	-	-	-	-	-	-	-	-	3	1	1	-	1	-	1	-	1	-	-	33%	8.0
Steve Bruce	2	-	1	1	-	-	-	-	-	-	-	-	3	1	1	-	-	-	1	-	-	-	-	66%	7.5
Ryan Giggs	1	-	-	2	-	-	-	-	-	-	-	-	3	-	-	-	-	-	-	-	-	-	4	-	8.0
Lee Sharpe	1	1	1	2	-	-	-	-	-	-	-	-	3	1	-	-	1	-	1	-	2	1	1	33%	7.0
David Beckham	1	-	-	-	-	-	-	-	-	-	-	-	1	-	-	-	-	-	-	-	-	-	-	-	7.0

▼ appearances/goals

appearances / apps as sub / goals	Premier League			FA Cup			Coca Cola Cup			European Cup			Total			left ft	right	header	inside/outside the area		^open play	set piece	assists	scoring rate	performance rating average
Gary Pallister	37	-	2	6	-	2	2	-	-	6	-	-	51	-	4	-	-	4	4	-	1	3	1	8%	7.5
Denis Irwin	35	-	1	6	-	3	2	-	-	5	-	-	48	-	4	-	5	-	3	2	1	4	2	8%	7.1
Paul Ince	32	-	5	5	-	-	1	-	-	5	-	-	43	-	5	1	4	-	1	4	4	1	3	12%	7.3
Mark Hughes	30	-	8	5	-	2	1	-	-	5	-	2	41	-	12	-	9	3	10	2	11	-	7	29%	7.2
Brian McClair	30	5	4	5	1	2	3	-	1	2	-	-	40	6	7	1	3	3	6	1	5	2	3	18%	7.2
Ryan Giggs	29	-	1	6	-	1	2	-	-	3	-	2	38	-	4	6	-	-	4	-	4	-	15	11%	7.4
Peter Schmeichel	28	-	-	6	-	-	1	-	-	3	-	-	37	-	-	-	-	-	-	-	-	-	-	-	7.4
Steve Bruce	32	-	2	4	-	2	1	-	-	5	1	-	36	1	4	1	-	3	4	-	2	2	-	11%	7.4
Andrei Kanchelskis	24	5	14	2	1	-	-	-	-	5	-	1	32	6	15	3	11	1	14	1	14	1	5	47%	6.7
Roy Keane	21	2	1	5	1	1	1	-	-	4	-	1	31	3	3	2	1	-	2	1	3	-	4	10%	7.5
Lee Sharpe	22	2	3	5	1	1	-	2	-	3	-	2	30	5	6	3	-	3	6	-	5	1	4	20%	7.0
Eric Cantona	21	-	12	1	-	1	-	-	-	2	-	-	24	-	13	4	5	4	13	-	9	4	10	54%	7.6
David May	13	5	1	1	-	-	2	-	-	4	-	-	20	5	2	-	2	-	2	-	1	1	-	10%	6.3
Nicky Butt	9	8	1	2	1	-	-	-	-	3	-	-	5	1	20	10	1	-	1	-	1	-	1	5%	7.0
Gary Walsh	9	-	-	-	-	-	-	-	-	3	-	-	3	-	16	-	-	-	-	-	-	-	-	-	7.1
Gary Neville	9	2	-	3	-	-	2	1	-	1	1	-	15	4	-	-	-	-	-	-	-	-	-	-	7.1
Andy Cole	13	1	9	-	-	-	-	-	-	-	-	-	13	1	9	2	6	1	9	-	7	2	-	69%	7.1
Simon Davies	3	1	-	-	-	-	-	-	-	5	-	1	8	1	1	1	-	-	1	-	1	-	2	12%	7.3
Paul Scholes	4	9	2	1	-	2	-	-	-	3	-	-	8	12	6	-	3	3	6	-	4	2	-	38%	7.8
David Beckham	2	1	-	1	1	-	-	-	-	3	-	1	8	2	1	-	-	1	1	-	1	-	1	13%	6.2
Keith Gillespie	3	6	1	-	-	-	-	-	-	3	-	-	6	6	1	1	-	-	1	-	1	-	1	15%	7.3
Paul Parker	1	1	-	-	-	-	-	-	-	2	1	-	3	2	-	-	-	-	-	-	-	-	-	-	6.8
Phil Neville	1	1	-	-	-	-	-	-	-	-	-	-	2	-	-	-	-	-	-	-	-	-	1	-	7.0
John O'Kane	-	-	-	-	-	-	1	-	-	1	1	-	2	1	-	-	-	-	-	-	-	-	-	-	7.0
Chris Casper	-	-	-	-	-	-	1	-	-	-	-	-	1	-	-	-	-	-	-	-	-	-	-	-	7.0
Kevin Pilkington	1	-	-	-	-	-	-	-	-	-	-	-	1	-	-	-	-	-	-	-	-	-	-	-	7.5
Graeme Tomlinson	-	-	-	-	-	-	2	-	-	-	-	-	2	-	-	-	-	-	-	-	-	-	-	-	7.0

league table

FA Carling Premiership 31 April 95

	P	W	D	L	F	A	Pts
Blackburn Rovers	39	26	8	5	78	35	86
Manchester United	39	24	9	6	73	26	81
Nottingham Forest	40	21	10	9	69	41	73
Liverpool	38	20	10	8	63	31	70
Newcastle Utd	39	19	11	9	61	41	68
Leeds United	39	18	12	9	53	35	66
Tottenham Hotspur	38	16	12	10	60	49	60
QPR	39	15	8	16	56	56	53
Wimbledon	39	15	8	16	46	63	53
Arsenal	40	13	11	16	51	47	50
Southampton	38	11	16	11	56	54	49
Chelsea	39	12	13	14	44	50	49
Manchester City	39	12	12	15	50	59	48
Sheffield Wed	40	12	12	16	45	55	48
Coventry City	30	11	13	15	41	59	49
Everton	38	10	14	14	40	48	44
Aston Villa	39	10	13	16	47	54	43
West Ham	37	11	9	17	38	46	42
Crystal Palace	38	10	12	16	29	40	42
Norwich City	40	10	12	18	35	51	42
Leicester City	40	6	9	25	42	77	27
Ipswich Town	39	6	6	27	33	88	24

time split

	0-10 mins	11-20 mins	21-30 mins	31-40 mins	41-50 mins	51-60 mins	61-70 mins	71-80 mins	81-120 mins
Andrei Kanchelskis	-	2	1	-	5	2	1	2	2
Eric Cantona	-	-	1	3	4	-	1	3	1
Mark Hughes	-	2	1	1	2	3	2	-	1
Andy Cole	-	3	-	1	-	2	1	2	-
Brian McClair	1	-	1	-	1	-	2	1	1
Paul Scholes	-	1	2	1	1	-	1	-	-
Lee Sharpe	-	-	1	-	-	-	-	2	-
Ryan Giggs	-	-	-	1	1	-	1	-	1
Paul Ince	-	-	1	-	-	1	1	-	1
Denis Irwin	-	-	-	-	1	-	-	-	1
Steve Bruce	-	-	-	-	-	-	-	-	2
Roy Keane	-	-	-	1	-	2	-	-	-
David May	-	-	-	-	-	-	-	1	-
Gary Pallister	-	-	-	-	-	-	2	-	-
David Beckham	-	-	-	-	-	-	-	-	-
Nicky Butt	-	-	-	-	-	-	-	-	-
Simon Davies	1	-	-	-	-	-	-	-	-
Keith Gillespie	-	-	-	-	-	-	-	-	-
own goal	-	-	2	-	1	-	-	-	-
TOTAL SCORED	5	10	9	11	17	11	11	18	13
TOTAL CONCEDED	4	3	4	4	5	4	5	6	6

✳ player of the month
Ryan Giggs
performance rating average: **8.0**

summary

	P	W	D	L	F	A
Premier League	39	24	9	6	71	24
FA Cup	6	6	1	1	16	7
Coca Cola Cup	3	2	0	1	4	3
Champions Lge	6	2	2	2	11	11
Total	54	34	12	10	102	45

notes

players must have played a minimum of three games in the month concerned to qualify for average performance ratings or scoring rate percentages; performance ratings are only awarded to players having played ten minutes or more in one match

manchester united v
SHEFFIELD WEDNESDAY
>Old Trafford

>Sunday 7 May 1995 / 4.00pm

[Att: 43,868]

1-0

[Last season :5-0]

team lineups

home team		rating
1.	Peter Schmeichel	7
3.	Denis Irwin	7
5.	Lee Sharpe	7
6.	Gary Pallister	7
8.	Paul Ince	7
9.	Brian McClair	7
10.	Mark Hughes	7
12.	David May	7
17.	Andy Cole	7
24.	Paul Scholes	7
27.	Gary Neville	7

24 mins — 52 mins

on the bench

19.	Nicky Butt
13.	Gary Walsh
23.	Phil Neville

visitors

1.	Chris Woods
2.	Peter Atherton
3.	Ian Nolan
10.	Mark Bright
11.	John Sheridan
12.	Andy Pearce
14.	Chris Bart-Williams
16.	Graham Hyde
17.	Des Walker
19.	Guy Whittingham
25.	Michael Williams

62 mins — 82 mins

on the bench

7.	Adem Poric
13.	Kevin Pressman
8.	Chris Waddle

Sparky and Des gurn for the ball

word up

Three points would be the sole requirement from today's game against a mid-table Sheffield Wednesday.

When **David May** stabbed the ball in early on, the players and fans alike celebrated like a third consecutive championship was on its way.

Another full-house sat back and waited for a rout that never came. **May's** feeling of elation was short lived as he left the field after twenty-four minutes with a torn back muscle. Youngster **Phil Neville** deputised well. United's pacy game died quicker than the rapturous atmosphere inside Old Trafford.

Although they seldom troubled **Schmeichel**, Wednesday's neat passing and an inspired **Des Walker** easily contained the reds as the tension set in both on the pitch and the terraces. However, **United** held the slender lead and although it wasn't a vintage display, points are more important than performances at this stage of the season. Today United got the three they needed and kept the pressure on Blackburn.

first aid box

> David May pulled back muscle

Andy shields it from his Sheffield marker

in the book

Referee:
P Durkin, Portland
Rating: 7

Bookings:
Hughes, Pearce, Walker

in the area

	time^	left ft	right	header	inside/outside the area	^open play	set piece
12. David May	5		*		*	*	

bite ⊂ this!

"United's edgy, untidy victory has narrowed the gap at the top to two points... United's latest performance was notable less for its inspiration than its perspiration. The return of Ince for Butt was the only change in the side that had attacked so fluently in winning at Coventry six days earlier, yet the perceptive passing that had won that match was almost totally lacking."

The Guardian

"Although a nervy performer at right-back, May has caught the eye when deputising for Steve Bruce as centre-half."

The Daily Telegraph

"Instead of easing the tension, the early goal appeared to increase it.
It came just after May had squandered a fine opportunity from close range when he headed too close to keeper Chris Woods, who was able to push the effort onto his right-hand post."

Today

"We got the result we wanted, that's the important thing.
I felt we lacked experience tonight, especially where keeping possession was concerned but with the team I picked there was not a lot we could do about it. There was a lot of anxiety amongst the team.
Sheffield Wednesday took advantage of that. They kept possession well and made us chase for the ball. In the end we just had to sit back and suffer a bit.
David May pulled a back muscle in the warm-up and he thought it would be okay. As it was, though, he had to come off. But he did get the goal."

ALEX FERGUSON

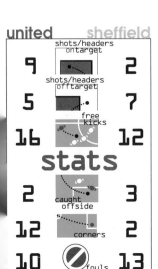

united   sheffield

shots/headers on target

9   2

shots/headers off target

5   7

free kicks

16   12

stats

caught offside

2   3

corners

12   2

fouls

10   13

Choccy shows that concentration is the key

>timeline

* **Fri 5 May** Tranmere Rovers' Jamie Hughes become the first professional player in Britain to be charged with taking performance-enhancing drugs.

> **YOU AIN'T GOT LONG JOHN — TORIES MASSACRED IN TOWN HALL ELECTIONS.**
> The Sun Fri May 5

* **Sat 6 May** Norwich City are relegated from the Premier League after losing 2-1 at Leeds United.

> **CLARKE PEGS INTEREST RATES AS MAJOR VOWS TO FIGHT ON.**
> The Independent Sat May 6

* **Sun 7 May** Celtic trounce Scottish Champions Rangers 3-0 in the Glasgow derby.

* **Mon 8 May** Blackburn Rovers win their crucial last home match with Newcastle United 1-0.

> **FOR THE SAKE OF ALL OUR FUTURES WE MUST REMEMBER THE PAST — VE DAY.**
> The Independent Mon 8 May

* **Tue 9 May** Crystal Palace's relegation fears increase with a 3-1 defeat by Leeds.

> **ALL QUIET — VE DAY.**
> Daily Mirror Tue 9 May

manchester united v
SOUTHAMPTON
>Old Trafford

[Att:43,479]

2-1

[Last season :2-0]

>Wednesday 10th May 1995 / 3.00pm

team lineups

home team | rating

1.	Peter Schmeichel	7
3.	Denis Irwin	7
4.	Steve Bruce	7
5.	Lee Sharpe	7
6.	Gary Pallister	7
8.	Paul Ince	7
9.	Brian McClair	8
10.	Mark Hughes	7
17.	Andy Cole	7
19.	Nicky Butt	7
27.	Gary Neville	7

76mins

on the bench

24.	Paul Scholes	7
13.	Gary Walsh	
28.	David Beckham	

visitors

13.	Dave Beasant	
3.	Francis Benali	
4.	Jim Magilton	
5.	Richard Hall	
6.	Ken Monkou	
7.	Matthew Le Tissier	
9.	Neil Shipperley	
10.	Neil Maddison	
14.	Simon Charlton	
15.	Jason Dodd	
16.	Gordon Watson	

57mins / 76mins

on the bench

12.	Neil Heaney	
1.	Bruce Grobbelaar	
21.	Tommy Widrington	

in the book

Referee:
P Danson, Leicester
Rating: 7
Bookings:
Neville, Le Tissier, Dodd

Butt punches the air in delight after Irwin's winner

word up

United ensured that the Championship wouldn't be decided until the final day of the season with a nail-biting victory over Southampton.

The game had started in the worst possible manner for the reds when **Charlton** put the Saints a goal up after five minutes. It was the first goal conceded by **Schmeichel** at Old Trafford for 13 months.

United's response was a tidal wave of attacks. **Pallister** hit the post after 16 minutes, **Hughes** and **Cole** came close too. After 21 minutes they equalised when **Cole** took an easy chance for his twelfth goal in 16 games.

United continued to press forward for a vital second goal but there were times when they left themselves exposed at the back. **Charlton** nearly added a second just after the interval.

United's dominance was not converting itself into goals and with nine minutes remaining the Championship seemed to be slipping away, but then **Cole** was brought down for a controversial penalty.

Irwin, probably the coolest head in the world, drove the ball into the corner of the net.

Amongst scenes of sheer elation United know they have to win at West Ham on Sunday and hope Blackburn don't beat Liverpool.

With black market tickets changing hands for three figures it's certainly the game every red wants to be at.

Pally leads the applause for United's faithful fans

>150
[Premier League #41]
Southampton
>10-5-95
Old Trafford
2-1
home * win

bite this!

"Another twist, another turn, another moment of nerve twanging tension in the kind of title run-in not seen in years. We should have known better because there was another footballing divinity within this famous stadium for the first time in almost four months. His name, of course, Eric Cantona.

Now, on what must be a Sunday bloody Sunday for either of the two title candidates, there is a fight to the death looming."

The Sun

"United laid siege to the Southampton goal, although they had to keep a wary eye on Southampton counters as the visitors revealed the confidence that had taken them on a six-game unbeaten run. Le Tissier, however, had lost his normal accuracy, several attempted volleys flying high and wide, and the greatest danger to Schmeichel came when Shipperley cut inside Bruce just after the hour. The Dane saved well."

The Times

"Just an hour before kick-off his partner Shirley gave birth to a bouncing - and no doubt kicking - baby boy.

Cole then put life back into Manchester United's faltering title hopes with possibly the most crucial goal and certainly the most important penalty award of his career."

Today

"We did well to get back into the game after the early disappointment.

The second half was always going to be one of huffing and puffing. I brought Scholes on to give Southampton a different problem. I wanted him to link up with Choccy behind Andy Cole.

If all else failed though I knew we always had the option of shoving Bruce and Schmeichel up front!

Sunday is going to be hard. We can only do so much, and if we are going to do anything we need a break. West Ham are a good side and we have a tough game in front of us."

ALEX FERGUSON

Saints' Dodd distracts Sharpey with his tickling stick

in the area

	time^	left ft	right	header	inside/outside the area	^open play	set piece
17. Andy Cole	21	*			*	*	
assist: Denis Irwin							
3. Denis Irwin	80		*		*		*
14. Simon Charlton	5						

stats

saints		united
7	shots/headers on target	4
10	shots/headers off target	3
18	free kicks	11
2	caught offside	5
14	corners	2
8	fouls	12

>time*line*

* **Mon 8th May** A two-minute silence is held at Ewood Park in respect for VE Day.

* **Tue 9th May** Alan Shearer announces he *will* win the title with Blackburn. Then he says, he will discuss a new contract with Blackburn.

* Kenny Dalglish warns his men that celebrating on Monday night could mean tempting fate for Rovers.

> **PEACE PARADE IN RUSSIAN STYLE** - Yeltsin celebrates VE day with doves of peace and street parties.
> DAILY MAIL Tue 9th May

* **Wed 10th May** United come back from a goal down against a Southampton side intent on ruining United's title dreams.

> **GROUP 4 SETS UP IMMIGRANT CONTROL SQUADS.**
> THE GUARDIAN Wed 10th May

* **Thu 11th May**

> **SACRIFICED - PERFECT MUM JOY, 29, BRAINWASHED BY BIBLE CULT, STABS HER CHILDREN TO DEATH AND DROWNS HERSELF.**
> THE SUN Thu 11th May

* **Fri 12th May** Jurgen Klinnsmann announces he is leaving Tottenham.

> **KNIFE MURDER OF CHEATED PROF'S WIFE - POLICE FIND BODY IN HOUSE WHERE SHE LIVED ALONE.**
> DAILY EXPRESS Fri 12th May

WEST HAM UNITED

v **manchester united:**

> **Upton Park**

[Att: 24,783]

1-1

[Last season] :2-2

[Premier League match #42]

team lineups

home team

1. Ludek Miklosko
2. Tim Breacker
8. Mark Rieper
4. Steven Potts
12. Keith Rowland
17. Michael Hughes
26. Don Hutchison
7. Ian Bishop
10. John Moncur
11. Matt Holmes
9. Trevor Morley

on the bench
30. Les Sealey
18. Simon Webster
6. Martin Allen

88 mins · 85 mins

visitors

#		rating
1.	Peter Schmeichel	8
27.	Gary Neville	8
4.	Steve Bruce	8
6.	Gary Pallister	8
3.	Denis Irwin	8
19.	Nicky Butt	8
16.	Roy Keane	8
8.	Paul Ince	8
5.	Lee Sharpe	8
9.	Brian McClair	8
17.	Andy Cole	8

on the bench
13.	Gary Walsh	
10.	Mark Hughes	9
24.	Paul Scholes	8

79 mins · 45 mins

word up

The most eventful of seasons could only finish in one manner - a dramatic one.

United had to beat West Ham, and hope that Blackburn didn't beat Liverpool. If this happened a third consecutive championship would be ours.

Things couldn't have started worse for the reds when ex-blue **Michael Hughes** put the Hammers a goal up. News also filtered through that Blackburn had taken the lead at Anfield. Despite the goal United were always the better of the two sides and battled with pride and passion. Their effort was rewarded when **McClair** levelled the scores afer 52 min. Liverpool had equalised against Blackburn - if we scored we would win the league.

A tidal wave of United attacks continued on the West Ham goal but 'keeper **Miklosko** was in excellent form, pulling off a string of fine saves.

When **Breacker** was seen to have handled the ball in his area and yet no penalty was awarded, you sensed it wasn't going to be United's day. Further frantic attacks yielded no goals and the championship went to Blackburn.

Just to consider that a team seemingly out of the championship race two months ago due to numerous set-backs was still in with a chance of lifting the trophy with seconds of the season remaining shows the quality of talent we have here at United.

We applaud your efforts lads and take heart from the fact that you'll be back... with Cantona.

Sportshot

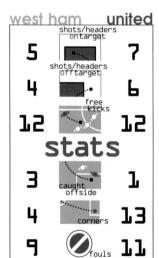

High-kicking Paul stretches Tim to breaking point

west ham   united

stats

west ham		united
5	shots/headers on target	7
4	shots/headers off target	6
12	free kicks	12
3	caught offside	1
4	corners	13
9	fouls	11

"If only we'd scored one more goal..."

in the area

		time^	left ft	right	header	inside/outside the area		^open play	set piece
9.	Brian McClair	52		*			*	*	
17.	Michael Hughes	31							

bite this!

"In one of the most dramatic conclusions to a league season, United did everything but score."   **DAILY EXPRESS**

"It was desperate storybook stuff with United being denied two possible penalties, one for handball, the other for a foul on Mark Hughes. We never knew that watching football could be so tiring.

The air had been electric with expectation once Brian McClair, that exemplary club servant for United, had levelled the score seven minutes into the second half and then, 11 minutes after that, the stadium shook with the news that Liverpool had equalised at home against Blackburn Rovers."

THE TIMES

"Hammers full-back Keith Rowland produced a perfect last ditch tackle, Ludek Miklosko a brave save, and then deep into injury time an overhead kick by Cole was blocked as United came forward for the winner that would have ripped the Premiership crown from Blackburn's grasp. As the outcome of the title went right to the wire, the Hammers were encamped inside their own half and there were a couple of crazy scrambles right in front of Miklosko's goal."   **DAILY MIRROR**

"But the difference, agonisingly, stayed at a single goal, a single point.

Each time the Hammers' goalkeeper, Ludek Miklosko, stood bravely in the way. Strange how this season of sleaze and scandal should turn in the end on the presence of one large Czech."   **THE INDEPENDENT**

"It has taken a good team to take the championship from us and I would like to congratulate Kenny and his players. Anyone that gets 89 points deserves to win the title.

Today's match saw a fantastic performance but it just did not go our way. The players were marvellous. We did more than we needed to win the game but maybe it was fate that was against us.

Still it has been a tremendous effort this season considering all the cautions, all the injuries, suspensions, and everything that has gone against us. People may be wondering about my decision to leave out Mark Hughes but I felt I had to take the wind out of West Ham's sails in the first half and I explained to Mark that he was always going to come on. We have done well in the past with only one up front. It was the right decision."

ALEX FERGUSON

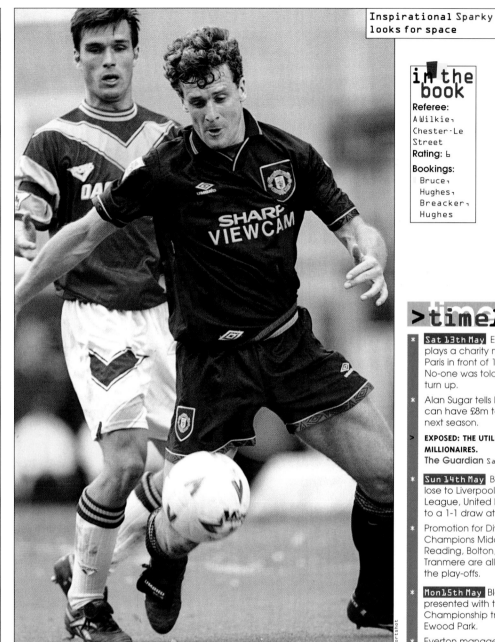

Inspirational Sparky looks for space

in the book

Referee:
A Wilkie, Chester-Le Street
Rating: 6

Bookings:
Bruce, Hughes, Breacker, Hughes

>timeline

* **Sat 13th May** Eric Cantona plays a charity match in Paris in front of 1,500 people. No-one was told he would turn up.

* Alan Sugar tells Francis he can have £8m to spend next season.

> **EXPOSED: THE UTILITY CHIEF MILLIONAIRES.**
The Guardian   Sat 13th May

* **Sun 14th May** Blackburn lose to Liverpool, but win the League, United being held to a 1-1 draw at Upton Park.

* Promotion for Division One Champions Middlesbrough. Reading, Bolton, Wolves and Tranmere are all through to the play-offs.

* **Mon 15th May** Blackburn are presented with the Championship trophy at Ewood Park.

* Everton manage to ensure their place in the Premiership for '95/96. Crystal Palace, Norwich, Ipswich and Leicester have all been relegated.

> **WE ARE THE CHAMPIONS-JOY OF THE ROVERS IN NAIL-BITING FINISH.**
Daily Express   Mon 15th May

* **Tue 16th May** Most players start their holidays. Manchester United and Everton start their training for the FA Cup Final.

* Brian Horton is sacked by Manchester City.

> **KILL ROGER COOK - AN EVIL CROOK HAS HIRED A HITMAN TO MURDER TV INVESTIGATOR ROGER COOK.**
Daily Star   Tue 16th May

Cole can't believe it's not the real thing...

player of the season 94/95

Paul Ince

performance rating average: 7.8

may 95

▼ appearances/goals →

	Premier League apps	apps as sub	goals	FA Cup	Coca Cola Cup	European Cup	Total	left ft	right	header	inside/outside the area	open play	set piece	assists	scoring rate	performance rating average
Gary Pallister	4	-	-	1 -	-	-	5 -	-	-	2	2 -	-	1	1		7.4
Peter Schmeichel	4	-	-	1	-	-	5	-	-	-	-	-	-	-		7.4
Mark Hughes	3	-	1	1	-	-	4 1	-	2	1	3 -	3	-	1		7.4
Paul Ince	3	-	-	1	-	-	4	-	-	-	1	1	1	-		7.0
Denis Irwin	4	-	1	1	-	-	5 1	1	-	-	1	1	1	-	20%	7.2
Gary Neville	4	-	-	1	-	-	5	-	-	-	-	-	-	-		7.5
Nicky Butt	3	-	1	1	-	-	4 1	-	-	-	-	-	-	-		7.5
Brian McClair	4	-	1	1	-	-	5 1	-	-	-	1	1	-	-	20%	7.4
Andy Cole	4	-	3	1	-	-	4 3	2	1	1	3 -	3	-	-	75%	7.5
Roy Keane	1	-	-	1	-	-	2	-	-	-	-	1	-	1		0.0
Steve Bruce	2	-	1	1	-	-	3 1	-	-	1	-	-	-	-		7.0
David May	2	-	1	-	-	-	2 1	-	-	1	-	-	-	-	50%	0.0
Lee Sharpe	4	-	-	1	-	-	5	-	1	-	1	-	2	-		7.2
David Beckham	-	1	-	1	-	-	2 -	-	-	-	-	-	-	-	50%	0.0
Paul Scholes	2	2	1	1	-	-	2 3 1	-	-	-	-	-	-	-	50%	0.0
Philip Neville	-	1	-	-	-	-	2	-	1	-	1	-	1	-		7.5
Ryan Giggs	-	-	-	1	-	-	2	-	-	-	-	-	-	-		0.0

94/95 season

▼ appearances/goals →

	Premier League apps	apps as sub	goals	FA Cup	Coca Cola Cup	European Cup	Total	left ft	right	header	inside/outside the area	open play	set piece	assists	scoring rate	performance rating average
Gary Pallister	42	-	2	7 - 2	2 -	6 -	57 - 4	-	-	4	4 -	-	1	3	1	7%	7.6
Denis Irwin	40	-	2	7 - 5	2 -	5 -	54 - 4	-	6	-	4	4 2	1	5	2	8%	7.2
Paul Ince	36	-	5	6 -	-	5 -	47 - 5	1	4	-	1	4	1	4	3	11%	7.8
Mark Hughes	32	1	6	6 - 2	-	5 - 2	43 1 11	-	9	3	10 2	13	1	3	26%	7.3
Brian McClair	35	5	5	6 1 2	3 - 1	2 -	46 6 8	1	4	3	7 1	6	2	3	38%	7.5
Ryan Giggs	29	-	1	6 1 1	-	3 - 2	35 1 4	6	-	-	4	-	4	15	11%	7.4
Peter Schmeichel	32	-	-	7 -	-	3 -	42 -	-	-	-	-	-	-	-	4%	7.4
Steve Bruce	35	3	2	5 - 2	1 -	6 1	46 1 4	1	-	3	4 -	2	2	-	47%	7.2
Andrei Kanchelskis	25	5	4	2 1	-	5 - 1	30 6 5	3	4	1	14 1	14	1	5	8%	6.7
Roy Keane	23	2	1	6 1 3	-	4 - 1	34 3 3	2	1	-	2 1	3	-	4	18%	7.5
Lee Sharpe	26	3	2	6 1 -	- 2	2 -	37 5 6	1	5	3	5 3	5	-	4	54%	7.1
Eric Cantona	21	-	12	1 - 1	-	4 -	24 - 13	4	5	4	13	9	4	10	14%	7.6
David May	5	4	2	1 -	2 -	4 -	22 5 3	-	1	2	3 -	2	1	-	4%	6.3
Nicky Butt	11	11	1	3 1	-	3 -	22 3 1	-	1	-	1 -	1	-	2		7.4
Gary Walsh	10	-	-	-	3 -	-	16	-	-	-	-	-	-	-	71%	7.1
Andy Cole	17	1	12	-	-	-	17 1 12	4	7	1	12	10	2	1	13%	7.3
Simon Davies	3	2	-	-	-	2 -	8 1 1	1	-	-	1 -	1	-	2	10%	7.3
Paul Scholes	6	11	3	1 -	3 - 2	1 -	10 4 3	-	4	3	7 -	5	2	-	13%	7.7
David Beckham	2	2	-	1 -	-	4 - 1	7 3 1	-	-	-	1 -	-	1	-	15%	6.2
Keith Gillespie	3	6	4	-	3 -	-	-	1	-	-	1	-	-	-		
Paul Parker	1	1	-	-	-	2 - 1	3 2	-	-	-	-	-	-	-		6.3
Phil Neville	1	1	-	1 -	-	-	2	-	-	-	-	-	-	2		7.0
John O'Kane	-	-	-	1 -	-	-	3 1	-	-	-	-	-	-	-		7.0
Chris Casper	-	-	-	-	1 -	-	2	-	-	-	-	-	-	-		7.0
Kevin Pilkington	-	1	-	-	-	-	1	-	-	-	-	-	-	-		7.5
Graeme Tomlinson	-	-	-	-	2 -	-	2	-	-	-	-	-	-	-		7.0
Gary Neville	16	2	-	4 -	2 1	1 1	23 4	-	-	-	-	-	-	-		7.3

league table

	P	W	D	L	F	A	Pts
Blackburn Rovers	42	27	8	7	80	39	89
Manchester Utd	42	26	10	5	77	28	88
Notts Forest	42	22	11	9	72	28	77
Liverpool	42	21	11	10	72	28	77
Leeds	42	20	13	9	59	38	73
Newcastle	42	20	12	10	67	47	72
Tottenham	42	16	14	12	66	58	62
QPR	42	17	9	16	61	59	60
Wimbledon	42	15	11	16	48	65	56
Southampton	42	12	18	12	61	63	54
Chelsea	42	13	15	14	50	55	54
Arsenal	42	13	12	17	52	49	51
Sheffield Wed	42	13	12	17	49	57	51
West Ham	42	13	11	22	44	48	50
Everton	42	11	17	14	44	51	50
Coventry	42	12	14	16	44	62	50
Man City	42	12	13	17	53	64	49
Aston Villa	42	11	14	16	51	56	48
Crystal Palace	42	11	12	17	34	49	45
Norwich	42	10	13	19	37	54	43
Leicester	42	5	11	25	45	80	29
Ipswich	42	7	6	29	36	93	27

⏱ time split

	0-10 mins	11-20 mins	21-30 mins	31-40 mins	41-50 mins	51-60 mins	61-70 mins	71-80 mins	81-90 mins
Andrei Kanchelskis	-	2	1	-	5	2	1	2	2
Eric Cantona	-	-	1	3	4	1	1	3	3
Mark Hughes	-	2	1	1	1	2	3	2	-
Andy Cole	-	3	-	1	1	1	3	1	1
Brian McClair	1	-	-	1	-	1	1	1	-
Paul Scholes	-	-	2	1	1	-	1	-	-
Lee Sharpe	-	-	-	1	2	-	1	1	-
Ryan Giggs	-	-	-	-	1	-	1	-	-
Paul Ince	-	-	1	-	-	-	1	1	1
Denis Irwin	1	1	-	-	-	1	-	-	-
Steve Bruce	1	-	-	1	-	-	1	-	-
Roy Keane	-	-	1	-	1	-	-	-	-
David May	-	-	-	-	1	-	-	-	-
Gary Pallister	-	-	-	-	-	-	1	2	-
David Beckham	-	-	-	1	-	-	-	-	-
Nicky Butt	-	-	-	-	-	-	-	-	-
Simon Davies	1	-	-	-	-	-	-	-	-
Keith Gillespie	-	-	2	-	-	-	-	-	-
own goal	-	-	2	-	-	-	1	-	1
TOTAL SCORED	5	10	11	11	17	11	12	16	12
TOTAL CONCEDED	4	3	4	4	5	6	6	5	6

* player of the season
Paul Ince
performance rating average: **7.8**

summary

	P	W	D	L	F	A
Premier League	42	26	10	6	77	28
FA Cup	7	6	1	0	16	6
Coca Cola Cup	3	2	0	1	4	3
Champions Lge	6	2	2	2	11	11
Total	58	36	13	9	108	48

notes

players must have played a minimum of three games in the month concerned to qualify for average performance ratings or scoring rate percentages; performance ratings are only awarded to players having played ten minutes or more in one match

manchester united v
EVERTON
> Wembley > Sunday 21 May 1995 / 3.00pm
[Att: 79,592]

0-1

team lineups

home team

		rating
1.	Peter Schmeichel	7
27.	Gary Neville	7
4.	Steve Bruce	6
6.	Gary Pallister	6
3.	Denis Irwin	6
19.	Nicky Butt	8
16.	Roy Keane	6
8.	Paul Ince	6
5.	Lee Sharpe	6
9.	Brian McClair	6
10.	Mark Hughes	6

on the bench

11.	Ryan Giggs	7
13.	Gary Walsh	
24.	Paul Scholes	6

45 mins / 72 mins

visitors

1.	Neville Southall
2.	Matt Jackson
3.	Andy Hinchcliffe
5.	Dave Watson
26.	David Unsworth
6.	Gary Ablett
16.	Anders Limpar
27.	Barry Horne
17.	Joe Parkinson
8.	Graham Stuart
14.	Paul Rideout

on the bench

10.	Daniel Amokachi
12.	Jason Kearton
9.	Duncan Ferguson

69 mins / 50 mins

Southall's super double-save from Scholes

first aid box

> Steve Bruce injured hamstring

in the book

Referee: G Ashby, Worcester
Rating: 7
Bookings: Neville, Horne

word up

Joe Royle's Everton won the 114th FA Cup Final in what was a flat day for United. The reds looked positive enough in the opening exchanges but after 30 minutes Everton went a goal up when Rideout headed home a rebound after **Stuart** had shot against the bar.

United looked drained and desperate, and although they came close to scoring on several occasions, you sensed it wasn't to be their day.

In the last 25 minutes of the game lively substitute **Giggs** crossed to **McClair** whose header hit the bar. experienced keeper Southall then made a tremendous double save from United's other sub **Scholes**. In the dying minutes **Schmeichel** went on one of his infamous attacks, but there was to be no reprieve.

It has been a dramatic season, not just for United but for football in general. We may not have a major trophy to polish at Old Trafford this summer, but to reach an FA Cup Final on top of taking the league to the last day of the season is by no means a failure. So near, yet so far, the old cliché couldn't have been more true.

Little Nicky out-jumps Amokachi

in the area

time^

14.	Paul Rideout	30

"We can recognise Neville Southall's courage, acknowledge Dave Watson's resilience, marvel at Anders Limpar's skills and salute Paul Rideout's goal. But what of Joe Royle? When the judgements are made on Everton's season, victory in the FA Cup Final will be seen not just as a single, quite astonishing accomplishment but more the fulfilment of an impossible dream."

DAILY EXPRESS

"Paul Rideout's goal won the battle but it was David Unsworth who won the war. The twenty-one year old Preston-born central defender stood head to head, toe to toe with Mark Hughes. Everyone knows how Hughes is the fiercest, most frightening attacking spearhead in English football.
His reputation alone is enough to scare defenders into raising the white flag.
But not Unsworth. He gave Hughes some of his own strong arm treatment, even beating him into retreat by the time the final whistle has sounded."

DAILY STAR

"Anders Limpar was last night hailed as football's answer to Michel Platini.
Joe Royle saluted Limpar for a royal command performance. His creativity illuminated Wembley and provided the winning strike.
Royle said: `He has the ability to be on the Platini level, the problem is he doesn't realise it as often as he could.'"

DAILY MIRROR

"I'd like to see this match again. I don't know if I did wrong, but I was doubtful as to whether Ryan would last the whole match if he came on at the beginning.
It's five years since we've won nothing. Sometimes our players forget what defeat is like. They know now."

ALEX FERGUSON

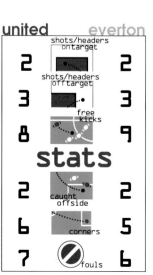

united   **everton**

2	shots/headers on target	2
3	shots/headers off target	3
8	free kicks	9

stats

2	caught offside	2
6	corners	5
7	fouls	6

Sideline scuffle: Neville locks arms with Stuart

Picking up the pieces...

> the video

MANCHESTER UNITED

OFFICIAL REVIEW
OF THE 94/95 SEASON

* Until next year...